ECHOES of GLORY

Echoes of Glory

ARMS AND EQUIPMENT OF

THE CONFEDERACY

By the Editors of Time-Life Books

TIME-LIFE BOOKS · ALEXANDRIA · VIRGINIA

Time-Life Books is a division of Time Life Inc.

TIME LIFE INC.
PRESIDENT and CEO: George Artandi

TIME-LIFE BOOKS
PRESIDENT: Stephen R. Frary
PUBLISHER/MANAGING EDITOR: Neil Kagan
Director of Finance: Christopher Hearing
Directors of Book Production: Marjann Caldwell,
 Patricia Pascale
Director of Publishing Technology: Betsi McGrath
Director of Photography and Research: John Conrad
 Weiser
Director of Editorial Administration: Barbara Levitt
Chief Librarian: Louise D. Forstall

Printed in 1998. © MCMXCI Time-Life Books.
First printing. Printed in U.S.A.

ISBN 0-7370-3159-X

The Library of Congress has catalogued the trade
version of this title as follows:

Arms and equipment of the confederacy / by the
 editors of Time-Life Books.
       p.   cm. — (Echoes of Glory)
    Includes bibliographical references and index.
    ISBN 0-8094-8850-7
    ISBN 0-8094-8851-5 (lib. bdg.)
    1. Confederate States of America. Army—
Firearms. 2. Confederate States of America. Army—
Equipment. 3. United States—History—Civil War,
1861-1865—Equipment and supplies.
    I. Time-Life Books. II. Series.
    UD383.5.A75   1991
    973.7'42—dc20   91-2278 CIP

ECHOES OF GLORY
Editor: Henry Woodhead
Administrator: Jane Edwin
Art Director: Herbert H. Quarmby
Deputy Editors: Harris J. Andrews, Kirk E. Denkler

Editorial Staff for *Arms and Equipment of the
 Confederacy*
Picture Editor: Kristin Baker Hanneman
Writers: Marfé Ferguson Delano, Barbara C. Mallen
Assistant Editor/Research: Karen C. Goettsche
Senior Copy Coordinator: Anne Farr
Editorial Assistant: Jayne A. L. Dover

Special Contributors: Kenneth C. Danforth, Stephen
G. Hyslop, Kimberly A. Kostyal, M. Linda Lee, John
Newton, Brian C. Pohanka, Jennifer J. Veech (text);
Anne K. DuVivier (art); Gail V. Feinberg (pictures);
Roy Nanovic (index)

Correspondents: Elisabeth Kraemer-Singh (Bonn),
Christine Hinze (London), Christina Lieberman (New
York), Maria Vincenza Aloisi (Paris), Ann Natanson
(Rome).

Photographs by Larry Sherer

Special thanks to: The Museum of the Confederacy,
Richmond, Virginia

The Cover: Members of the Richmond Grays, a
company of the 1st Virginia Infantry, pose early in
the war.

Credit: Courtesy of The Cook Collection, The
Valentine Museum, Richmond

Consultants and Special Contributors:

Earl J. Coates, a historian and museum curator for the
U.S. Department of Defense, has studied Civil War
arms and equipment for the past 30 years, specializ-
ing in supply operations. He has written numerous
articles on the subject and is the coauthor of *An
Introduction to Civil War Small Arms.* He is a member of the Company of Military Historians and the
North-South Skirmish Association, which he serves as
deputy commander.

Mark Elrod is a historian and musicologist with an
interest in 19th-century America. He organized the
Federal City Cornet Band of Washington, D.C., a re-
creation of a mid-19th-century United States military
band. A fellow in the Company of Military Historians,
he has coauthored *A Pictorial History of Civil War Era
Musical Instruments and Military Bands.*

Col. John R. Elting, USA (Ret.), former associate pro-
fessor at West Point, has written or edited some 20
books, including *Swords around a Throne, The
Superstrategists,* and *American Army Life,* as well as
Battles for Scandinavia in the Time-Life Books World
War II series. He was chief consultant to the Time-
Life series The Civil War.

Les Jensen, museum curator with the U.S.
Department of the Army, specializes in Civil War arti-
facts. A fellow of the Company of Military Historians
and a contributor to *The Image of War* series, he is
also a consultant for numerous Civil War publications
and museums and author of the 32d Virginia Infantry
volume in the *Virginia Regimental Histories Series.* He
was for eight years the curator of collections of the
Museum of the Confederacy in Richmond, Virginia.

Michael McAfee specializes in military uniforms and
has been curator of uniforms and history at the West
Point Museum since 1970. A fellow of the company
of Military Historians, he coedited with Col. John
Elting *Long Endure: The Civil War Years* and collabo-
rated with Frederick Todd on *American Military
Equipage.* He is the author of *Artillery of the
American Revolution, 1775-1783,* and has written
numerous articles for *Military Images Magazine.*

Howard Michael Madaus, curator of the history sec-
tion of the Milwaukee Public Museum since 1968, is
a noted authority on Civil War flags and firearms. In
addition to supervising exhibits of military equipment, he is the author of two books, *The Battle Flags
of the Confederate Army of Tennessee* and *The
Warner Collector's Guide to American Longarms.* He
has also published numerous articles relating to military equipage in such journals as *Military Collector &
Historian* and *The Flag Bulletin.*

Chris Nelson, a former journalist, has been a Civil
War collector and reenactor for more than 30 years.
He is a member of the company of Military
Historians, a contributing editor to *Military Images
Magazine,* and the coauthor of *Photographs of
American Civil War Cavalry.*

Contents

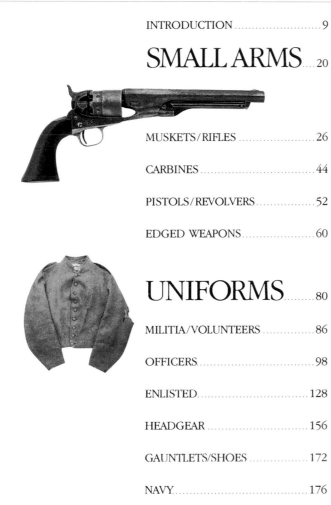

Led by their mascot hound *(right, background)*, Confederate soldiers of the 1st Maryland charge the Federal defenders of Culp's Hill at Gettys-

burg on July 3, 1863. Union troops *(right, foreground)* **repulsed the assault, killing the dog along with 31 Rebels.**

The Honorable Campaign

America was in the second year of bloody civil war when, in September 1862, a British colonel named Garnet Wolseley took advantage of a leave of absence from his post in Canada to visit the Confederate troops in the field. Like many Englishmen, Wolseley was sympathetic to the cause of Southern independence; and, as a battle-scarred veteran of campaigns in Burma, the Crimea, India, and China, he was eager to see for himself if the Rebel soldiers of the Army of Northern Virginia measured up to the professional standards of their European counterparts. After a brief sojourn in the Confederate capital of Richmond, Wolseley headed for Winchester in the Shenandoah Valley of Virginia. Robert E. Lee's forces were encamped several miles north of the town, recuperating from an inconclusive foray into Maryland that had cost the South some 16,000 casualties in battles at South Mountain, Harpers Ferry, and Antietam.

The first Confederate soldiers Wolseley encountered were a less-than-impressive sight. "Each day we passed batches of sick and wounded going to the rear," he recalled, "weakly men struggling slowly home, many of them without boots or shoes, and all indifferently clad." The motley attire of a passing cavalry detachment stood in sharp contrast to the uniform appearance of the Federal prisoners whom the horsemen were escorting into captivity. Nevertheless, the mounted Confederates seemed unconcerned about their dishevelment, according to Wolseley. "Many rode along in their shirt-sleeves as gay and happy as if they were decked with gold and the richest trappings."

The Englishman was cordially received by Lee, Stonewall Jackson, and other senior Confederate officers, and he was pleasantly surprised at the absence of the sort of pomp and circumstance that he had observed around the headquarters of European armies during wartime. The generals and their staffs lived simply, in regulation canvas tents, and there was "no crowd of aides-de-camp loitering about" as would have been the case with European commanders.

Colonel Wolseley accepted Lee's invitation to attend a large-scale military review and inspection. As thousands of Confederate troops filed past, the British officer cast a critical eye on the lines of marching troops. He observed that some units were to a man outfitted in short jackets, caps, and trousers of gray cloth, while others presented "a harlequin appearance, being dressed in every conceivable variety of coat, both as regards color and cut." Some sported captured Yankee forage caps, and others "gray wideawake hats, looped up at one side." The fastidious Englishman thought that the long hair worn by many of the soldiers was "most unmilitary."

But despite their untidy appearance and shabby garb, the colonel did not fail to notice a sure sign that these Rebels were serious soldiers: Their rifles were clean, well cared for, and ready to use. Above all, it was the proud bearing of the Confederates—"an unmistakable look of conscious strength"— that won Wolseley's undying respect. Never had he seen an army, he said, that "looked more like work."

The lean and self-reliant veterans at Wolseley's review scarcely resembled the enthusiastic but inexperienced volunteers who had flocked to the colors in the spring of 1861, eager to risk their lives repelling the despised Yankee. The bombardment of Fort Sumter and the secession of the Southern states had spurred close to 500,000 men to sign up in the cause of the fledgling Confederate nation. In courthouse towns throughout the South, they enlisted in companies and chose their officers, often after spirited election campaigns. They drilled in town squares and set off for assembly points where they joined other companies to form regiments. The men were supremely confident and utterly convinced of the righteousness of their cause. "Excitement was at white heat," the Texan John W. Stevens recalled, describing the highly charged atmosphere of the time. "Our patriotism was just bubbling up and boiling over and frying and fizzing."

Most of the homegrown volunteer companies marched bearing flags made by wives or sweethearts and wearing their own distinctive regalia. At the beginning of the War the Confederates had no central system of supply, much less identical uniforms to distribute to the troops. As a result, the volunteers drilled in a striking variety of dress. Although gray was from the outset the preferred color, some Confederate units wore blue, and uniforms covered the spectrum from the green-clad Emmett Guard of the 17th Virginia Regiment to the scarlet fez and baggy red trousers of the Louisiana Zouave Battalion. Just as flamboyant as the dress were the names of the militia companies, grand-sounding titles such as the Southern Rights Guards, the Charleston Zouave Cadets, the Sussex Light Dragoons, or, even more boastful and defiant, the Tallapoosa Thrashers,

"One drill was hardly over before another was called. It was arduous labor, harder than grubbing, stump-pulling, or cracking rocks on a turnpike."

PRIVATE ALEXANDER HUNTER
17TH VIRGINIA INFANTRY
REGIMENT

Sporting the exotic trappings of the French-colonial Algerian light infantry, Colonel Gaston Coppens' Louisiana Zouaves line up for a drink from a pretty provisioner, or *vivandière (left)*. Only two Confederate regiments adopted the gaudy Zouave uniform as their standard attire.

the Cherokee Lincoln Killers, and the Barbour County Yankee Hunters.

The volunteers went to war with fire in their eyes but a motley collection of firearms on their shoulders. A couple of the Confederate states had their own arsenals, and the Rebels were able to confiscate arms from Federal repositories in the South. But many recruits had to bring their own from home, and the firearms that they carried ranged from antiquated flintlocks to rifle muskets of recent manufacture. Some weapons dated from ancient times and bordered on the ludicrous. In his zeal to arm his men to the teeth, the mayor of Memphis, Tennessee, ordered the manufacture of 64 pikes for an Irish company being recruited in his city. These medieval weapons were described as "about 10 feet long, with a bayonet head for thrusting and a hook for cutting."

Confederate cavalrymen—most of whom enlisted with their own mounts and rode them to war—generally carried a hodgepodge of military hardware. "The men procured what they could in the way of arms," wrote the historian of the 4th Virginia Cavalry. "Some had shotguns and some had pistols." Throughout the South, the new companies and regiments faced shortages of leather accouterments—belts and cartridge boxes—and sufficient numbers of haversacks, canteens, and knapsacks were likewise hard to come by.

Once mustered, the volunteer regiments were drilled in rigidly choreographed, close-order tactics that had changed little since Napoleon's time. Officers and privates alike had to familiarize themselves with a complex, often bewildering litany of commands that maneuvered their blocks of troops with geometrical precision—from column into line and back again; facing by the front, flank, or rear; forming a square to resist cavalry. "One drill was hardly over before another was called," the Virginian Alexander Hunter remembered. "It was arduous labor, harder than grubbing, stump-pulling, or cracking rocks on a turnpike." The goal of all the complex drilling was the fulfillment of a simple maneuver: When the moment of truth came, the men of the regiment, standing elbow to elbow in two ranks, were expected to blast their way through the Federal line with massive volleys of musketry, or to carry the position at bayonet point.

Despite the fact that the Confederate army was built from scratch, mostly with raw recruits unschooled in the soldier's art, it was blessed from the first with an exceptional officers' corps that boasted a high number of military professionals. More than a third of the Confederacy's general officers were graduates of West Point and former officers in the U.S. Army who chose to "go South." Other notable military schools, such as the Virginia Military Institute and The Citadel in Charleston, South Carolina, furnished a pool of talented young officers who chose to fight for the South. Being brand-new, the Confederate army offered a chance for quick advancement, and it proved especially alluring to daring and energetic young officers spoiling for a fight and eager to make their mark in their generation's war.

In their first stabs at molding raw recruits into a polished fighting force, however, the Southern army's young officers often found the responsibilities of leadership less than glorious. "To appreciate fully the truth that men are but children of a larger growth, one must have commanded soldiers," wrote John S. Wise, a VMI cadet who abandoned his studies to accept a commission in the Confederate army. "Without constant guidance and government and punishment, they become careless about clothes, food, ammunition, cleanliness, and even personal safety."

"I think I am dirtier than I ever was before. I have not changed clothes for two weeks, and my pants have a hole in each leg nearly big enough for a dog to creep through. I am afraid the dirt is striking in, as I am somewhat afflicted with the baby's complaint—a pain under the apron."

MAJOR FRANK PAXTON
27TH VIRGINIA INFANTRY
REGIMENT

Discipline did not always come easily to soldiers whose regimental superiors had frequently been prewar neighbors and equals. The difficulty was compounded by the fact that most volunteer officers had been voted into positions of authority by their men. Colonel Asbury Coward of the 5th South Carolina complained that at first his troops "refused to appreciate the fact that the wearing of a star, a bar, or a chevron made any change in the man they had known at home." Nonetheless, unit pride ran strong, in no small part because of the infectious enthusiasm of the young Confederate officers. And as the early battles of the War would indicate, the daring and sheer aggressiveness of these officers, along with the dedication of the men, had much to do with Confederate successes.

For the most part, Confederate troops had the benefit of sufficient rations during the first months of the War. Few units went hungry. The Federal naval blockade had yet to close the door on Southern ports, and supplies moved freely across the South by river and rail. In some locations, there was even too much food. "Commissary stores were plentiful," according to Daniel Smith of the 1st Alabama, "and there was shameful waste." Smith saw wagonloads of fresh beef that had spoiled being hauled away and buried, while "flour, molasses, and sugar were issued in larger quantities than could possibly be eaten." Many of the volunteers tended to excess in other ways, for it proved difficult to relinquish the habitual luxuries of home. An artillery officer observed that some of his gunners had hauled trunkloads of spare clothing off to war with them; one man's luggage included "a dozen face towels and a smaller number of foot and bath towels." Such niceties turned out to be more burden than asset, the new soldiers quickly learned. "The

Among the Confederacy's best and brightest was Colonel Micah Jenkins of South Carolina, an 1854 graduate of The Citadel in Charleston. A respected military authority who established his own military academy before the War, Jenkins distinguished himself in battles from First Manassas to the Wilderness, eventually rising to the rank of brigadier general. A misdirected Confederate volley ended his life in May 1864.

knapsack was a terror," said Private John Robson of the 52d Virginia, "loaded with 30 to 50 pounds of surplus baggage."

The days of plenty for the Confederate troops would come to a quick end. Winfield Scott, the general in chief of the Union army, had likened the ever-tightening stranglehold on Confederate resources to the grip of an anaconda—the South American serpent that crushes its prey—and his analogy was not far wrong. The ability of the South to maintain its troops in the field would vary from theater to theater and from campaign to campaign, but early on the Confederates learned to make do with less, so that the decreased availability of supplies was not as much of a hardship as it might have been. "Wisdom is born of experience," Robson recalled, explaining how the exigencies of war eventually compelled every soldier, no matter how cosseted he might have been at home, to value a light load over an elegant turnout. Veterans came to pride themselves on their ability to travel light, outmarching as well as outfighting their Yankee foes. Burdensome knapsacks crammed with gear never entirely disappeared from the Southern ranks—they were issued periodically to both the Eastern and Western armies—but the typical Confederate soldier chose to pare down his load, carrying his bedding in a blanket roll that was slung across the body from the left shoulder. To further reduce weight, veterans generally favored the rubberized poncho over the canvas dog tent and let their woolen blankets substitute for heavy overcoats. Southerners, particularly those in the Western armies, tended also to discard the regulation headgear, a forage cap or kepi, in favor of a civilian-style slouch hat, which was more comfortable and provided more relief from the sun.

No matter what the gear, Civil War campaigning was a rough business for Yank and Reb alike, and there was decidedly little glamour for the men in the field. In camp or on the march, the soldiers of the Civil War were mostly filthy, uncomfortable, generally unhealthy, and often ill. "I think I am dirtier than I ever was before," the 27th Virginia's Major Frank Paxton wrote his wife. "I have not changed clothes for two weeks, and my pants have a hole in each leg nearly big enough for a dog to creep through. I am afraid the dirt is striking in, as I am somewhat afflicted with the baby's complaint—a pain under the apron." On the march back south from Pennsylvania, where at the Battle of Gettysburg the Confederates lost 28,000 men killed, wounded, or missing, Chaplain Florence McCarthy noted that his uniform was "coming all to flinders." He complained that his socks had disintegrated and added, "I can buy none, beg none, steal none, and it is a matter of impossibility to get a piece of clothing washed." In order to ease his blistered feet the chaplain was eventually compelled to don a pair of women's stockings, taken from a Maryland shop. But these, too, soon wore out.

Virtually every soldier was on all-too-familiar terms with *pediculus corporis,* the common louse. "We could not avoid the bug," one Texan stated. "He was everywhere, and he was no respecter of person. He could wear the gray or the blue, he was at home in both armies, was loyal to both flags." In every camp, at every halt, men could be seen picking the pests from their bodies and the seams of their clothing; but even steeping uniforms in boiling water proved ineffective in ridding the troops of the vermin.

Perhaps more than about the ravages of lice, the Confederate soldier fretted, with good reason, about the condition of his feet. With regiments frequently called upon to cover 20 miles in a single day's march, the deterioration of footgear was a constant concern. Soldiers would typically wear out two or more pairs of shoes in a single campaign, and a not-uncommon sight was that of improvised units of the shoeless—men marching across the relatively soft farm fields, paralleling the main columns on the hard-packed turnpikes, to protect their bare feet. When the troops settled into camp for the winter, men who had been shoemakers in civilian life were told to write home for their tools, then put to work making repairs. Some soldiers were able to patch their brogans with strips of leather cut from belts and cartridge boxes.

When supplies wore thin, Yankee prisoners became the unwilling providers of much-needed ordnance, clothing, and equipment. Strict disciplinarians such as General Stonewall Jackson occasionally issued orders prohibiting this pillaging, but the practice was well-nigh universal. In the wake of a Confederate victory at Hartsville, Tennessee, John Green of the Kentucky Orphan Brigade appropriated the braided overcoat of a captured Union colonel. The Federals "were bountifully supplied with everything a soldier could wish," Green reported, "so we ransacked their camp for good clothes." Another prime source of shoes, trousers, and overcoats was the corpse-strewn battlefields. The artillerist Henry Berkeley described how, by dawn of the day following the 1862 engagement at Fredericksburg, Virginia, "all the Yankee dead had been stripped of every rag of their clothing." Berkeley compared the bloodied, naked dead to "hogs which had been cleaned."

The carnage of Civil War battlefields was truly horrific. At Antietam the 1st Texas sustained 82 percent casualties, and at Gettysburg 588 of the 800 men in the 26th North Carolina fell. Behind the dry statistics published in the newspapers and magazines of the times lay nightmare scenes of agony and desolation unfathomable to those who waited at home. A soldier of the 6th Georgia rendered his personal indictment of the slaughter: "The dead lying all around, your foes unburied to the last, horses and wagons and troops passing heedlessly along. The stiffened bodies lie, grasping in death the arms they bravely

A column of Confederate troops pauses during its march down a street in Frederick, Maryland, in this rare photograph taken from above a dry-goods store. "They were the dirtiest men I ever saw," a witness noted, "a most ragged, lean and hungry set of wolves. Yet there was a dash about them that the northern men lacked."

bore, with glazed eyes and features blackened by rapid decay. Here sits one against a tree in motionless stare. Another has his head leaning against a stump, his hands over his head. They have paid the last penalty. They have fought the last battle. The air is putrid with decaying bodies of men and horses. My God, my God, what a scourge is war."

In an age when even the most senior commanders were expected to lead their troops into battle, losses among the Confederate officers' corps were proportionately higher than those among the enlisted men. Seventy-seven Confederate generals were killed in action or died of wounds, and in the Seven Days' Battles alone, Lee's army lost 10 brigade commanders and 66 regimental commanders. This steady attrition of Southern leadership contributed significantly to the eventual decline in Confederate fortunes on the battlefield.

As deadly as the battles were, more soldiers died from disease than from bullets. The unsanitary conditions of camp life triggered epidemics of typhoid fever and dysentery that claimed thousands of lives. Measles and malaria dogged the ranks of both armies. As the War ground on, Confederate regiments that once had numbered nearly a thousand men shrank to a couple of hundred. Despite the institution of a conscription act that authorized the draft of all white males between the ages of 18 and 35, the numerical strength of Southern forces continued inexorably to decline. The more populous Union was largely able to make good its losses, by means of both the draft and the enlistment of 179,000 black soldiers.

Even though the Confederates were outmanned, their inspired leadership and personal audacity made them formidable foes. The Rebels were "careful to keep their bayonets bright and their lines of battle well dressed," said the Union general Joshua Chamberlain; they were "rough and rude, yet knew well how to make a field illustrious." Another Federal veteran stated simply, "Their splendid courage and military precision will command our admiration forever." Time and again, Southern armies defeated numerically superior Federal forces—surging forward to the attack and screaming the "rebel yell," their eerie, high-pitched battle cry. An Ohio soldier described the sound as a "peculiar, uncanny yelping, a succession of jerky, canine cries, which, at a distance, from its shrillness seemed like the sound of boys' voices, but when near it was terror-striking from its savageness."

In June 1864, Lieutenant Colonel Theodore Lyman of the Union army took the opportunity of a temporary lull during the fighting at Cold Harbor in Virginia to meet with the enemy—a not-unusual occurrence on the battlefields of the Civil War. As officers from the opposite sides discussed the course of the conflict under a flag of truce, Lyman was impressed by the dignity and reserve of the Confederate commanders. "They have an absence of all flippancy," he noted, "an earnestness of manner which is very becoming to

"The stiffened bodies lie, grasping in death the arms they bravely bore, with glazed eyes and features blackened by rapid decay. They have paid the last penalty. They have fought the last battle. The air is putrid with decaying bodies of men and horses. My God, my God, what a scourge is war."

A SOLDIER, 6TH GEORGIA INFANTRY REGIMENT

On October 5, 1864, Rebel troops under the command of General Samuel French *(foreground, above)* attack the Federal outpost at Allatoona, Georgia, a depot containing supplies desperately needed by the Confederates. The attackers surrounded the Union garrison, "filling every hole and trench, seeking shelter behind every stump and log that lay within musket range," reported the Union commander John Corse. But in the end, the Rebels were repulsed by Federal artillery.

them." Lyman speculated that their solemnity derived from "a sense of their ruin if their cause fails."

Even after the tide of war had irrevocably turned in favor of the North, Southern soldiers fought on with grim defiance. "As long as we have two great armies in the field our cause is full of hope," stated the Virginia artilleryman Ham Chamberlayne. "A people cannot be conquered by occupying its territory. Its armies must be whipped, beaten and broken up. Their 'anaconda' will have a slow meal—our armies will be indigestible."

In the end, of course, the proud Southern armies were swallowed up, and their demise was spurred by an erosion of morale born of hunger and despair. The old military maxim that an army travels on its stomach proved all too true for the armies of the Confederacy.

As the War continued, both the quality and the quantity of rations declined. The corn bread that became the standard fare for Southern soldiers was made

from coarse, unsifted meal, and it was invariably overcooked and frequently wormy. The bread would get "so hard and moldy," complained a man of the Stonewall Brigade, "that when we broke it, it looked like it had cobwebs in it." The cherished coffee issue that Federal troops continued to take for granted all but disappeared from Southern ranks. The deprived Rebels attempted to concoct a variety of imitation coffees, including brews of burnt rice or of acorns, crushed and boiled. Perhaps the most popular substitute was what one Louisianan described as "a decoction made from the roots of the sassafras tree."

Unlike the Northern armies, the Confederate forces were seldom followed into the field by sutlers—the traveling vendors whose delicacies of canned meat, cakes, and pies helped to alleviate the tedium of the soldiers' standard fare of hardtack and salt pork. More importantly, the Confederate commissariat was never able to efficiently coordinate the management and shipment of foodstuffs to armies in the field.

Confederates bought and occasionally stole what they could from local farmers; but in time the Federal blockade, the occupation of the South's agricultural heartland, and the severing of lines of supply reduced the Southern soldiers to a chronic state of hunger. In the wake of General Braxton Bragg's retreat from Kentucky, a Confederate officer watched his famished men gathering corn from the ground where the horses had fed. For days, he reported, such pick-

With the indefatigable resolve that saw them through four years of bloody conflict, Confederate troops commanded by Brigadier General E. Porter Alexander organize a last line of defense in an apple orchard northeast of Appomattox Courthouse. It was "a fairly good position," Alexander recalled, "but I knew that Lee would not approve an unnecessary shot, and not one was fired from our line."

ings were the "sole diet of all." Confederate commissaries tried to make up for the lack of vegetables by advising the soldiers to eat wild onions, and at least one general, Isaac Trimble, issued an order instructing his brigade to gather edible wild plants such as dandelion and watercress.

While supplies of uniforms and equipment remained adequate, although barely so, food shortages steadily sapped the Southern soldiers' strength and will to fight. "Despondency, like a black and poisonous mist, began to invade the hearts before so tough and buoyant," recalled Captain John Esten Cooke, a staff officer in Lee's army. "Feed a soldier well, and let him sleep sufficiently, and he will fight gaily. Starve him, and break him down with want of sleep and fatigue, and he will despond." When it became apparent that victory was impossible, many Confederates thought it senseless to continue the struggle. "I am in hopes that this campaign will close the war," a South Carolinian wrote from the trenches at Petersburg in October 1864. "I don't see what we are made to suffer so much for."

Doleful letters from home further crippled the morale of the Southern soldiers. Men were torn between their duty to a dying cause and the needs of their families, left destitute in the wake of marauding Yankee armies. Lee's aide, Walter Taylor, estimated that in the final months at Petersburg the Army of Northern Virginia was losing more than 100 men a day from desertion.

When all hope had evaporated, the final collapse of the Confederate armies came quickly. In the battered Army of Tennessee, falling back before General Sherman's inexorable advance, whole brigades numbered less than the regulation strength of a regiment. Some units ceased to exist altogether. "Soldiers whom I knew had been soldiers of steadiness and courage were straggling and sleeping, unarmed and apparently unconcerned," wrote an army surgeon during Lee's retreat from Petersburg to Appomattox. "Gaunt hunger had at last overcome their manhood, and they had scattered through the country to any house or hut that promised a piece of bread."

Three days after Lee surrendered 28,000 troops to Grant at Appomattox, the defeated Confederates held a last parade, a coda to four years of carnage and heroism. In a formal ceremony, General John B. Gordon led a long column of Rebels past lines of Federals commanded by General Joshua Chamberlain. The two sides exchanged salutes—a gesture that Gordon called "a token of respect from Americans to Americans." Union soldiers wept as they watched the pitiful fragments of famous regiments pass before them, the brokenhearted survivors stacking their arms and furling their tattered colors for the last time.

Chamberlain found himself unable to view those lean and bearded soldiers in butternut and gray as enemies. Rather they seemed to him "the embodiment of manhood; men whom neither toils and sufferings, nor the fact of death, nor disaster, nor hopelessness could bend from their resolve." The Confederate soldier could have asked for no finer tribute.

"They were the embodiment of manhood; men whom neither toils and sufferings, nor the fact of death, nor disaster, nor hopelessness could bend from their resolve."

BREVET MAJOR GENERAL
JOSHUA L. CHAMBERLAIN
U.S. ARMY

SMALL ARMS

On April 15, 1861, while the shock waves of the Federal surrender at Fort Sumter were still reverberating across the land, a former U.S. Army ordnance officer named Caleb Huse sailed for England on a mission for the new Confederate War Department. Not long after his arrival, Huse procured the services of one Archibald Hamilton, a London businessman said to be "acquainted with every gunmaker in England." With Hamilton as his agent and money to burn, Huse proceeded to make deals that opened a transatlantic conduit of English arms to the Confederacy.

The quick-thinking, aggressive Huse stole a march on his competition in the contest for foreign arms. His Union counterpart, Colonel George L. Schuyler, the U.S. government's purchasing agent, did not arrive in London until mid-August, whereupon he had great difficulty procuring British arms. Schuyler ultimately resorted to buying in bulk from the Continent—inferior weapons that Huse dismissed as "the merest rubbish in the world."

Huse's initial success had such an impact that in October 1861, the U.S. consul in London wrote to Washington in distress: "Of Enfield rifles the Confederates have thousands now ready for shipment, and have all the armories here at work for them. With these and what they are getting at Birmingham, they must be receiving not far from 1,500 per week." The news of Huse's achievement was warmly received back in Richmond, Virginia, where Major Josiah Gorgas, the Pennsylvania-born chief of the Confederate Bureau of Ordnance, faced the immense task of arming an agrarian society at a time in history when weapons technology was rapidly advancing.

Gorgas was not worried about the immediate future. Thanks to the swift seizure of Federal armories and arsenals located within the boundaries of the Confederacy, prewar purchases from profit-hungry Yankee traders, and the sizable stocks that had been accumulated over the years in state and local repositories under the Militia Act of 1808, the Confederate government possessed from 285,000 to 300,000 military firearms—an ample supply, provided that the war was a very short one.

That supply had been rapidly amassed following the unsuccessful raid on the United States Armory and Arsenal at Harpers Ferry, Virginia, by the radical abolitionist John Brown in October of 1859. Brown's action, which created the specter of slave revolt, had a profound psychological effect on the South. Southern governors began petitioning the Federal government to speed up delivery of the militia arms due them in 1860 and even 1861. They found a sympathetic ear in the United States secretary of war, John B. Floyd of Virginia, who authorized the advance of several thousand of the best arms in production and approved the sale of older weapons at bargain prices.

Still, the majority of weapons available to the fledgling Confederate army were heavy, clumsy, outdated relics. And some Southern governors were reluctant to allow any weapons allocated for home defense to leave their states. If the struggle with the North lasted more than a few months, as knowledgeable military men expected, the new nation would be hard-pressed to arm its volunteer army. The Confederate soldier could fight without a fancy uniform and even without regular food rations, but not without weapons—despite the popular boast, "We can whip them with cornstalks!"

The Confederacy had precipitated a civil war at a time when the United States reigned as the leading firearms producer in the world, especially in techniques of mass production and standardization of parts. But with the notable exception of the machinery seized by Virginia state troops at Harpers Ferry on April 17, 1861, the majority of the modern arms-manufacturing equipment and most of the raw materials were located in the industrialized North.

Until the decade prior to the War, the standard infantry weapon had been the flintlock smoothbore musket. All models had to be loaded in the same laborious way: A paper cartridge containing a powder charge and a lead ball, or several tiny lead balls called buckshot, was torn open with the teeth (at the command "Tear cartridge"); powder, then ball was dropped into the gun's muzzle, followed by the paper, which served as wadding, and the whole load was driven the length of the barrel with a metal ramrod.

To fire the weapon, a soldier ignited the powder charge by an unreliable flintlock mechanism: A chip of flint on the weapon's hammer created a spark in a shallow pan primed with a little powder from the paper cartridge. The gun would not fire when the powder was wet or even damp. When it did fire (about 80 percent of the time), the ball was unstable in flight and accurate only at short range: 200 yards against formations, up to 100 yards against individuals. By 1861, the smoothbores had become more reliable, primarily because the temperamental old flintlock mechanism had been replaced by new percussion caps—tiny caplike copper casings containing a small amount of an explosive such as fulminate of mercury.

A far more critical improvement had transformed the musket into a rifle, whose bore was no longer smooth but scored with spiral grooves. The rifling gave the lead ball a stabilizing spin when it was fired, dramatically increasing accuracy and range. A skilled marksman could hit a target 600 yards away.

But forcing a hard, round ball down the lands and grooves of the rifled bore was much more difficult and time-consuming than loading a smoothbore musket, especially in the heat of battle when even experienced soldiers became clumsy. Rifles were thus impractical for general infantry use until 1849, when a French army captain named Claude A. Minié came up with an ingenious yet simple solution to the problem.

Minié developed a cartridge that contained an elongated, soft lead projectile with a hollow, cone-shaped base. He cast the conical bullet slightly smaller than the diameter of the rifle bore, which enabled the projectile, popularly known as the Minié ball, to slide easily down the rifling. The hollow base of the bullet rested on top of the gunpowder; when the weapon was fired, the ignition of the powder caused the soft lead of the bullet to expand into the lands and grooves of the barrel. Minié's invention was later perfected by James H. Burton of Virginia, the master armorer at the federal installation in Harpers Ferry who later became Gorgas' right-hand man as the superintendent of Confederate armories.

Using Minié's invention, a trained soldier could load and fire three shots a minute—not very fast for men advancing across several hundred yards of open terrain, but fast enough to make the accurate, long-range rifle a lethal weapon in the hands of skilled marksmen in sheltered positions.

In the late 1850s, gunsmiths devised methods of updating the old smoothbore muskets by cutting rifling into their barrels, making what were called rifle muskets. The rifling process worked well on arms of .58 caliber or less; the smaller bullet increased accuracy without forfeiting stopping power. Cutting grooves into the bores of .69-caliber arms was not as successful because the process weakened the barrels.

In the mid-1850s, ordnance experts at the national armory in Springfield, Massachusetts, developed a new rifle musket and rifle (the latter having a shorter barrel) called the Model 1855, after the year the design was developed. The basic pattern soon became the mainstay of the American infantryman.

The Model 1855 was equipped with a rear sight for better aiming, and an innovative priming system that ignited the charge by automatically feeding a percussion tape under the hammer of the weapon. The percussion tape, developed by a Maryland dentist named Edward Maynard, resembled a roll of paper caps for a modern cap pistol. It consisted of small pellets of fulminate cemented in a row between two strips of paper and then varnished to make it moisture resistant. In practice, however, the Maynard tape

primer proved complex to use and somewhat unreliable. Shortly before the outbreak of the War, the U.S. Army introduced an improvement on the Model 1855—the Springfield Model 1861 rifle musket. Instead of employing the Maynard primer, the Model 1861 reverted to the earlier and simpler percussion-cap system of ignition.

Armorers made other significant improvements in weapons intended to be carried by cavalrymen. Muzzleloading shoulder weapons, the staple of foot soldiers, had always been extremely awkward for mounted men. As early as 1819, an inventor from Portland, Maine, named John H. Hall developed a breechloading rifle with totally interchangeable parts. Hall shortened his creation to carbine size (about 38 inches in length, as opposed to the 49 to 57 inches of a musket or

How to Load a Rifle

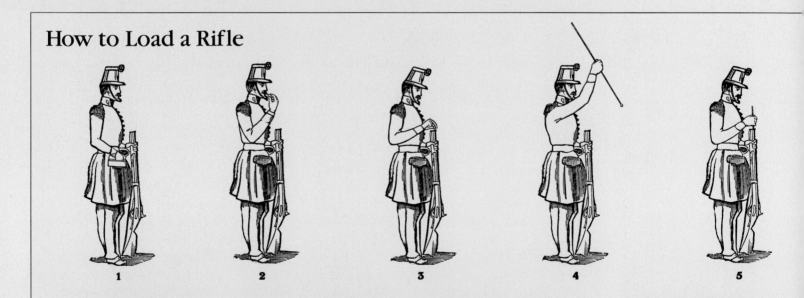

1 LOAD: Grasp the rifle with the left hand. Place the butt between the feet, the barrel toward the front. Seize the barrel with the left hand close to the muzzle, which should be held three inches from the body. Carry the right hand to the cartridge box on the belt.

2 HANDLE CARTRIDGE/TEAR CARTRIDGE: Seize a cartridge between the thumb and the next two fingers. Place it between the teeth. Tear the paper. Hold the cartridge upright between the thumb and first two fingers in front of and near the muzzle.

3 CHARGE CARTRIDGE: Empty the powder into the barrel. Disengage the ball from the paper with the right hand and with the thumb and first two fingers of the left. Insert the ball, with its pointed end up, into the muzzle and press it down with the right thumb.

4 DRAW RAMMER: Draw the rammer out by extending the arm. Turn the rammer. Keeping the back of the hand toward the front, place the head of the rammer on the ball.

5 RAM CARTRIDGE: Insert the rammer. Steady it with the thumb of

rifle). But technical difficulties and the U.S. Army's reluctance to abandon muzzleloading arms prevented the Hall carbines and rifles from gaining general acceptance. Still, many of them existed in state armories in 1861, and some early Confederate volunteers carried them into battle.

The most popular breechloading arms of the period were made by the Sharps Rifle Manufacturing Company of Hartford, Connecticut. In 1861, the reliable and accurate Sharps carbine was standard issue for the United States cavalry. It used a cartridge with a powder chamber made of linen. Upon firing, the linen burned away, making the weapon easy to reload.

The world-renowned Colt Patent Arms Manufacturing Company, also located in Hartford, dominated the handgun field. Its six-shot revolver had been adopted as a sidearm for cavalrymen in 1847. The weapon's popularity in the civilian market made the name of its inventor, Samuel Colt, a household word.

Some 60 companies in New England, New York, and Pennsylvania also manufactured handguns. Like the famous Colt six-shooter, all of these weapons were rifled and had effective ranges of between 50 and 75 yards.

By the fall of 1861, just as the Confederate arms stocks were running low, blockade-runners brought in the first trickle of arms from Caleb Huse's purchases in England. They included several thousand top-quality Enfield rifles and rifle muskets that were the equal of any of the Springfields.

During his tour, Huse was in continual competition with Northern agents. He was as

6　　　**7**　　　**8**　　　**9**

the left hand. Seize its small end with the thumb and forefinger of the right hand. Press the ball home, holding the elbows near the body.

6 RETURN RAMMER: Draw the rammer halfway out. Grasp it near the muzzle with the right hand. Clear it from the bore by extending the arm. Turn it and insert it in the carrying groove. Force the rammer home by placing the little finger of the right hand on the head.

7 PRIME: With the left hand, raise the piece until the hand is as high as the eye. Half-face to the right, with the right foot at right angles to the left. Half-cock the hammer with the thumb of the right hand. Remove the old percussion cap. Take the new cap from the pouch. Place it on the nipple. Press the cap down with the thumb.

8 READY/AIM: Fully cock the hammer and seize the small of the stock with the right hand. Place the butt against the right shoulder. Incline the head to align the right eye with the sight. Close the left eye.

9 FIRE: Press trigger with forefinger.

successful fighting the Yankees on the commercial front as any Southern general was on the battlefields back home. From 1861 to 1865, between 300,000 and 325,000 European firearms were run past the Union blockade into the South, most of them purchased by Huse.

The imported weapon favored by Confederate officers, including the legendary generals Jeb Stuart and Pierre Gustave Toutant Beauregard, was the Le Mat revolver. Created by Dr. Jean Alexandre François Le Mat, a New Orleans physician, the weapon held nine .42-caliber rounds in a cylinder that revolved around an upper barrel, and a single load of buckshot that fired through a lower barrel of .63 caliber. A hammer that shifted up and down fired both the revolving cylinder and the buckshot barrel. Le Mat signed a contract to produce 5,000 of the weapons for the Confederacy, although nowhere near that number ever made it into the hands of Southern soldiers. When he was unable to secure the necessary machinery at home, Le Mat traveled to France and set up a factory in Paris.

Meanwhile, Southern agents scoured the countryside in search of civilian arms suitable for military use. One such agent was an itinerant minister in Louisiana named Ballard S. Dunn. Traveling in the area outside New Orleans during November and December 1861, the Reverend Dunn made his contribution to the Rebel cause by snapping up 946 weapons of various sorts. They included venerable flintlock and percussion-cap muskets, short-barreled muskets called musketoons, Kentucky and Mississippi rifles, and several varieties of shotgun.

Although the rural South was a nation of firearm owners, most families were reluctant to part with their weapons. Many people used them for hunting, and with most of the able-bodied young men away at war, the people at home preferred to keep their weapons handy to protect themselves against possible slave uprisings. Still, the use of privately owned sporting rifles and shotguns became so prevalent in the Confederate army that President Jefferson Davis approved a bill authorizing a monthly payment to any soldier who provided his own weapon.

Major Gorgas' great hope was to develop a weapons industry in the South with the arms-making equipment captured at Harpers Ferry as a foundation. The Confederate ordnance chief ordered the rifle-musket machinery seized there to be shipped to Richmond and installed in the armory, under the supervision of James Burton. In 1802, the building had been the site of a weapons factory for the state of Virginia. After a few decades of production, the factory fell into disuse, but the building continued to function as a small-arms repository and repair shop.

Under Burton's leadership, the Richmond Armory produced the lion's share of weapons turned out by the Confederate government. In addition, it refurbished many of the tens of thousands of weapons captured from Federal arsenals and on the battlefields.

Gorgas selected the former U.S. Arsenal at Fayetteville, North Carolina, as the site for the Harpers Ferry rifle-making machinery. Production began in the spring of 1862 and soon rose to about 350 rifles a month. The weapons were brass mounted, and most of them were designed to hold a saber bayonet. Each rifle's lock plate was stamped with the eagle from the old Harpers Ferry die, with the letters "U.S." cut out and "C.S.A." stamped in.

Gorgas also established a smaller rifle-making facility in Asheville, North Carolina, with machinery the government had purchased from a private armsmaker. In November of 1863, Gorgas, now a colonel, reported that "the armories at Richmond, Fayetteville, and Asheville have produced an aggregate of about 28,000 small arms within the year."

Later in the War, Gorgas set up several more government factories, including one in Richmond that produced about 3,000 copies of the Sharps carbine for the Confederate cavalry. In the fall of 1864, he moved its machinery to Tallassee, Alabama, to prevent capture by the Federals. He also set up a factory in Tyler, Texas, as a means of supplying the Confederate armies fighting west of the Mississippi River. But production there was extremely limited.

Meanwhile, Southern entrepreneurs scrambled to get into the arms business. In June of 1861, a private factory was established in New Orleans by two English brothers named Ferdinand and Francis Cook. Using steel from the Shelby Iron Works near Selma, Alabama, the Englishmen were soon producing 20 rifles a day. The September 26, 1861, issue of the *Memphis Daily Appeal* proudly wrote: "The rifle manufactory of Cook & Brother at New Orleans seems to have proved a complete success. Last week they shipped 50 rifles to the Sunflower Guards in Virginia with sword bayonet attachment, which were pronounced by competent judges to be far superior in strength, accuracy, and range to the original Enfield pattern after which they were made."

By the War's end, no fewer than 18 different firms were producing rifles and rifle muskets in the South and another 7 were making revolvers. But production was plagued by the chronic shortage of raw materials. Iron often had to be used in place of steel—a substitution that caused frequent delays in delivery, to say nothing of degrading the quality of the weapons that resulted. When iron ran low, brass—some of it melted down from donated church bells—was used to substitute for certain gun parts. When brass became scarce, the manufacturers used a combination of pewter and lead.

As the Union armies carried the war deeper and deeper into the South, many weapons manufacturers had to move their factories to safer locations. One of them, Charles H. Rigdon, shifted his revolver-making factory no fewer than four times. In New Orleans in 1862, the Cook brothers painstakingly dismantled their rifle-making machinery, loaded it on steamers, and headed up the Mississippi to Vicksburg. From there they journeyed to Alabama and then to Athens, Georgia, where they reestablished their business, only to find themselves, two years later, directly in the path of Sherman's march to the sea.

Given the almost unbelievable assortment of firearms circulating in the Confederacy, it is not surprising that few Confederate infantry units ever went into battle with all of the men carrying the same type of weapon. A typical regiment, the 10th South Carolina, armed one company with Enfield rifles, a second with Mississippi rifles, a third with Harpers Ferry rifle muskets made in Richmond, and the others with smoothbore muskets. The companies assigned to protect the regiment's flanks carried the best weapons, those in the center the less desirable ones.

Despite the heroic efforts of men like Gorgas, Burton, Huse, and others, in the end the rural South simply lacked the resources to compete in the field of arms technology with the much more populous, industrialized North. In 1863, Christopher Miner Spencer in Boston introduced a magazine-fed, breechloading rifle that was far better than anything the South could hope to produce. Called the Spencer, the weapon gave Federal armies an advantage only dreamed about by Southern commanders. As a Confederate major commented wistfully late in the War: "With a good breechloading rifle that cleans itself, a well-made tape cap and sword bayonet, our boys would prove invincible."

Shown brandishing a short bowie knife and clutching a flintlock altered for percussion firing, William B. Ott, a volunteer in the 4th Virginia Infantry, was killed on July 21, 1861, at First Manassas.

"Popguns and Cornstalks"

The raw recruits who rushed to serve the Confederacy in April 1861 boasted of being able to whip their Yankee counterparts with nothing more than "popguns and cornstalks." Little did they know that the weapons they would be issued were scarcely more effective than mock guns. Southern arsenals at the War's outset contained a mere 296,000 shoulder arms—largely a vintage assortment of antiquated flintlock muskets and altered percussion smoothbores. Only 24,305 modern rifles were available for the troops.

Most of the Confederates who saw early action were armed with .69-caliber muskets. Though deadly at close quarters, these unwieldy smoothbore weapons were notoriously inaccurate at distances of 100 yards or more. The unfortunates who toted them into battle were sometimes taunted by Federals who, recognizing the musket's limitations, cavorted brazenly just beyond their opponents' range of fire.

By late 1862, after a furious effort by the Confederacy to upgrade its outmoded stock of longarms, many of the Rebel soldiers had been issued a far-superior rifle musket, whose grooved barrel spun the bullet and gave it greater accuracy and a longer range than the ball shot from a smoothbore. Armed with a rifle musket, a Confederate marksman could hit a target as far as 600 yards away—making him a much more formidable enemy.

RICHMOND RIFLE MUSKET

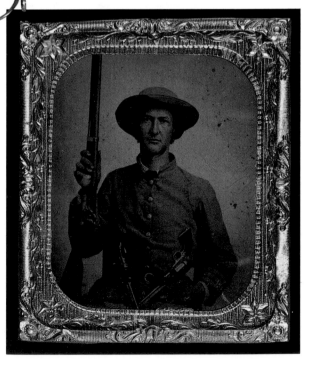

U.S. MODEL 1842 MUSKET

Retired as the standard infantry firearm in 1855, the U.S. Model 1842 musket was returned to service with the onset of hostilities in April 1861. Thousands of the .69-caliber smoothbores—the first regulation percussion muskets ever made—were stored in Southern arsenals before the War. Like the Confederate soldier at right, countless Confederates went into battle carrying Model 1842 muskets, even as late as December 1863. The muzzle of the weapon's 42-inch-long barrel could be fitted with a socket bayonet, as shown at far right.

D. NIPPES MODEL 1840 FLINTLOCK CONTRACT MUSKET

Some 5,600 of these antiquated Nippes—the last of the .69-caliber smoothbore flintlocks produced under government contract—were stored in the nation's arsenals at the War's outset. Although most were upgraded to percussion, others, like the one shown here, were issued with their flint firing systems still intact. Several thousand Confederates relied on these guns in the War's early years.

U.S. MODEL 1822 MUSKET, .69 CALIBER

The longarm that a majority of Confederate volunteers first carried into battle was likely to have been this smoothbore musket, originally a flintlock but altered to percussion by the thousands between 1843 and 1861. The ungainly weapon weighed more than 10 pounds and measured 57 inches long.

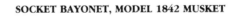

SOCKET BAYONET, MODEL 1842 MUSKET

Arms for Volunteers

The Confederacy's meager cache of modern firearms was snatched up by the South's regular state militias within weeks of the start of the War. The leavings—obsolete flintlocks and percussion smoothbores—were distributed among the throngs of impassioned volunteers who, initially at least, accepted them with little complaint.

It was not long, however, before infantrymen began to chafe at fumbling with flints and smoothbores while their Yankee counterparts carried percussion rifles. Even those Rebels familiar with the intricacies of firing a flintlock were hard-pressed to overcome the smoothbore's appalling inaccuracy.

So loath were Confederate foot soldiers to bear smoothbores that, in May 1861, several companies of the 28th Virginia mutinied, and, in the words of Jubal A. Early, Colonel of Volunteers, "declared that they would not take muskets." Only Early's dire threats of summary discharge and public disgrace persuaded the men to accept the weapons—all except eight holdout soldiers, who were hooted out of camp.

The Best of the Arsenal

Rebel soldiers who found themselves equipped with any of the newer weapons in the Confederacy's collection counted themselves lucky indeed. These fortunate few—most of whom were established state militiamen and early volunteers—enjoyed the slight edge afforded by the greater accuracy, longer killing range, and superior handling of guns like the much-prized "Harpers Ferry" and "Mississippi" rifles shown below.

This edge was turned to keen advantage at First Manassas in July 1861 by the 4th Alabama, a regiment outfitted with Mississippi rifles. According to one Confederate's account, the doughty Alabama men were shoring up the Confederate left flank when a Federal force, including the New York Fire Zouaves, advanced on the Rebel line. "Our Alabamians allow them to approach within 50 yards," the observer wrote, "when they deliver a volley from 800 Mississippi rifles, and scatter the Zouaves beyond all recall. Advance they will not. The morale of these braves was destroyed."

Two infantrymen of the ragtag 9th Mississippi display their brightly burnished Mississippi rifles while gathered around a campfire with compatriots in Pensacola, Florida.

U.S. MODEL 1855 RIFLE MUSKET

One of two standard arms listed in the Confederate officers' field-duty manual, the U.S. Model 1855 rifle musket was found in Southern arsenals in limited numbers before the War. Although Rebel infantrymen generally favored the .58-caliber firearm, they disliked its temperamental firing system, which substituted a roll of fulminate-studded primer tape for the familiar percussion cap.

U.S. MODEL 1855 RIFLE—"HARPERS FERRY" RIFLE

Confederate troops captured hundreds of these well-crafted, .58-caliber rifles when they seized the U.S. Armory at Harpers Ferry in 1861. The single-shot, muzzleloading weapon weighed just over 10 pounds and was seven inches shorter than its rifle musket predecessor, shown at top. Like the rifle musket, it was fitted for the Maynard tape primer percussion system.

U.S. MODEL 1841 "MISSISSIPPI" RIFLE

The Mississippi, considered one of the handsomest firearms of the Civil War, was a great favorite of the Confederate infantry and cavalry alike. Especially prized for its deadly long-range accuracy, the weapon was originally issued in .54 caliber, but many were rerifled after 1855 to the .58-caliber U.S. standard.

New Guns from Old

The individual states of the Confederacy supplemented their secessionist governments' efforts to arm Rebel forces by opening state arm reserves and by soliciting citizens for private firearms—double-barreled shotguns, sporting rifles, and old fowling pieces. In addition, the states awarded many contracts to small-gun manufacturers and repair shops for the fabrication and alteration of muskets and rifles.

On occasion, states retained private gunsmiths to refurbish small arms for a single state regiment. Such was the case with Thomas Riggins of Tennessee. At his Knoxville workshop, Riggins and 60 assistants labored day and night to convert country rifles and flintlocks into handy large-bore percussion carbines for the East Tennessee Squirrel Shooters, a volunteer cavalry regiment. By all accounts, Riggins' craftsmanship was excellent; a Riggins carbine, it was said, "got the beef."

.69-CAL. BUCK-AND-BALL CARTRIDGE

.69-CAL. ROUND BALL CARTRIDGE

MODEL 1842 "PALMETTO" MUSKET

South Carolina outfitted its militia with this well-made percussion musket, which was fabricated in the early 1850s by William Glaze & Company of Columbia. The distinctive insignia forward of the hammer—a palmetto tree—gave the .69-caliber smoothbore its nickname and marked it as uniquely Southern. The weapon was a virtual copy of the U.S. Model 1842 percussion musket.

VIRGINIA MANUFACTORY FLINTLOCK MUSKET, ALTERED

One of thousands of .69-caliber smoothbore flintlocks altered to percussion under state contract, this firearm was originally manufactured for the state militia in 1808 at the Virginia Manufactory in Richmond. Some 58,428 of the antiquated flintlocks were stored in the state arsenal until the War's onset, when Confederate authorities farmed them out to gun shops for emergency retooling.

ALTERED KENTUCKY RIFLE

The hard-pressed Confederate states transformed civilian hunting arms, such as the Kentucky rifle shown above and with the soldier at left, into serviceable military weapons by shortening their barrels, reboring them to a standard caliber, and fitting them with bayonets.

.69-CAL. MUSKET OR SHOTGUN AMMUNITION PACK

Weapons
from Yankee Land

SHARPS MODEL 1859 RIFLE

The .52-caliber Sharps rifle, fabricated
by the Sharps Rifle Manufacturing
Company of Hartford, Connecticut, was
the best-liked breechloading arm of the
Civil War. The rifle's breechblock dropped
down when the trigger-guard lever was
pulled down, exposing the bore. A
cartridge covered with linen *(below)* was
inserted. Southern arsenals managed to
acquire about 1,600 of these weapons in
the months leading up to the War.

.52-CAL. C.S. SHARPS CARTRIDGE

WHITNEY ENFIELD RIFLE MUSKET

Less than a year before the outbreak of hostilities, Mississippi and Georgia contracted with the Northern armsmaker Eli Whitney of New Haven, Connecticut, for the delivery of some 2,000 of these .58-caliber rifle muskets. Other Southern states purchased an unknown number of Whitney Enfields before May 1861, when Federal intervention finally halted the illicit arms trade.

ROBBINS & LAWRENCE MODEL 1841 CONTRACT RIFLE

Among the better-made contract rifles on the market prior to the War were those patterned on the Model 1841 Mississippi rifle, such as this .54-caliber Robbins & Lawrence. Two thousand of the 15,000 manufactured for the U.S. Ordnance Department were stored in the Baton Rouge Arsenal *(below)* at the outbreak of hostilities.

Only a month before it was seized by Louisiana state authorities, the Baton Rouge Arsenal was still receiving Federal-issue arms from the Springfield Armory in Massachusetts. Such weapons transfers resulted from a standing order issued in 1859 by U.S. Secretary of War Floyd to periodically supply Southern arsenals with arms from Northern inventories. Accordingly, some 18,500 percussion muskets, 11,420 altered muskets, and 2,000 rifles were shipped to the Baton Rouge Arsenal in 1860 and 1861.

1853 ENFIELD RIFLE MUSKET
The standard weapon of the British army, the .577-caliber Enfield weighed more than nine pounds and measured 55 inches. It was reasonably accurate up to 1,000 yards.

ENFIELD RIFLE
The Enfield rifle, eight inches shorter than the rifle musket, was a favorite of the Confederate light infantry. Its blued barrel had a spring clasp that secured a sword bayonet *(right)* to the gun's muzzle.

AUSTRIAN LORENZ RIFLE MUSKET
The Lorenz, the most frequently imported weapon after the Enfield, was issued in calibers from .54 to .59 inches. The .54-caliber version was heavily used by the Army of Tennessee and units in the Western theater.

Arms from the Old World

To supplement its limited store of armaments, the Confederacy dispatched Captain Caleb Huse to Europe in April 1861 to purchase foreign weapons. Huse's efforts unleashed a westward flood of small arms, which a French military observer labeled "the refuse of all Europe."

In truth, the quality of imported Confederate guns varied greatly. The 400,000 British Enfield rifle muskets smuggled past Federal blockades ranked as Confederate favorites, second in popularity only to the much-coveted Springfields.

Other imports performed less admirably. Most of the Austrian firearms—the Lorenz *(above)* excepted—were horrors of shoddy workmanship. Likewise, the uneven bores and crooked barrels of Belgian imports earned them the dubious epithet of "pumpkin slingers."

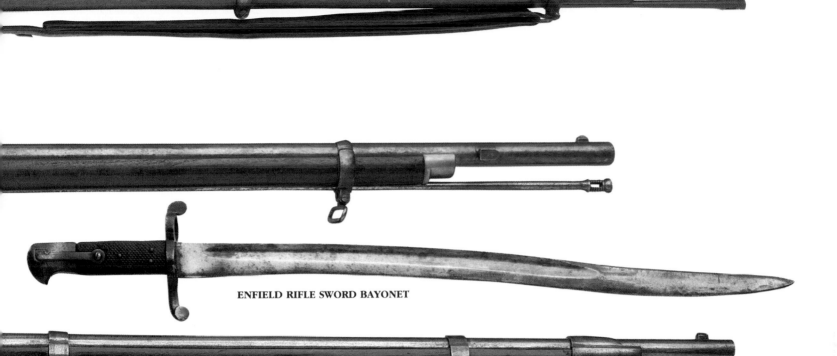

ENFIELD RIFLE SWORD BAYONET

Confederate infantryman Hugh Lawson Duncan of the 39th Georgia proudly displays a British Enfield rifle musket in this photo, most likely taken at the time of his enlistment in March 1862.

Bolstering the Enfield rifle musket's broad popularity was its .577 caliber, which permitted the Rebels to use American- or British-made cartridges *(top)* housing either the .58 Confederate bullet *(middle)* or the custom English slug *(bottom)*.

RICHMOND ARMORY LOCK PLATES, 1861-1863

The lock plate of a longarm *(above)* fabricated at the Richmond Armory bears the pronounced hump characteristic of metalwork struck from captured Harpers Ferry dies. Its peculiar shape was designed to support the Maynard tape primer system, which the Confederates—for reasons of economy or expedience—chose to leave off. When the Federal tooling wore out, armory mechanics made new dies that minimized the hump, as shown in the lock plate at right. A "C.S." was added to the "Richmond, Va." marking on lock plates forged after 1862.

A Federal Bounty

"Although we have upon our side the best engineers and artillerists of the old service, we have never yet succeeded in making pieces equal to those brought into the field by the enemy. In fact, it is dangerous to use guns of our own manufacture," bemoaned one Confederate in his memoirs.

The soldier's lament was, unfortunately, true—with the exception, that is, of the longarms produced at the Rebel armories in Richmond, Virginia, and Fayetteville, North Carolina. Just a week into the War, the Confederacy seized the U.S. Armory at Harpers Ferry and transferred what amounted to more than one-third of the Federal government's stock of arms-producing machinery to these arsenals. Using the superior Union equipment, Confederate gunsmiths turned out more than 64,000 of the exceptionally fine firearms featured below.

.58-CAL. GARDNER CARTRIDGE

.58-CAL. AMMUNITION PACK, CONFEDERATE-MADE

SOCKET BAYONET FOR RICHMOND RIFLE MUSKET

RICHMOND RIFLE MUSKET AND FAYETTEVILLE RIFLE

Near-exact replicas of the U.S. Model 1855/61 rifle musket and the U.S. Model 1855 rifle, these weapons were produced on machinery taken from the Harpers Ferry armory. The lock plate of the .58-caliber Richmond rifle musket *(top)* was cast from Richmond Armory dies that reduced the hump found on early-production Richmond arms and Model 1855 rifle muskets. Unlike its Union forerunner, the 56-inch-long gun employed a percussion cap. Similarly, the Maynard primer hump on the Fayetteville rifle lock plate was eliminated entirely from this late-production arm *(bottom)*, which also featured a butt plate and nose cap of brass rather than iron.

From Southern Shops

TYLER TEXAS RIFLE

This .58-caliber rifle is one of only 4 that remain from the approximately 3,000 made at the Tyler Ordnance Works in Tyler, Texas. Assembled from castoff parts of country rifles, Enfields, Hall carbines, and sundry musket barrels, Tyler Texas rifles share only one commonality: the single screw fixing the lock plate to the stock *(right)*. This feature, characteristic of hunting rifles, is traceable to the armory's original owner, J. C. Short, who manufactured sporting arms before turning to military ordnance. In fall 1863, the Confederate government purchased Short's firm and transferred additional equipment from defunct armories at Little Rock, Camden, and Arkadelphia, Arkansas, to the Tyler facility.

COOK & BROTHER RIFLE

Modeled on the British Enfield, this .58-caliber rifle was distinguished by its Stars and Bars trademark. It was one of 7,200 weapons manufactured at the New Orleans-based Cook & Brother Armory, the Confederacy's largest private arms producer. Union occupation forced the Cook brothers, Ferdinand and Francis, to relocate the firm to Athens, Georgia, in 1862, where production continued until July 1864.

COOK & BROTHER MUSKETOON

The .58-caliber barrel of this muzzleloading, Enfield-type musketoon was nine inches shorter than its rifle counterpart. The number of musketoons manufactured by Cook & Brother is not known, but was probably fewer than a thousand. The barrels of most, if not all, of the guns were finished with brown lacquer.

By and for
the States

DAVIS & BOZEMAN RIFLE

Under state contract, Davis & Bozeman in Central, Alabama, manufactured about 900 of these Mississippi-model arms between October 1863 and November 1864. The .58-caliber rifles had 33-inch, brass-mounted barrels and brass butt plates. On the breech was stamped "D. & B. ALA." and the date. The armorers Henry Davis and David Bozeman also repaired and altered firearms for Alabama.

GEORGIA ARMORY RIFLE

"The 'Georgia Rifle' is a beautiful piece of workmanship, not surpassed by any arm manufactured in the United States or in Europe," boasted the Milledgeville *Southern Recorder* of August 12, 1862. During the War, 125 rifles a month were fabricated at the Georgia Armory in Milledgeville. The guns varied in design, but, like the rifle above, were typically .58 caliber with brass fittings.

GREENWOOD & GRAY/J. P. MURRAY RIFLE

This .58-caliber rifle took its name from the English superintendent of the Greenwood & Gray gun factory, J. P. Murray, who advertised in the *Columbus Sun* of March 31, 1863, for "50 good gunsmiths and machinists, to whom as good wages as is given in the Southern Confederacy will be paid." The Georgia firm produced 262 of these Mississippi-pattern arms for Alabama from 1863 to 1864.

MENDENHALL, JONES & GARDNER RIFLE

Some 80 gunsmiths toiling in a former flour mill on Deep River in Jamestown, North Carolina, produced 2,000 of these Model 1841 Mississippi-style rifles on contract to the state of North Carolina between April 1862 and November 1864. The Mendenhall, Jones & Gardner contract originally called for the delivery of 10,000 such arms, each .58 caliber with an iron butt plate and bayonet lug.

SAWED-OFF SHOTGUN

One of the principal arms of the Confederate cavalry was the sawed-off, double-barreled shotgun. This sporting gun's 12-gauge barrels have been shortened to allow for easier handling on horseback. Each barrel fired a 12-pellet round of buckshot.

RICHMOND CARBINE
Like other "Richmond" longarms, this .58-caliber rifle muzzleloader was manufactured at the Richmond Armory on machinery captured from the Harpers Ferry arsenal. Five thousand were made.

COOK CARBINE
Cook & Brother Armory, initially of New Orleans and later of Athens, Georgia, produced a limited number of these Model 1853 British Enfield-pattern muzzleloaders for the Confederate government. The .577-caliber cavalry weapon was 37 inches long.

BILHARZ, HALL & CO. CARBINE
This .58-caliber muzzleloader, patterned on the Model 1855 Springfield rifle carbine, was made in 1863 by Bilharz, Hall & Company of Pittsylvania Courthouse, Virginia, under a Confederacy contract.

Cavalryman's Choice

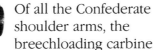

Of all the Confederate shoulder arms, the breechloading carbine was the hardest to come by. This short-barreled weapon, prized by cavalry for its handiness, was never produced in quantity, even in Federal armories; only a few thousand were stockpiled in Southern arsenals prior to the War.

Except for this scanty allotment—and the few thousand breechloaders bought on the Northern market in 1860 or scavenged off the battlefield—Southern cavalry was largely limited to unwieldy, muzzleloading arms. Of these, cavalrymen preferred carbines, but many had to carry the longer infantry rifles. Even born-in-the-saddle Rebels found it next to impossible to load such weapons on a moving horse while under hostile fire—and live to load again.

Many Confederate cavalrymen came to rely on sawed-off shotguns. At close range, a regiment armed with 12-gauges was a formidable force indeed; according to one Confederate account, such a force of horsemen once scattered with a single discharge "400 of the enemy whom three of our regiments had vainly tried to dislodge."

MAYNARD CARBINE, EARLY MODEL

"Nothing to do with Maynard but load her up, turn her North, and pull the trigger. If 20 of them don't clean out all Yankeedom, then I'm a liar," reported a Confederate private in the *Intelligencer* of Oxford, Mississippi. Georgia, Florida, and Mississippi bought 2,369 of these .35- and .50-caliber breechloaders from the Massachusetts Arms Company between 1860 and 1861. A trigger guard released the breech *(right)*, which accepted a custom metallic cartridge.

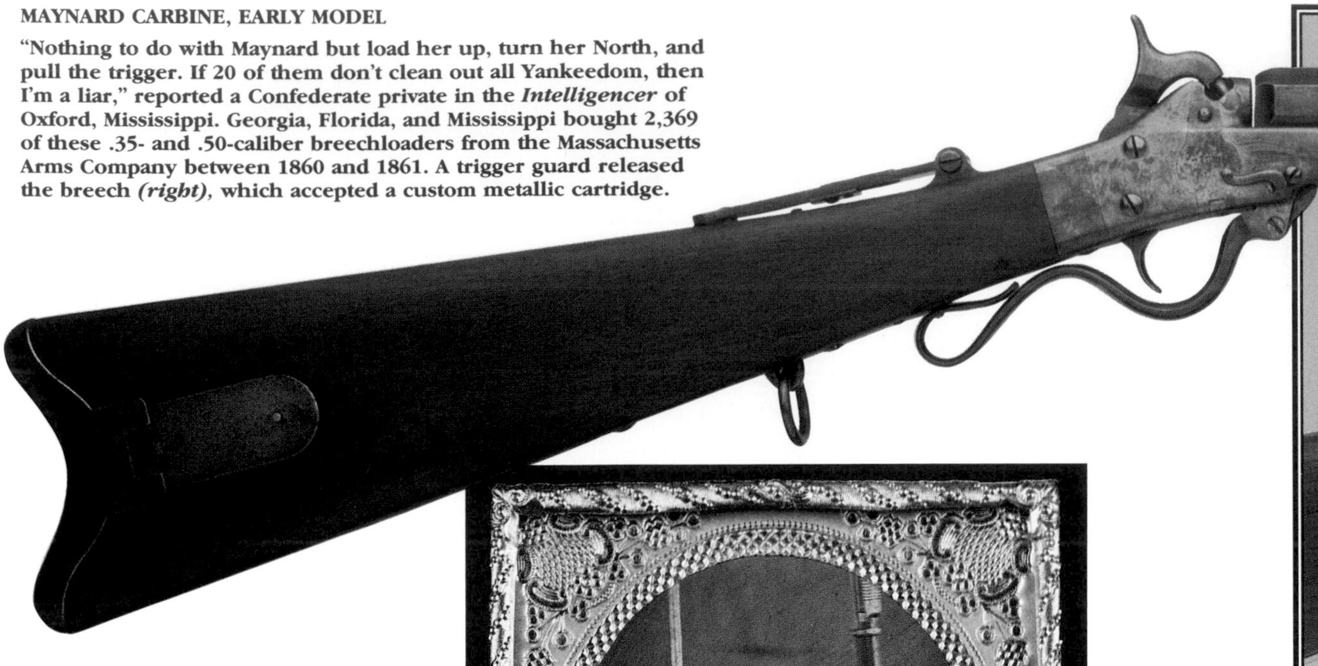

FIRST SERGEANT CHARLES POWELL, 24TH NORTH CARO-LINA, WITH COLT CARBINE

U.S. MODEL 1833 HALL CARBINE

At the outset of the War, Southern arsenals contained 1,881 Hall breechloading carbines. The .52-caliber smoothbore Model 1833 shown here was produced exclusively by Simeon North of Middletown, Connecticut. So well made that its parts were interchangeable from one gun to another, the Hall smoothbore had a spur-release lever that opened the breech *(right)* to receive a paper cartridge.

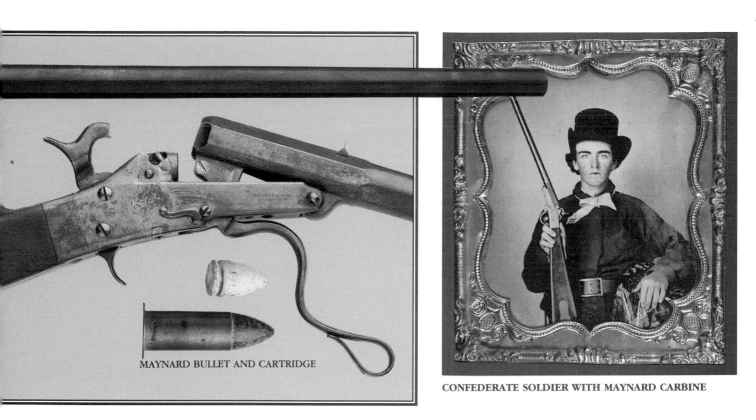

MAYNARD BULLET AND CARTRIDGE

CONFEDERATE SOLDIER WITH MAYNARD CARBINE

COLT REPEATING PERCUSSION CARBINE, MODEL 1855

Despite its rapid-fire design, the Colt repeating carbine was not popular with the Confederate troops because of its complex and unreliable construction. The Colt Patent Arms Manufacturing Company of Hartford, Connecticut, fabricated 4,435 of these breechloading six-shooters in .36, .44, and .56 calibers, some of which were purchased by Southern states before the War. Above is a typical .56-caliber arm.

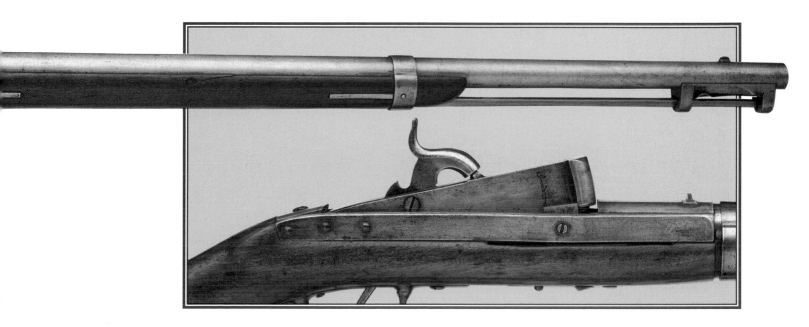

48

RICHMOND SHARPS CARBINE

The Richmond Sharps, the commonest of the Confederate breech-loaders, was a copy of the Sharps carbine. Some 5,000 of these .52-caliber firearms were produced between late 1862 and the War's end by S. C. Robinson Company and the Confederate government.

Southern Breechloaders

Confederate attempts to manufacture breechloading carbines were severely hampered by the South's lack of technical expertise and its dearth of tools and materials. The few armories that undertook production of these sought-after cavalry arms were plagued with complaints about their quality and peformance.

General Robert E. Lee wrote of the Richmond Sharps carbine that it was "so defective as to be demoralizing to our men." The *Richmond Whig* of March 30, 1863, reported that during a test firing of nine Confederate Sharps, seven barrels burst.

Later research revealed, however, that such failures were more often the result of improper handling than of poor workmanship.

Ironically, the one breechloader whose operation was largely beyond reproach—the Morse—used specialized ammunition that was difficult to make and was always in short supply.

KEEN, WALKER & CO. CARBINE

In 1862, Keen, Walker & Company of Danville, Virginia, manufactured 282 of these well-crafted, .52-caliber carbines, known variously as "Confederate Perry" or "Tiltling Breech" carbines. When the serpentinc lcvcr in front of the trigger was pulled down, the forward end of the breechblock rose, permitting easy loading.

BILHARZ, HALL & CO. CARBINE

Among the rarest of the Rebel-made breechloaders was the "Rising Breech" carbine manufactured by Bilharz, Hall & Company of Pittsylvania Courthouse, Virginia. Unlatching and lowering the trigger guard *(left)* forced the breechblock, with its loading chamber, above the bore. A .54-caliber paper or sheepskin cartridge could then he inserted into the chamber. Closing the trigger guard reseated the breechblock and readied the gun for firing.

MORSE CARBINE

The Morse carbine, made at the Greenville Military Works to arm the South Carolina State Militia, was the most advanced of the Confederate breechloaders. Opening the hinged lever over the breech slid the breechblock backward, revealing the loading chamber. The carbine accepted only a special center-fire, .50-caliber Morse cartridge, which housed bullet, powder charge, and primer inside a single metallic casing. Fewer than 1,000 of these fine weapons were produced.

LEONARD TARGET RIFLE

This sniper rifle, handcrafted by George O. Leonard, Jr., of New Hampshire, was found on July 5, 1863, at Gettysburg in the Devil's Den near Round Top. The hefty 36-pound percussion target rifle was fitted with a precision telescopic sight for hairsplitting accuracy up to 1,000 yards. The engraving "H.C.P. CSA, 1862" on the stock's silver plate identified the gun as Confederate.

The Sharpshooter's Pride

"From a distance of nearly half a mile, the Rebel sharpshooters drew a bead on us with a precision that deserved the highest commendation of their officers, but that made us curse the day they were born," wrote the Union soldier William Henry De Forest. Indeed, Rebel snipers—often perched in trees or concealed in rocky outcroppings—fired their sharpshooting rifles with deadly effect.

Only crack shots were selected to be-come Confederate sharpshooters. In many regiments, soldiers chosen as sharpshooters were exempted from all camp and guard duty; instead they drilled six hours a day on distance estimation and marksmanship using special, superaccurate rifles such as the ones shown above. Confederate snipers served as part of regular infantry regiments until the final year of the War, when they were drafted into sharpshooter battalions.

BRITISH-MADE WHITWORTH BULLET

BRITISH WHITWORTH RIFLE

When outfitted with a telescopic sight, the Whitworth had a killing range of 1,500 yards, making it the undisputed favorite of Rebel sharpshooters. Its twisting hexagonal bore imparted a lethal steadiness to the flight of the bullet and gave the .45-caliber rifle phenomenal accuracy. Beginning in late 1862, the Confederacy imported a small number of them from the Whitworth Rifle Company of Manchester, England.

BRITISH-MADE WHITWORTH TUBE CARTRIDGE

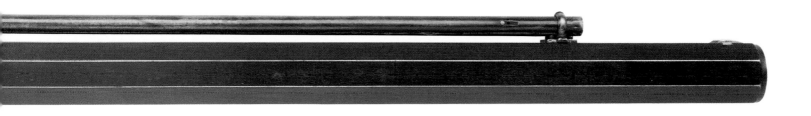

A Fateful Boast at Spotsylvania

Major Charles Whittier cradles the head of Union General John Sedgwick as Captain Richard Halstead vainly feels for a pulse. Sedgwick and members of his VI Corps were overseeing the placement of Union front-line artillery at Spotsylvania when Confederate sharpshooters some 800 yards distant spied them. As sniper fire began whizzing overhead, Sedgwick strode boldly over to a cowering soldier, saying, "Why, what are you dodging for? They could not hit an elephant at that distance." No sooner had Sedgwick spoken than a bullet from a Rebel's Whitworth ripped into his left cheek, killing him instantly. "His loss to this army is greater than the loss of a whole division of troops," lamented U. S. Grant on hearing of Sedgwick's death.

Handguns for Rebels

One of the first things a Southern volunteer grabbed as he left home to join the Rebel forces was the family handgun.. Given the choice, he picked a revolver with a rifled bore over an old single-shot, smoothbore "horse pistol." Revolvers with rifled barrels were more accurate, faster firing, and easier to load. But, as many volunteers soon discovered, they were useless to an infantryman, dangerous in camp, and an encumbrance on the march.

Cavalrymen, however, found the easy-handling, short-range handguns perfectly suited to the close confines of cavalry warfare. Unfortunately, not enough of them could be acquired in the weapons-poor South to arm the mounted ranks.

Early in the conflict, a Confederate ordnance officer came up with a practical approach to the problem, which he presented to Secretary of War Benjamin in March of 1862. "I respectfully suggest that you disarm the infantry," he wrote. "In this way enough pistols could be obtained for all the cavalry and the infantry could get money for an arm that is of no service." Benjamin obliged.

To supply most of its handguns, the Confederacy captured thousands of Northern pistols, imported others, and manufactured some of its own, most of which were copies of the famed Colts.

COLT "ARMY" REVOLVER
The preferred sidearm of the Rebel soldier was this .44-caliber 1860 Colt "Army," a six-shot revolver made by the Colt Patent Arms Manufacturing Company. The Army's percussion ignition system was among the most reliable and efficient ever devised.

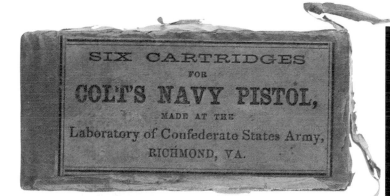

.44-CAL. CARTRIDGE

Colt cartridges of paper, foil, or sheepskin were issued in ammunition packs of six.

William B. Todd of Company E, 9th Virginia Cavalry, posed for this photograph with his Colt Army revolver.

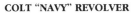

COLT "NAVY" REVOLVER

The Colt "Navy" Revolver differed from the Army model in several aspects, including its .36 caliber. A great many of the Colt models used by Confederates were privately owned, although some had been bought by Confederate agents early in 1861. The weapons had attached loading levers for tamping down cartridges in each of the six chambers.

Early Sidearms

Tucked into the belt of this 1st Virginia Cavalry soldier is a Massachusetts Adams revolver. The unidentified Confederate was among the volunteers who received one of the coveted Adams handguns purchased by the state of Virginia before the War.

MASSACHUSETTS ADAMS REVOLVER

A number of these .36-caliber, double-action revolvers were purchased by Southern states before the War and were issued to Confederate volunteers. Around 700 of them had been produced by the Massachusetts Arms Company of Chicopee Falls and acquired by the Federal government between 1857 and 1861. Patterned on the British Adams & Deane pistol, each weighed a little over two and a half pounds and had a six-inch-long rifled barrel.

U.S. ASTON HORSE PISTOL, MODEL 1842

Considered one of the best military single-shot percussion pistols ever made, the U.S. Aston was produced for the Federal Ordnance Department by the armsmaker Henry Aston of Middletown, Connecticut. Between mid-1840 and mid-1850, Aston crafted 30,000 of the .54-caliber smoothbore pistols at a cost of $6.50 each. Many were carried by Southerners.

PALMETTO ARMORY PISTOL, MODEL 1842

Except for the distinctive "Palmetto Armory" stamp on the lock plate and the absence of a rear sight, the Palmetto pistol was identical to the U.S. Aston horse pistol (above). In 1851, the state of South Carolina authorized the metalworker William Glaze and the Massachusetts armory superintendent Benjamin Flagg to produce 2,000 of the pistols at the Palmetto Armory in Columbia. They were used extensively by South Carolina troops.

ADAMS & DEANE REVOLVER

The .44-caliber, double-action Adams was highly regarded by Confederate officers. Exceptionally well made, the five-shooter was imported from the London Armoury Company in England. Ordnance records indicate that the state of Virginia received a shipment of 999 of the handguns as early as January 21, 1861.

KERR REVOLVER

The .44-caliber Kerr, imported from the London Armoury Company, saw more action in the hands of more Confederate cavalrymen than all Southern-manufactured handguns combined. Touted as the equal of any Northern-made revolver, the five-shot Kerr could be fired single or double action. Several thousand were run through the blockade between 1861 and 1865.

Prized Arms from Abroad

Many of the finest Confederate handguns were imports. Major General James Ewell Brown ("Jeb") Stuart was said to have favored his French Le Mat, a formidable nine-shooter. Moments before he was felled at Yellow Tavern, Virginia, Stuart reportedly fired a volley from his Le Mat into the 5th Michigan's troopers, helping to scatter their ranks and check the Federal advance. Unfortunately for him, his spirited salvo was answered by the shot that would kill him.

The largest single producer of imported handguns for the South was the London Armoury Company, manufacturer of the Adams & Deane and the Kerr revolvers. Beginning in 1861, thousands of these high-quality arms were shipped from London through the Federal blockade to numerous Southern ports.

LE MAT REVOLVER

Capable of delivering nine successive shots followed by a single burst of buckshot, the .40-caliber Le Mat packed greater firepower than any other Civil War handgun. Its cylinder revolved around a .63-caliber shotgun barrel beneath a conventional rifled pistol barrel. The Confederacy imported 1,500 Le Mats from Paris and London.

.41-CAL. LE MAT BULLET

.41-CAL. LE MAT CARTRIDGE

.63-CAL. LE MAT BUCKSHOT
CARTRIDGE

Made in the South

At the outbreak of war, not a single pistol manufacturer existed anywhere in the South. Within a year, however, many patriots and opportunists, lured by the Confederacy's promise of interest-free loans and lucrative contracts, had started up handgun factories.

Only three, Griswold & Gunnison, Leech & Rigdon, and Spiller & Burr, ever achieved credible production quotas. By all accounts, the pistols they manufactured—replicas of Northern Colts and Whitneys—were well-made arms. But the weapons did suffer from inferior metal castings. In the Civil War South, steel was nearly impossible to come by. Confederate gunsmiths substituted weaker metals such as brass and iron, which they obtained by hook or crook—often by melting candlesticks and church bells.

An unidentified Rebel soldier poses with a Colt Navy revolver or a Confederate look-alike.

GRISWOLD & GUNNISON REVOLVER

Twenty-two slaves and two overseers working at a converted cotton-gin factory in Griswoldsville, Georgia, turned out 3,606 of these Colt-model, .36-caliber revolvers between 1862 and 1864. Brass was substituted for hard-to-get steel in the pistol's frame.

SPILLER & BURR REVOLVER

Spiller & Burr of Atlanta, and later of Macon, Georgia, manufactured about 760 of these .36-caliber revolvers, copies of the Federal Whitney, between 1863 and 1864. The gun's brass frame extended over the breech to prevent the iron barrel from cracking when fired.

LEECH & RIGDON

Considered the finest of the Confederate-made Colts, the Leech & Rigdon revolver had a .36-caliber, dragoon-type iron barrel and an iron frame with brass back straps and trigger guard. Some 1,500 of these six-shot percussion pistols were produced during the War.

EDGED WEAPONS

Brigadier General Samuel Garland, Jr., was killed in the battle for South Mountain, in Maryland, on September 14, 1862, as he tried to rally his North Carolina regiments against a Federal division attacking Fox's Gap. His commander, General D. H. Hill, said that Garland had "no superiors and few equals in the service."

A Waning Tradition of Swords and Sabers

The hallowed weapon of the great classical warriors, the sword held a romantic appeal for many Confederates. In the Civil War, it served both as weapon and symbol of rank. In the prewar era, many cavalrymen considered the traditional saber their principal weapon. But since cavalry charges were seldom practical in the overgrown terrain of the eastern United States, nearly all cavalrymen came to rely on pistols and carbines. Artillerymen were often issued short swords to defend themselves, but they too turned to revolvers in increasing numbers.

Infantry officers wore swords but used them in combat only as weapons of last resort. Staff officers and generals carried swords mainly as a badge of office. (Stonewall Jackson's sword was drawn so seldom that it eventually rusted in its scabbard.)

Most Confederate swords were variations on U.S. Army models and were made in the South by a number of manufacturers. Many officers, however, wore imported sabers, some carried family heirlooms, and others who had served in the prewar army retained their U.S. swords.

BRIG. GEN. SAMUEL GARLAND, JR.
The grip and blade of this foot officer's sword worn by Garland at the time of his death are etched with a floral design. As the inscription on the scabbard records, the sword was presented to Garland in 1860 by the Lynchburg Home Guard, a militia company he organized that was mustered into Confederate service as Company G of the 11th Virginia Infantry.

Prewar Officers' Swords

GEN. THOMAS J. "STONEWALL" JACKSON
Jackson carried his old U.S. Army field and staff officer's sword with him throughout the Shenandoah Valley campaign.

1840 U.S. LIGHT ARTILLERY SABER
Based on a Prussian pattern, the 1840 saber was common in the Confederate army.

BRIG. GEN. MICAH JENKINS
The throat of Jenkins' scabbard was struck by a bullet the same day he was fatally shot by a Confederate soldier at the Wilderness—May 6, 1864. Ironically, Jenkins had once commented that no Yankee bullet could kill him.

GEN. ISAAC R. TRIMBLE
Made by Ames Manufacturing of Chicopee, Massachusetts, Trimble's sword is an example of the 1850 U.S. foot officer's sword.

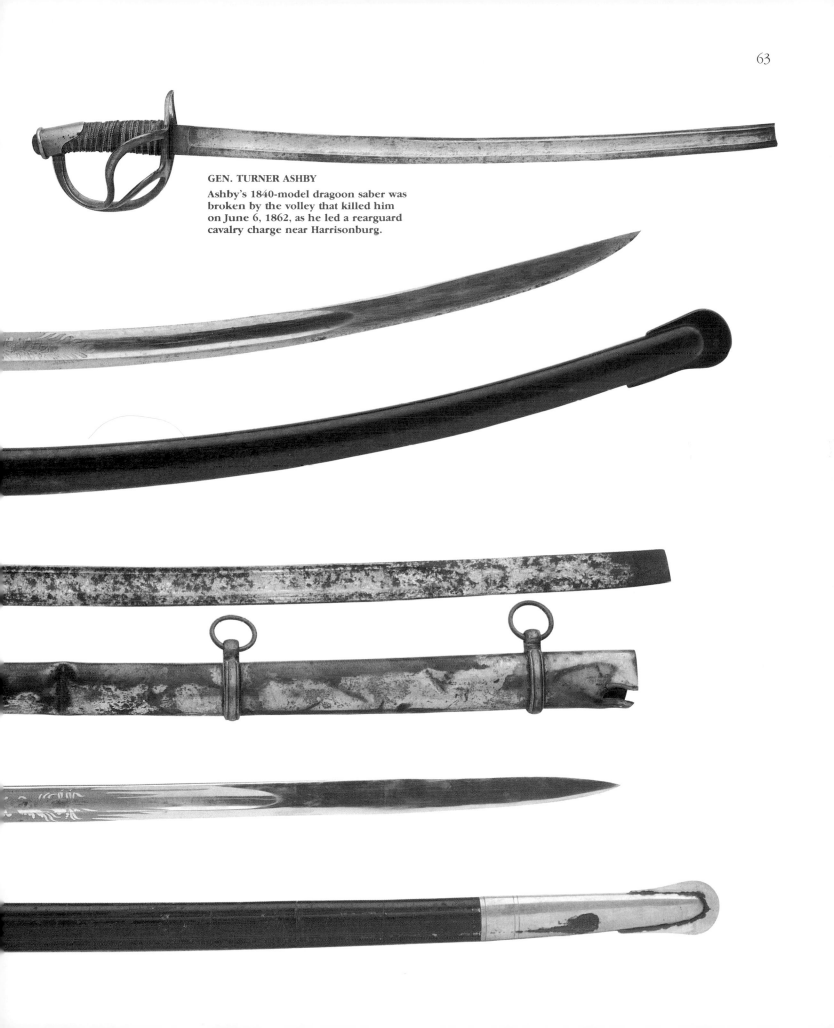

GEN. TURNER ASHBY

Ashby's 1840-model dragoon saber was broken by the volley that killed him on June 6, 1862, as he led a rearguard cavalry charge near Harrisonburg.

Militia Blades

GEN. BRAXTON BRAGG

The city of Mobile presented the sword and scabbard below to Bragg upon his return from the Mexican War.

BRIG. GEN. WILLIAM BARKSDALE

An eagle's head pommel—a popular motif of the early 19th century—adorns General Barksdale's militia officer's sword.

CAPT. W. M. BECKHAM

The cross-guard design of this ornate sword and scabbard owned by Captain Beckham of the 24th South Carolina was widely popular on the eve of the War.

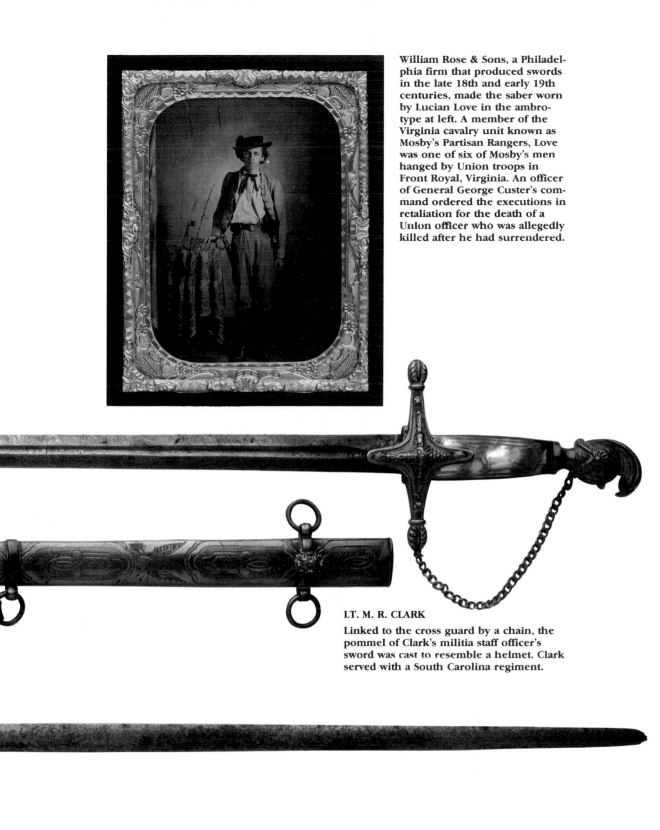

William Rose & Sons, a Philadelphia firm that produced swords in the late 18th and early 19th centuries, made the saber worn by Lucian Love in the ambrotype at left. A member of the Virginia cavalry unit known as Mosby's Partisan Rangers, Love was one of six of Mosby's men hanged by Union troops in Front Royal, Virginia. An officer of General George Custer's command ordered the executions in retaliation for the death of a Union officer who was allegedly killed after he had surrendered.

LT. M. R. CLARK

Linked to the cross guard by a chain, the pommel of Clark's militia staff officer's sword was cast to resemble a helmet. Clark served with a South Carolina regiment.

Virginia Swords

SWORD OF CAPT. JOHN R. JOHNSON

CAPT. JAMES M. CARRINGTON

Commander of the Charlottesville Artillery, Carrington wore this sword made by McKennie & Company of Charlottesville.

MAJ. EDWARD S. MARSH

The counterguard of Marsh's sword, crafted by Boyle & Gamble of Richmond, bears the letters "CS." Marsh fought with the 4th North Carolina Infantry.

COL. WILLIAM R. AYLETT

An officer of the 53d Virginia, Aylett lost this sword and scabbard, made by Boyle, Gamble & McFee, at the Battle of Gettysburg.

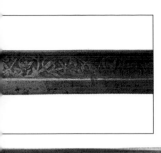

Inscribed with his name and an artillery scene, Captain Johnson's sword was made by Burger & Brothers of Richmond. Johnson was captured at Gettysburg.

Sporting a top hat captured from a Union soldier, Luther Hart Clapp of the 37th Virginia Infantry posed with sword and scabbard for the camera. Clapp's sword was made by the Richmond firm of Boyle & Gamble.

Southern-Made Swords

Regulation saber in hand, this unknown cavalry lieutenant with the Army of Northern Virginia struck a formal pose for the camera.

STAFF AND FIELD OFFICER'S SWORD

The Confederate States Armory in Kenansville, North Carolina, produced the sword above. Despite its name, the firm had no official ties to the government.

LT. HAMILTON BRANCH

This foot officer's sword carried by Lieutenant Branch, who fought with the 54th Georgia Infantry, was made by William J. McElroy & Company of Macon, Georgia.

BRIG. GEN. DANIEL W. ADAMS

Crafted by Leech & Rigdon of Memphis, the field officer's sword above was presented to General Adams on July 1, 1861.

CAVALRY OFFICER'S SABER

The weapon above was made by the Nashville Plow Works, a firm that turned plowshares into swords once the War began.

Swords from New Orleans

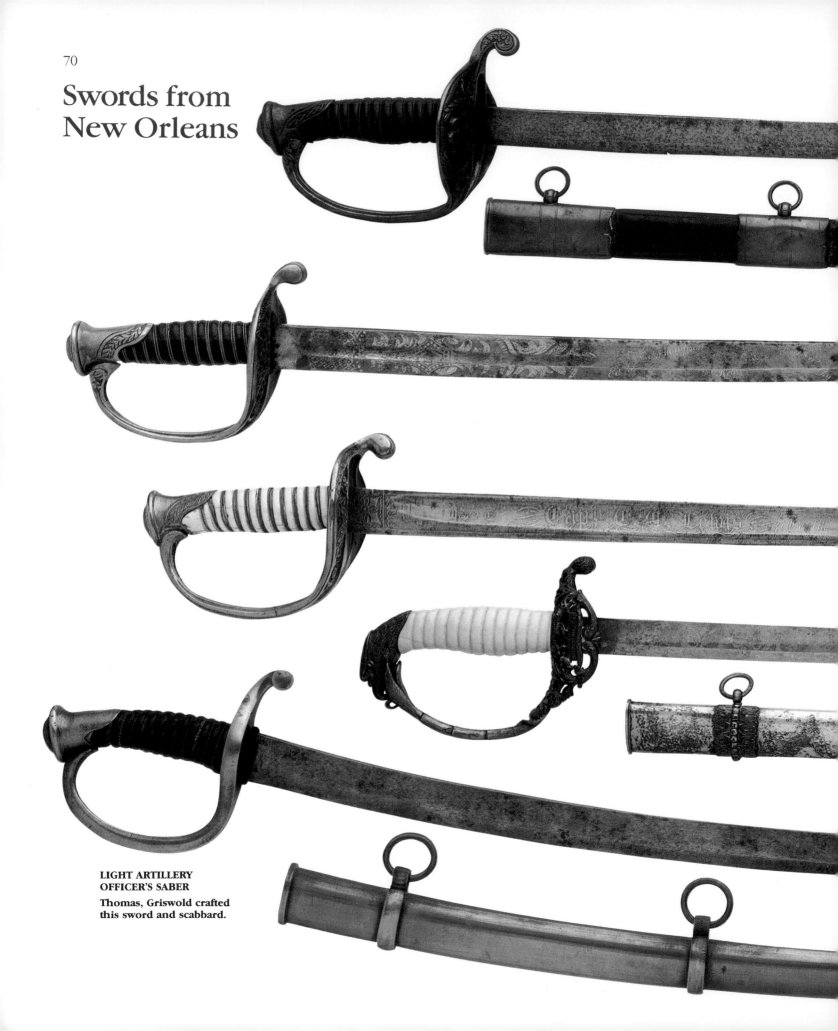

**LIGHT ARTILLERY
OFFICER'S SABER**
Thomas, Griswold crafted
this sword and scabbard.

LT. R. C. BOND
Bond's saber was made by A. H. Dufilho.

CAPT. EDWARD PORTER THOMPSON
A member of the 6th Kentucky, Thompson carried this Thomas, Griswold & Company sword.

CAPT. C. C. LEWIS
Dufilho made this sword worn by Captain Lewis, who served with the Confederate Guards Artillery.

CAPT. JOHN ROY
Roy's weapon was made by Thomas, Griswold.

Presentation Models

GEN. STERLING PRICE

Crafted by Thomas, Griswold & Company, the fancifully decorated sword at right was awarded to Price by the city of New Orleans in early 1862 after his victory at Lexington, Missouri. The ivory grip takes the form of an ear of corn; its gold guard combines a stalk of hemp, a tobacco leaf, grapes, and a cotton boll.

BRIG. GEN. JOHN McCAUSLAND

This filigree sword with scabbard was given to McCausland by the citizens of Lynchburg, Virginia, for his role in defending the city in June 1864. A newspaper, soliciting public subscriptions to pay for the gift, suggested, "Let the individual contributions be small, so that all may contribute something to this memento of our gratitude."

**MAJ. GEN.
PATRICK R. CLEBURNE**

A shamrock adorns the hilt of this sword *(right)* given to the Irish-born Cleburne by the 15th Arkansas in 1863. Engraved on the scabbard is the "Harp of Erin."

GEN. BRAXTON BRAGG

Made by L. Bissonnet of Mobile, Alabama, the sword at left was presented to General Bragg by the men of his escort guard, a Louisiana cavalry company led by Captain Guy Dreux. The sword features a beaded and scalloped guard.

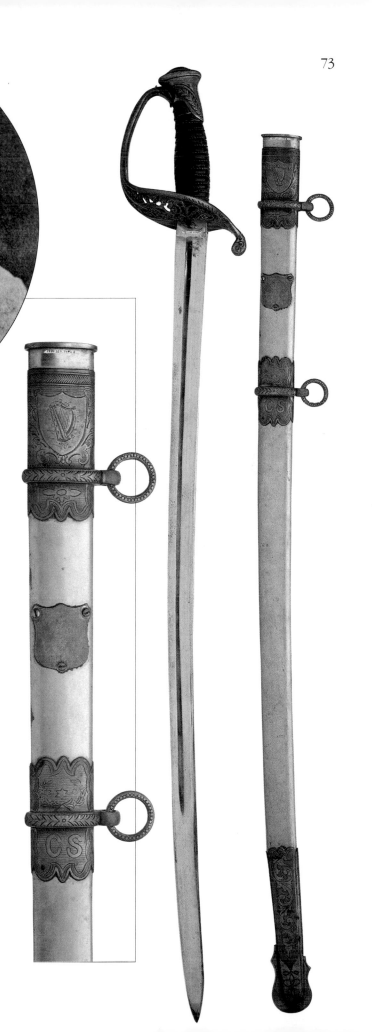

Blades from Abroad

CAPT. L. A. WEBRE
The hilt of this French-made foot officer's sword worn by Captain Webre of the 26th Louisiana Volunteers is engraved with his name, his regiment, and the year 1862—in December of which he died in battle at Chickasaw Bluffs.

BRITISH CAVALRY SABER
This cavalry sword with an iron scabbard is of the type produced by the government armory at Enfield, England.

A Prussian Giant and His Sword

In battle, Johann August Heinrich Heros von Borcke was an astonishing sight. "A giant, mounted on a tremendous horse, and brandishing wildly over his head a sword as long and big as a fence rail" is how a Northern journalist described this one-man juggernaut. Born in Prussia and an officer in the 2d Brandenburg Dragoons, the six-foot-four-inch, 240-pound von Borcke (*left*) set sail for America to seek adventure—and to evade his creditors—shortly after the Civil War began. He soon attached himself to General Jeb Stu-

**A mounted von Borcke warns Jeb Stuart of
the attack on Brandy Station in June 1863.**

art's entourage as a volunteer aide and was
promoted to major for his "fearless and un-
tiring" service.

Von Borcke's sword *(above)* was made in
Solingen, Germany, a town renowned for its
swordsmiths since the 10th century. The
weapon measures an impressive 42 inches
long overall, with a blade 1⅝ inches deep.
Solingen swords and blades of more modest
proportions were widely imported by both
the Confederacy and the Union during the
War. Von Borcke fought with his Solingen
in most of the Virginia cavalry skirmishes
and battles in Virginia until a neck wound
received at Middleburg in June 1863 put
him out of action for the rest of the War.

Enlisted Men's Swords

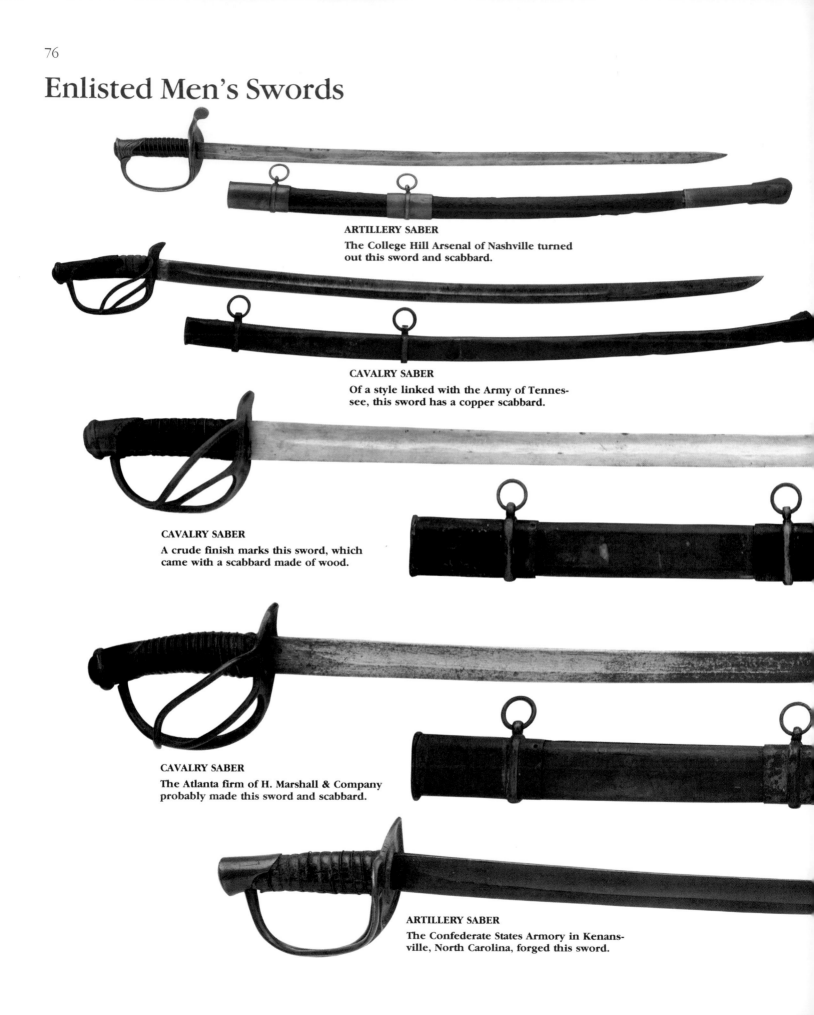

ARTILLERY SABER

The College Hill Arsenal of Nashville turned out this sword and scabbard.

CAVALRY SABER

Of a style linked with the Army of Tennessee, this sword has a copper scabbard.

CAVALRY SABER

A crude finish marks this sword, which came with a scabbard made of wood.

CAVALRY SABER

The Atlanta firm of H. Marshall & Company probably made this sword and scabbard.

ARTILLERY SABER

The Confederate States Armory in Kenansville, North Carolina, forged this sword.

A member of the Partisan Rangers led by John S. Mosby, the soldier at left grips an 1840 cavalry saber—the model that set the pattern for American cavalry sabers for the next 75 years.

FOOT ARTILLERY SWORD

This short sword worn by a Confederate artilleryman was copied from the Roman-style weapon of Napoleon's gunners. The leather scabbard was hung from the belt.

LOUISIANA KNIFE, SHEATH, AND BELT
This weapon was stripped from the body of a dead Confederate at Shiloh.

CONFEDERATE STATES ARMORY BOWIE KNIFE

BOWIE KNIFE WITH D-SHAPE KNUCKLE GUARD

BOWIE KNIFE, SHEATH, AND BELT
Captain Richard Gatlin of the North Carolina Edgecombe Guards carried this bowie.

Fighting Knives

Many Confederate soldiers carried a large side knife named the bowie after James Bowie, the Alamo hero who is said to have originated the type. The majority of these knives were made by local blacksmiths to sell to men entering the service, although many were forged in Southern factories. The blades of the knives ranged from 6 to more than 18 inches long.

Some bowies came equipped with D-shape knuckle guards.

Bowie knives served a variety of utilitarian purposes, from skinning rabbits to scaling fish. Although they were rarely used as weapons, the knives were primarily regarded as such by Confederate soldiers: A single chop with a heavy bowie could easily sever a man's arm.

CROSS-GUARD SIDE KNIFE

Brandishing bowie knives and revolvers, brothers Daniel, John, and Pleasant Chitwood link arms and glower at the camera after enlisting in the Barstow County Yankee Killers, later designated Company A of the 23d Georgia. Pleasant Chitwood died of dysentery in 1862, but Daniel and John soldiered on in Hardee's Corps, resisting Sherman's advance through Georgia and the Carolinas.

BOWIE KNIFE

BOWIE KNIFE

DAGGER

BOWIE KNIFE PRESENTED TO SGT. CHARLES BEERMAN

UNIFORMS

"We were a motley-looking set," recalled Private Valerius Giles of the regiment he joined in Austin, Texas, in the spring of 1861. The Confederate army had not yet adopted a particular style of uniform, he noted, and no two companies were dressed alike; Giles' own company was turned out in "four different shades of gray." Yet the lack of consistency did nothing to dampen the pride of the troops or of the civilians who helped outfit them. "The citizens of Austin and the surrounding neighborhood bought the cloth," Giles recollected. "A tailor took our measurements and cut out the uniforms. Then the ladies made them up. Oh, we were fine!"

Giles' regiment was by no means atypical. Although the vicissitudes of four years of war waged amid a tightening Union blockade would foster an impression of the Rebel soldiers as a ragged lot, many units were reasonably well attired, even late in the conflict. But the emphasis was on practicality rather than on conformity, and what the Confederates wore varied according to location and time period.

A civilian writing of Lee's Army of Northern Virginia in September 1862 noted that the men had no uniforms to speak of, and added: "I have never seen a mass of such filthy, strong-smelling men. Three of them in a room would make it unbearable, and when marching in column along the street the smell from them was most offensive." These fetid troops appeared to have become "so inured to hardships that they care but little for any of the comforts of civilization."

Other observers reported similar conditions, but suspected that there was something deliberate about the dishevelment. As an English witness, Colonel Sir Arthur Fremantle, put it: "The Confederate has no ambition to imitate the regular soldier at all. He looks the genuine Rebel; but in spite of his bare feet, his ragged clothes, his old rug, and

toothbrush stuck like a rose in his buttonhole, he has a sort of devil-may-care, self-confident look, which is decidedly taking."

Still other witnesses told of troops who were not only jaunty but spiffy. A Confederate who joined the Army of the Mississippi in 1862 wrote that his comrades were "not so badly clothed and equipped as I had expected to see, quite the reverse. They were splendidly armed and very well clad. All I saw had good shoes, too." Another recruit marveled at the sight of General Richard Taylor's Louisiana Brigade around that time. The brigade stood more than 3,000 strong, he recalled, and "each man, every inch a soldier, was perfectly uniformed, wearing white gaiters and leggings, marching quick-step, with his rifle at 'right-shoulder shift.' "

In the autumn of 1863, a Union soldier remarked that prisoners taken from Lee's army—the same throng disparaged for its untidiness the year before—were "better clothed than any we had before seen; all were provided with overcoats and jackets of much better material than our own." These admirable outfits were "of English manufacture," the Yankee added, "and they furnished conclusive evidence of successful blockade running." Plainly, the story of the Confederate army was not strictly a riches-to-rags tale.

That Confederates' uniforms varied so widely in detail and quality reflected the extemporaneous nature of their cause. Evoking the spirit of the American Revolution, the Southerners were ever distrustful of centralized authority. By necessity, the government in Richmond set certain standards for the outfitting of troops. But the regulations amounted to little more than a vaguely stated theme, one on which the soldiers and their providers rang a thousand variations.

A certain resistance to uniformity was embedded in American military tradition. In the early days of the Republic, Americans looked with skepticism on the idea of a large permanent military force and purposely kept the Regular Army small and weak. The larger needs of national defense were to be met by the common militia, made up of all able-bodied white males, who were required to attend local musters once or twice a year. Penalties for failing to appear were seldom enforced, however. Participation lagged, and the common militia was all but moribund by the time of the Civil War. Only a few such militia regiments served during the conflict.

The gap left by the decline of the common militia was filled by volunteer militia companies, whose recruits adopted colorful names and wore fancy uniforms. Some were working-class organizations and others were ethnic; but many, particularly in urban areas, were made up of the well-to-do. For all intents and purposes, they were social and political men's clubs, but they proved to be valuable military assets when the War began.

Some of these units had a long history. The Richmond Light Infantry Blues, for example, formed in 1789. The Washington Artillery of New Orleans, one of the oldest military units in Louisiana, was raised in 1838. But most such companies in the South sprouted up in the late 1850s, many as a response to the specter of slave rebellion evoked by John Brown's raid on Harpers Ferry in 1859.

Although a few Southern states had dress regulations for their militia, most of them authorized the governor to grant companies the right to choose their own style. In general, companies picked a uniform first and asked permission later, and few governors cared to deny them after the fact. As a result, Southern militia units on the eve of the Civil War were eclectic in the extreme. Among them were contingents decked out as Scottish highlanders, French chasseurs and Zou-

aves, Continental soldiers, and frontiersmen in fringed hunting frocks. Many of these companies adhered to their exotic dress even after they had been incorporated into the Confederate army.

With the start of hostilities, thousands of volunteers flocked to the colors, either joining prewar militia companies or forming their own units. Many of these new companies also chose distinctive uniforms. The proud Irishmen of the Emerald Guards of Mobile departed for Virginia wearing dark green, while the Granville Rifles of North Carolina went to war in black pants and red flannel shirts. The red shirts hardly made the riflemen inconspicuous to the Yankees, but perhaps the greatest risk was run by those Confederate volunteers who entered the War's early contests dressed in blue and drew friendly fire. Captain James M. Williams of Mobile, whose newly formed militia company was folded into the 21st Alabama Regiment, forswore his accustomed blue uniform after learning that some of his similarly attired comrades were fired on by Confederates at the Battle of Shiloh. "When I get my gray coat," he assured his wife, "I intend to sell the blue one and be done with everything that looks in the least Yankee-ish."

Such calamitous confusion underscored the need for consistency, but when it came to uniforms, the Confederates remained remarkably loose-knit. Although the bulk of the troops at the start of the War belonged to the so-called Provisional Army—made up of men drawn from the prewar militia and new volunteer companies—the only soldiers who were issued uniforms directly by the Confederate government were the enlisted men of that government's small, embryonic Regular Army. Nevertheless, what the regulars wore set the pattern in terms of uniform color and rank designations.

By the best evidence, credit for designing

that basic scheme belongs to a Prussian artist named Nicola Marschall, then living in Marion, Alabama. In April 1861, the Confederate congressional committee assigned to conceive a design for the regular uniform reached an impasse. Alabama Governor Andrew B. Moore, eager to help, referred the problem to a friend and relative, Mrs. Napoleon Lockett, who in turn asked Marschall to draw up a plan.

The peripatetic Marschall had been impressed with a group of Austrian army sharpshooters he had seen in Verona, Italy, in 1857. They had worn a short gray tunic with green facings, with the ranks of the officers distinguished by different-size stars. Marschall incorporated these elements into his design. A uniform board appointed by the Confederate Congress modified Marschall's system of ranking, but his basic scheme was instituted for the Regular Army in June. It consisted of a double-breasted gray tunic for all ranks, with seven buttons in each row. Made like a frock coat, it had a skirt that reached halfway between the hip and the knee, much shorter than conventional frock coats. There was a standing collar and pointed cuffs, the latter with three small buttons along the underside.

Colored trim was used to indicate which arm of the service a man belonged to—staff (buff), artillery (red), cavalry (yellow), infantry (light blue), or medical (black). The tunics of all ranks were edged throughout in the appropriate color, with collars and cuffs of that same color. Stars, bars, and braid were used to denote specific ranks (see accompanying chart). Officers were further distinguished by silk net sashes, in buff for generals and in other colors for lower-ranking commissioned officers (red for staff, engineers, artillery, and infantry; green for medical; and yellow for cavalry). Noncommissioned officers wore worsted sashes (red for artillery and infantry, and yellow for cavalry).

Trousers were light blue for all enlisted men and regimental officers, dark blue for higher-ranking officers. All were appropriately trimmed in the service color for the line units and in gold for staff. Headgear posed a problem from the start. Originally, a shako was contemplated, but the quartermaster in New Orleans assigned to obtain the first Regular Army uniforms was unable to find a contractor who could meet the requirements. Instead, a cap, in the form of the French kepi, was adopted.

Finally, special buttons were prescribed for officers. Those worn by staff had an eagle surrounded by stars, while the other branches were distinguished by letters: "E" for engineers, "A" for artillery, "R" for rifles, "C" for cavalry, and "I" for infantry.

Officially, this detailed plan was altered in only one particular during the course of the War. The thigh-length tunic was deemed unconventional and proved universally unpopular, and in 1862, the new edition of the regulations specified a longer "frock coat." Some improvisation was inevitable, however, since the Regular Army uniform was adopted by most volunteer officers, who were required to buy their own uniforms. As a result, materials, buttons, linings, and other features varied with the inclinations and pocketbook of the wearer.

For the Confederate rank and file—the volunteers with the Provisional Army—the elaborate specifications of the Regular Army plan meant little. Versions of the regular outfit were acquired by some ordinary enlisted men, but there was no concerted effort to make that uniform the standard. At the beginning of the War, the volunteers were expected to provide their own clothing, for which they were to be reimbursed, generally at the rate of $50 a year. Known as the com-

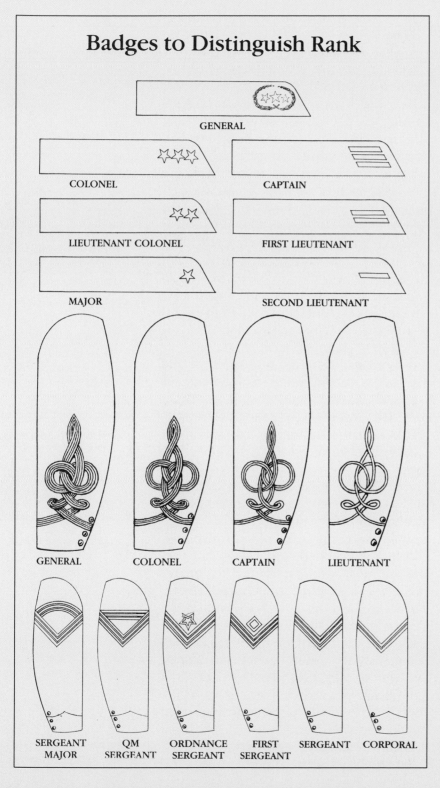

Badges to Distinguish Rank

GENERAL

COLONEL

CAPTAIN

LIEUTENANT COLONEL

FIRST LIEUTENANT

MAJOR

SECOND LIEUTENANT

GENERAL COLONEL CAPTAIN LIEUTENANT

SERGEANT MAJOR QM SERGEANT ORDNANCE SERGEANT FIRST SERGEANT SERGEANT CORPORAL

mutation system, this practice dated from the War of 1812. Adopted by the Confederacy before hostilities began, it constituted the easiest and quickest way to clothe the troops and saved the cash-poor Confederacy from having to stockpile mountains of clothing that might be wasted if there was no war.

Once the fighting started, however, the defects of the commutation system became apparent. The bewildering variety of outfits was part of the problem. The volunteer militia companies wore their old uniforms, while the new volunteer companies provided themselves with everything from fancy gilt and plumes to serviceable field clothing. Some units, mainly from Mississippi, North Carolina, and Georgia, conformed to state regulations, whereas others were mustered wearing civilian clothes. The army had little choice but to make provision for soldiers who enlisted without uniforms or who wore out their clothing. By early June 1861, the quartermaster general, Colonel A. C. Myers, acknowledged that what the volunteers brought with them to camp was fraying and that "in a few weeks they will be destitute of most of the articles of clothing. The law requires volunteers to furnish themselves, but as they cannot do so in the field, we must look after their comfort in this respect."

Thus came a major shift in Confederate policy, with the government in Richmond taking on the responsibility for supplying at least some of the 100,000 volunteers. The new policy was in effect by mid-July 1861, with the most ragged of the volunteers being supplied first. By September, a clothing factory had been set up in Richmond, to be followed by others in cities throughout the South; the major depots were in Richmond, Athens, Atlanta, and Columbus. These operations were modeled after the uniform production center at the U.S. Army's Schuylkill Arsenal, although none approached the output of that thriving concern. Each depot employed a small group of tailors to cut out the pieces for uniforms. Those pieces, along with trim, buttons, and thread, were then issued to seamstresses, who sewed them together and were paid by the completed piece. Most depots employed about 40 men in-house and around 2,000 to 3,000 women in the town, who did the sewing in their homes.

The new system proved surprisingly successful; only the availability of raw materials limited output. By April 1863, for example, the Atlanta depot, a typical operation, was producing roughly 35,000 uniforms a year, and was projecting 130,000 for the next year.

The uniforms these factories turned out bore little resemblance to the one prescribed for the Regular Army. Spurning the long tunic, the depots produced short, waist-length jackets in a variety of configurations. Such jackets had a long and honorable history, having been worn by troops in the War of 1812, during the Mexican conflict, in the Seminole War, and on the frontier. More importantly, they could be made quickly and without great expenditure of cloth.

Although one or two depots produced jackets of gray and pants of sky blue, most of them cut the jackets and trousers from material of the same color for as long as that material happened to be on hand. Thus a single depot might produce jackets and pants of gray broadcloth one month, and of jean, a mixed cotton-wool weave, the next. Indeed, none of the patterns devised at the various locations were approved or even recorded by a central authority.

By October 1862, the depot system was strong enough that the government began to take over the responsibility for supplying all clothing. This new issue system, instituted gradually, set annual allotments for various articles of clothing as well as prices that were to be charged for items drawn in excess of the allotment. If a soldier underdrew his allotment, he was paid the difference. If he overdrew, the difference was taken out of his pay. During a three-year enlistment, for example, a soldier could expect to receive four pairs of shoes a year, with extra pairs costing $6 each. He was owed two jackets the first year and one each for the following two years, with the value established at $12 per garment. He was given one overcoat for the three-year stint; another would cost him $25. So the wardrobe went, down to cap (four at $2 each), socks (12 at $1 a pair), and drawers (seven in all, $3 each).

The allotments were not sufficient to meet all the needs of soldiers on campaign. A man in a hard-marching unit might easily wear out four pairs of shoes in a matter of months; he was sure to exhaust his ration of socks. One solution short of drawing on one's pay was to appeal to friends and family. A soldier from Alabama implored his wife to "send me either two pairs of woolen socks or some yarn and a needle to darn those I have. They no longer keep my toes in confinement as they used to, but let them out incontinently." Another option was to scavenge clothing from the dead.

The government frequently had difficulty meeting the allotments. The shortage of domestic wool in the South posed a particular problem; Confederate mills could not provide the thick woolens needed for winter clothing. Thanks to the abundance of cotton, there were large quantities of shirts, underwear, and other lightweight articles; and the substitution of jean for pure wool cloth helped in other respects. But certain articles, like overcoats and blankets, were either prohibitively expensive or unattainable in the South. As a result, the Confederacy turned to foreign suppliers.

Major J. B. Ferguson was sent to England in September 1862 as the official quartermaster purchasing agent there. At his instigation, large quantities of English army shoes, as well as bulk woolen cloth, began to arrive in Confederate ports. In addition, private speculators contracted to run uniforms and cloth from various European ports through the blockade, with mixed success.

Finally, some Southern states supplemented the efforts of the government in Richmond by producing considerable quantities of clothing, mainly to meet the needs of their own. Georgia and North Carolina did particularly well by their troops.

Despite such exertions, the troops were often less than impressed with what they received. Lieutenant J. F. J. Caldwell of McGowan's South Carolina Brigade wrote just after the War: "The quality was more to be complained of than the quantity. Most of the men rubbed out a jacket in two or three months—a pair of pantaloons in one. It was coarse, stiff, and flimsy. Sometimes, even, cotton pants were offered us in mid-winter.

Scarcely a particle of flannel was to be had. The cut was worst of all. Anybody could put on the clothing, but scarcely any object in nature, except a flour barrel, would find a fit. Shoes were scarce, blankets curiosities, overcoats a positive phenomenon."

The troops met such trials with resignation leavened by occasional grumbling and healthy doses of humor. After soldiers of the 2d Texas Infantry entered the fight at Shiloh wearing ghostly uniforms of undyed wool, a story circulated among the Texans that a Federal prisoner had inquired of his captors, "Who were them hellcats that went into battle dressed in their graveclothes?"

Understandably, few Confederates waxed sentimental about their clothing at the time. But after the struggle, the fading uniforms were prized by many veterans and their descendants. They testify today to the improvised nature of the Confederate rebellion—a cause that slighted consistency but put a premium on adaptability and resourcefulness.

Sergeant George Kurtz *(left)* belonged to the Morgan Continental Guards of Virginia, a militia company that joined the 5th Virginia Infantry.

Uniforms from Peacetime

The U.S. Militia patterned its uniform after the tight swallowtail dress coat and tall shako common in Europe prior to 1848. In that year, Europe experienced a radical change in military dress, adopting the frock coat introduced earlier by the French army. But Americans were slow to relinquish the more conservative style. Militia companies, like the Warrenton Rifles of Virginia (whose uniform is pictured here), were still wearing the outmoded swallowtail coat and shako in 1861.

Also called "spiketails" and "claw hammers," the swallowtail coat was the oldest style of upper garment used by the military between 1851 and 1872. American militias favored gray—their traditional dress color and the cheapest color to produce at that time.

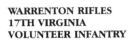

**WARRENTON RIFLES
17TH VIRGINIA
VOLUNTEER INFANTRY**

Private Richard A. Weaver wore this gray wool non-regulation tail coat *(left)* when he served with the Warrenton Rifles. Rows of braid known as false buttonholes connect the buttons. The shako *(below)* belonged to John Quincy Marr, captain of the Warrenton Rifles. Marr was shot while defending Fairfax Courthouse on June 1, 1861, becoming the first Confederate soldier to be killed in combat.

HAMILTON BRANCH, OGLETHORPE LIGHT INFANTRY

OGLETHORPE LIGHT INFANTRY

Based in Savannah, Georgia, the Oglethorpe Light Infantry (OLI) was made up of wealthy planters' and merchants' sons. In January 1861, before Georgia seceded, the 1st Regiment Georgia Volunteers (which included Company B of the OLI) seized Fort Pulaski, near Savannah. Oglethorpe Light Infantry members wore coats like this one, which belonged to a Corporal Branch.

CAPT. JAMES L. CLARK MARYLAND GUARD BATTALION

The dress uniform of the Maryland Guard included a dark blue Zouave jacket trimmed with yellow cord in the French style. Organized by Baltimore's "best citizens" in 1859, the Maryland Guard disbanded in May 1861 when Federal troops occupied Baltimore. Clark, like most other Guard members, joined the Confederate army. He served as an aide to Jeb Stuart and was later promoted to captain in the 12th Virginia Cavalry.

Owned by Captain Edwin W. Branch, commander of the Richmond Grays, this shako exemplifies the stock militia dress hat. The number "1" identifies it as the first regiment, the Virginia Volunteers. Wealthy militia units commissioned special cap insignia; others bought a standard badge and inserted their own regimental numbers.

LT. DAVID HENRY ANSLEY CLINCH RIFLES

Members of the Clinch Rifles, who later joined the 5th Georgia Infantry, wore this dress uniform coat and shako from 1850 to 1860. Lieutenant Ansley, the uniform's owner, sustained a wound shortly before the Battle of Missionary Ridge that rendered him an invalid for the rest of his life.

This militia swallowtail coat, owned by a sergeant in the Morgan Continental Guards, was modeled after the 18th-century uniform worn by the company's namesake, Daniel Morgan. During the Revolutionary War, Morgan earned a reputation as one of George Washington's best riflemen.

Bolivar Buckner's Legacy

During the years before the Civil War, most Southern states instituted no official dress regulations for their militia companies. Even when uniforms were specified, these companies tended to adopt parts rather than the whole: In Mississippi, the only prescribed item worn consistently was the three-cornered black felt hat.

The best surviving examples of a state militia uniform belonged to General Simon Bolivar Buckner. Although Buckner attempted to standardize the dress of the Kentucky State Guard, which he organized in March 1860, he never got further than providing uniforms for himself, his staff, and the battalion officers.

General Buckner designed his frock coat in the West Point colors of gray, black, and gold. Early in 1861 the Northern press misconstrued this Kentucky uniform as being Confederate army regulation.

KEPI, SIMON BOLIVAR BUCKNER

A Kentucky original, Buckner's pleated fatigue jacket was widely copied by other states. General Leonidas Polk once said of this jacket, "I like it, sir, it looks comfortable, it looks soldierly, in fact, sir, it looks rebellious!"

Sporting bearskin shakos, members of the Kentucky State Guard settle into camp at the Louisville Fair Ground after a parade in August 1860. Simon Bolivar Buckner *(inset)* commanded the Guard, whom he pronounced to be "admirably drilled in rifle tactics, handsomely uniformed, and fully armed and equipped."

SOUTH CAROLINA MILITIA

Resembling the color of Federal uniforms, this N.C.O.'s blue frock coat may have endangered its owner when he wore it in battle early in the War. Other militia troops experienced similar problems. The Orleans Guard Battalion arrived at Shiloh wearing their blue dress uniforms. They were forced to turn their coats inside out after fellow Rebels mistook them for the enemy.

Captain John Thomas Wheat offers his resignation to Colonel James B. Walton of the Washington Artillery of New Orleans. Wheat resigned from the militia unit to take command of a battery at Pensacola, Florida, in 1861. He was killed at Shiloh the following April.

Dressing Up for War

A great variety of uniforms appeared on the battlefield in 1861 as members of state militia companies, the first men to see active combat, were dispersed to different units. Soldiers in the field found it difficult to distinguish between friend and foe, given the fact that as many as 10 different uniforms may have existed within one state regiment.

The diversity of dress, noted one Rebel, ranged from "the dirty gray and tarnished silver of the Carolinian" to the "dingy butternut of the Georgian, with its green trimming and full skirts, and the Alabamians nearly all in blue of a cleaner hue and neater cut."

WASHINGTON ARTILLERY OF NEW ORLEANS

The "handsomely French" frock coat and kepi worn by the Washington Artillery "made them very fine beside our homespun infantry fellows," remarked one Confederate soldier upon seeing the New Orleans outfit for the first time. The Washington Artillery employed New Orleans' leading tailors to fashion their uniforms.

SOUTH CAROLINA

NORTH CAROLINA

VIRGINIA

MARYLAND

Southern soldiers and civilians showed support for the Confederacy by pinning state secession cockades to their hats and jackets. Although these badges were usually made of ribbon, South Carolina's cockade was woven from leaves of the state's abundant palmetto tree.

These two members of General Harry Hays' Louisiana Tiger Brigade sport the uniform shirts they wore in combat.

PVT. KENNEDY PALMER 13TH VIRGINIA INFANTRY

Nellie Palmer made this blue flannel battle shirt for her brother Kennedy. Early in the War, when Confederate soldiers had no standard uniform, officials instituted the wearing of wool battle shirts to create a uniform appearance.

FORAGE CAP, PVT. PALMER

FIELD SIGNS

On the eve of First Manassas, General Beauregard devised a system of so-called field signs—reversible wing badges and colored armbands *(right)*—to identify Southern troops in combat. He discarded the plan when he learned that the Union forces intended to use the same system. White cap bands *(above)* were also tried but were unsuccessful because they were used inconsistently.

Militia officers wore shoulder straps as part of their standard "undress," or everyday, uniforms prior to 1861. Originally designed so that the men could remove them and substitute epaulets for dress occasions, straps were later sewn directly to coat shoulders. The number of stripes on each side of the strap designated rank. Background color denoted the branch of service.

Although epaulets remained popular with officers, regulars, and state troops in the years before the Civil War, they were rarely seen thereafter. The rank devices—two bars for a captain, an embroidered eagle for a colonel, and one star for a brigadier general—were borrowed from U.S. Army regulations.

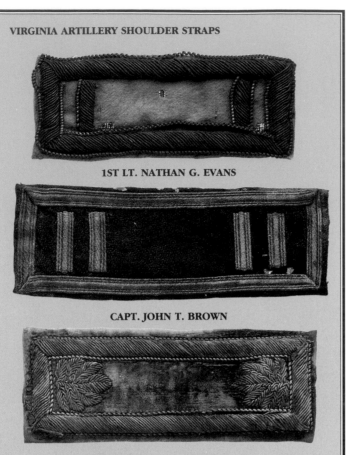

VIRGINIA ARTILLERY SHOULDER STRAPS

1ST LT. NATHAN G. EVANS

CAPT. JOHN T. BROWN

MAJ. JOHN T. BROWN

A Miscellany of Insignia

Before the Confederacy devised a cohesive system of insignia for identifying rank and branch of service, each state militia prescribed its own insignia. Regulations provided for shoulder straps, epaulets, and hat insignia.

In many cases, as exemplified by the Virginia militia system of shoulder straps and epaulets *(left and below),* these items were patterned after those prescribed by U.S. Army regulations. The bugle cap insignia called for in North Carolina state regulations *(above, right)* was worn by infantry officers in the Union and Confederacy alike.

To further distinguish their units, individual militia companies often designed additional pins or badges. Even though Maryland did not secede, Confederate soldiers from that state wore a variety of pins adapted from the Calvert heraldic cross *(right).*

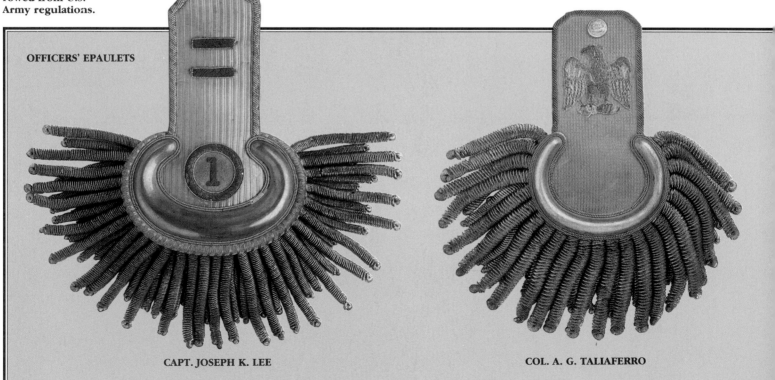

OFFICERS' EPAULETS

CAPT. JOSEPH K. LEE

COL. A. G. TALIAFERRO

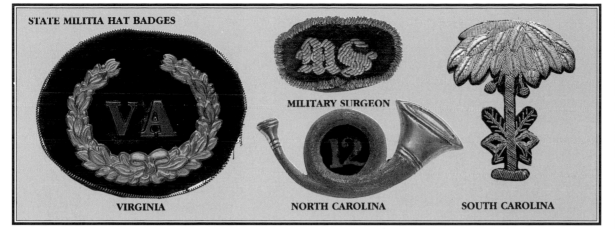

STATE MILITIA HAT BADGES

VIRGINIA

MILITARY SURGEON

NORTH CAROLINA

SOUTH CAROLINA

States authorized their own cap badges *(left)*, including a facsimile of the badge designated for Virginia in 1858 and South Carolina's palmetto tree.

Texans wore the "lone star" *(below, left)*, the state's emblem. Lieutenant John Rust's sweetheart embroidered his Laurel Brigade badge *(below)*.

SPECIALIZED INSIGNIA

TEXAS

LOUISIANA

WASHINGTON LIGHT ARTILLERY

2 Md

MARYLAND

LAUREL BRIGADE VIRGINIA

BRIG. GEN. CARNOT POSEY

THE LAUREL BRIGADE BADGE ADORNS THIS PRIVATE'S HAT.

ALABAMA

STATE SEAL

ALABAMA
VOLUNTEER CORPS

ALABAMA
VOLUNTEER CORPS

MOBILE
VOLUNTEER CORPS

MOBILE CADET

STATE SEAL
(LOCAL)

FLORIDA

TERRITORIAL SEAL

VARIANT STATE EMBLEM

ARKANSAS

STATE SEAL

2D ARKANSAS REGIMENT
(LOCAL)

GEORGIA

STATE SEAL

STATE SEAL

STATE SEAL
(LOCAL)

STATE SEAL
(LOCAL)

IRISH
JASPER GREENS

LAMAR
MOUNTED RIFLES

LOUISIANA

STATE SEAL

STATE SEAL

STATE SEAL
(LOCAL)

NEW ORLEANS
VOLTIGEURS

NEW ORLEANS GUARDS

NEW ORLEANS BATTALION
OF ARTILLERY

VIRGINIA

STATE SEAL

STATE SEAL

STATE SEAL

STATE SEAL

STATE SEAL
(LOCAL)

STATE SEAL
(LOCAL)

KENTUCKY

STATE SEAL

MARYLAND

STATE SEAL

State Buttons

Aside from their mundane utility, ornamented uniform buttons were an essential element of Civil War military insignia. Used to indicate branch of service and rank as well as national, state, and unit loyalties, they also added the gleam of polished metal to the unadorned fronts of most uniforms.

Before the War, virtually all Southern state buttons were made in the North. When the fighting broke out, the Confederacy found itself without a single button factory and had to import European-made varieties. Later, as the blockade gradually choked off this supply, a number of small Southern firms turned out crude versions known as locals.

The dress regulations written by the Confederate War Department in 1861 specified eagle buttons for general and staff officers, branch-of-service letter buttons for other officers *(see following pages),* and regimental-number buttons for enlisted ranks (these last, however, were never issued). But many soldiers, officers and men alike, chose to proclaim their first loyalty by wearing the buttons of their state.

NORTH CAROLINA

STATE SEAL

STATE SEAL (LOCAL)

STATE SEAL (LOCAL)

VARIANT STATE EMBLEM

VARIANT STATE EMBLEM (LOCAL)

VARIANT STATE EMBLEM (LOCAL)

VARIANT STATE EMBLEM (LOCAL)

HORNET'S NEST RIFLE CORPS

SOUTH CAROLINA

STATE SEAL

STATE SEAL

STATE SEAL

STATE SEAL

MODIFIED STATE SEAL

STATE SEAL (LOCAL)

TENNESSEE

STATE SEAL (LOCAL)

STATE SEAL (LOCAL)

MISSISSIPPI

MILITIA

ARTILLERY

CAVALRY

INFANTRY

MILITIA (LOCAL)

MILITIA (LOCAL)

TEXAS

MODIFIED STATE SEAL

STATE SEAL

CAVALRY

MODIFIED STATE SEAL (LOCAL)

MODIFIED STATE SEAL (LOCAL)

WACO GUARDS

OFFICERS

Revered for his "coolness, good disposition, and contagious courage," General James Longstreet *(below)* wore his tunic when other officers "would have none of it." Although critically wounded at the Wilderness in 1864, Longstreet outlived all the other members of the Confederate high command.

LT. COL. ARCHER ANDERSON

Lieutenant Colonel Anderson, who served on the staffs of Generals D. H. Hill, Theophilus Holmes, and Joseph E. Johnston, wore this tunic faced with white wool. As published in July 1861, C.S.A. army regulations called for a "double-breasted tunic of gray cloth, with the skirt extending halfway between the hip and knee." The tunic, with its short skirt copied from an Austrian infantry uniform, proved both uncomfortable and unpopular.

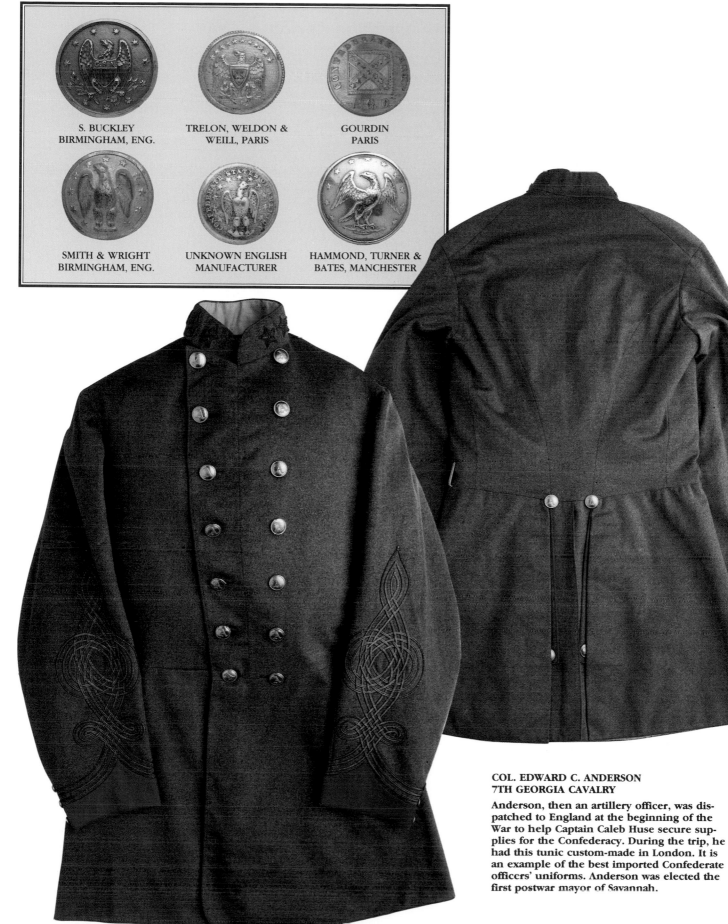

S. BUCKLEY
BIRMINGHAM, ENG.

TRELON, WELDON &
WEILL, PARIS

GOURDIN
PARIS

SMITH & WRIGHT
BIRMINGHAM, ENG.

UNKNOWN ENGLISH
MANUFACTURER

HAMMOND, TURNER &
BATES, MANCHESTER

COL. EDWARD C. ANDERSON
7TH GEORGIA CAVALRY

Anderson, then an artillery officer, was dispatched to England at the beginning of the War to help Captain Caleb Huse secure supplies for the Confederacy. During the trip, he had this tunic custom-made in London. It is an example of the best imported Confederate officers' uniforms. Anderson was elected the first postwar mayor of Savannah.

The Favored Frock Coat

Despite regulations, after 1861 the tunic practically disappeared. Officers took instead to "the familiar cut of the frock coat with good length of tail," as one Confederate staff officer put it. This change marked the introduction of a more comfortable and practical style of military cloth-ing. Yet the basic structure of Confederate frock coats—a close-fitting body sewn to a separate skirt that fell below the hips—remained their only common element. Officers interpreted the regulations according to their access to tailors, their financial resources, and their individual taste. Although many frock coats were inspired by official regulations, they rarely copied standard uniforms exactly.

**LT. COL. ROBERT RANDOLPH
4TH VIRGINIA CAVALRY**

The yellow facings on Randolph's frock coat identified him as cavalry; the cuff piping was a break from regulations. Commissioned as a first lieutenant, Randolph reached the rank of major before he was killed near Meadow Bridge, Virginia.

The Tennessee officer in this hand-colored ambrotype wears the light blue infantry version of a regulation-inspired frock coat.

**CAPT. JAMES L. CLARK
2D MARYLAND CAVALRY**

Clark's coat, vest, and cap followed Confederate regulations as closely as did any officer's uniform. He substituted a dark blue infantry kepi for the yellow-crowned cap authorized for the cavalry since yellow wool was hard to procure during the War.

Garb of the High Command

**GEN. ROBERT E. LEE
ARMY OF NORTHERN VIRGINIA**

Promoted to brigadier general in 1861, Lee posed for this 1863 portrait in the coat he always wore, which had a colonel's collar insignia and a general's button arrangement. A group of women from Maryland who supported the Confederate cause sent Lee the gray English broadcloth coat *(left)*. Once described as "beaming the highest intelligence and unvarying kindness, yet with command so firmly set in his features that all knew him for the unquestioned chief," Lee attained the highest rank of any officer in the Confederate service.

GEN. BEAUREGARD'S KEPI

**GEN. BRAXTON BRAGG
ARMY OF TENNESSEE**

General Bragg, whose frock coat is shown below, replaced Beauregard as commander of the Army of Tennessee. Plagued by chronic migraine headaches, Bragg was notorious for his irascibility. While one historian credits him with "the highest moral character and skill in planning military maneuvers," he notes that the general's "unpopularity with practically everyone he encountered greatly diminished his effectiveness."

**GEN. PIERRE GUSTAVE TOUTANT BEAUREGARD
DEPARTMENT OF SOUTH CAROLINA AND GEORGIA**

The wide button spacing on Beauregard's elaborate frock coat *(above)* reflects a trademark of Charleston tailors. Although Beauregard *(left)* considered his assignment to Charleston in 1862 a demotion, he accepted it, saying, "I shall rely on the ardent patriotism and unconquerable spirit of the men under my command to sustain me successfully."

Coats for the Army's Generals

Confederates distinguished officers' ranks by the use of the "Austrian knot"—an arrangement of gold braid worn by French officers on the sleeves of their undress coats. Each rank received one braid, ranging from one strand for a lieutenant to four for a general.

Whereas generals were further characterized by a pattern of three stars surrounded by a wreath on their collars, the Confederacy never officially differentiated between different grades of general officers. Unofficially, however, officers adopted the Federal system of button spacing: double-breasted rows of two buttons for brigadier generals. Since no regulations existed for ranks higher than this, the Rebels used rows of three buttons to signify major generals.

GEN. JAMES PETTIGREW
SOUTH CAROLINA
Pettigrew, whose close-fitting frock coat is pictured at left, accepted a commission as brigadier general in 1862. He was fatally wounded at Falling Waters, West Virginia, while commanding a portion of the rear guard during the retreat to the Potomac.

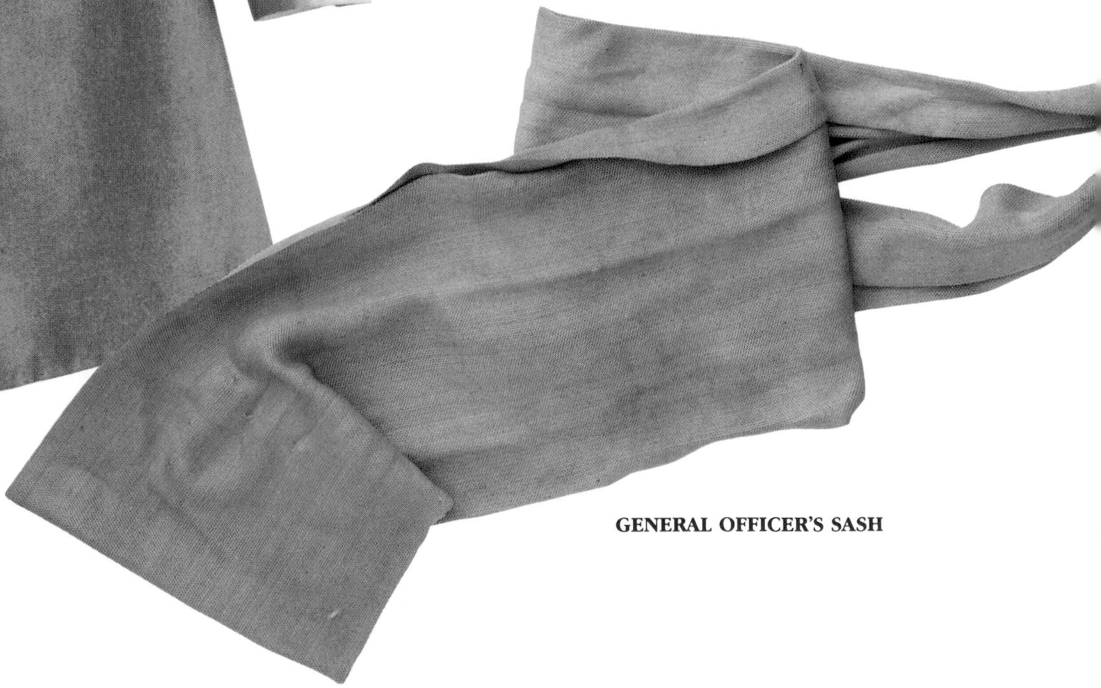

GENERAL OFFICER'S SASH

105

**GEN. THOMAS M. LOGAN
SOUTH CAROLINA**

Logan wore this coat at Johnston's surrender to Sherman in North Carolina. Sherman expressed amazement that this "slight, fair-haired boy" had commanded a brigade.

**GEN. JAMES CONNER
SOUTH CAROLINA**

Conner owned this wide-skirted frock coat lined with yellow silk. At Mechanicsville, during the Seven Days' Battles, a rifle ball broke Conner's leg. Two years later he was wounded again in the same leg, and it had to be amputated. Despite his handicap, Conner continued to command in the field.

STAFF, GENERAL OFFICERS', AND GENERAL SERVICE BUTTONS (LOCAL)

**GEN. BENJAMIN G. HUMPHREYS
MISSISSIPPI**

During the War, Humphreys wore this wool jean uniform, presented to him by a society of patriotic women from Woodville, Mississippi. The wool used to make this set was raised, spun, woven into cloth, and sewn in Wilkinson County, Mississippi. Although he could have afforded finer cloth, Humphreys wore this uniform out of allegiance to his home state, where he was elected governor after the War.

**GEN. WILLIAM DORSEY PENDER
NORTH CAROLINA**

A perfect example of an officer's field uniform, Pender's general's coat served him in combat. He modified it for field wear by adding padding under the arm and a strap on the shoulder so he could carry a knapsack. His British imported enlisted man's trousers were rent by the shell fragment that wounded him at Gettysburg in May 1863. Although his injury did not appear to be fatal, Pender was evacuated to a hospital in Staunton, Virginia. During the long, dusty trip, his leg became infected and had to be amputated upon his arrival. He died hours after the operation.

Homespun Frock Coats

At the beginning of the War, making uniforms from homespun cloth, like the one worn by this Confederate major from Richmond, became popular as a symbol of Southern self-sufficiency.

**COL. ELLISON CAPERS
24TH SOUTH CAROLINA INFANTRY**

Capers served most of the War with the 24th South Carolina Volunteers, whom he helped to recruit. His uniform's brown-and-white checked lining more typically appeared in civilian clothes. Paroled as a brigadier general in 1865, Capers entered the Episcopalian ministry.

**1ST LT. FRANCIS P. FLEMING
1ST FLORIDA CAVALRY**

Fleming's coat bears his rank insignia on the collar but lacks sleeve braid. This variation echoes an 1862 general order specifying no braid for officers' coat sleeves. By dispensing with prominent signs of rank, officials hoped to make officers less conspicuous on the battlefield.

**CAPT. AUGUSTUS JONES
17TH GEORGIA INFANTRY**

Captain Jones *(above)* was killed at Second Manassas. His black servant combed the field for Jones' body, finally finding it in a heap of corpses gathered for burial. He removed Jones' coat *(right)*, belt, and sword and trekked back to Georgia to return them to the family.

**CAPT. JOSEPH M. STOREY
43D GEORGIA INFANTRY**

The bullet that pierced Storey's lung in August 1864 at Lovejoy's Station near Atlanta entered through the patched hole in the left breast of his coat. Assumed dead on the field, Storey was discovered by one of his men, who carried him—using his blanket for a stretcher—to a train bound for the Macon hospital where he recovered. The holes—now repaired—on the left arm of the coat came from slugs that wounded Storey the year before and caused the amputation of one of his fingers.

The Personal Touch

Resplendent in his elaborately styled frock coat, Brigadier General Frank Armstrong fought with the Union army at First Manassas. He resigned in August 1861 to join the Confederate forces, eventually assuming command of a cavalry brigade in the West.

**COL. LAURENCE M. KEITT
20TH SOUTH CAROLINA
INFANTRY**

A wealthy South Carolinian, Keitt commissioned the finest Charleston tailors to design his frock coat *(right)*. Custom touches include the electric blue fabric behind the sleeve braid and on the faced lapels. Put in command of Kershaw's Brigade in May 1864, Keitt was leading it into the fray at Cold Harbor the following month when he was shot and killed.

**SGT. THOMAS W. BLANDFORD
8TH KENTUCKY MOUNTED INFANTRY**

Blandford's coat *(above)* displays an unusual arrangement of a single strand of gold braid paralleling the sleeve seam beginning at the wrist and forming a trefoil at the elbow. The rows of 16 tiny ball buttons on each sleeve echoed a conceit of French fashion at the time. As originally designed, the buttons enabled the wearer to roll his sleeves all the way back.

OFFICER'S SASH

GEN. BRYAN GRIMES, NORTH CAROLINA

In his account of the Battle of Chancellorsville, Grimes wrote to his wife, "My sword was severed by a ball, my clothes perforated, and a ball embedded in my sword belt." He survived the War, only to be assassinated at his plantation in 1880. Grimes *(below, flanked by his staff)* chose a frock coat devoid of rank insignia and a blue kepi *(below)*.

Contrasts in Quality

MAJ. JOHN HUGHES, 7TH NORTH CAROLINA INFANTRY

Quartermaster in General Robert Hoke's division, Hughes imported his uniform from S. Isaacs, Campbell & Company in England, and it came through the blockade at Wilmington, North Carolina. When no one else would take the risk, S. Isaacs, Campbell offered credit to Confederate customers. By the end of 1862, Rebels had purchased nearly $5 million worth of supplies from the firm and had paid only half of the amount due.

**CAPT. WILLIAM H. CLEAVER
7TH TEXAS MOUNTED RIFLES**

In contrast to the fine English wool broadcloth from
which John Hughes' uniform was crafted, Cleaver's
was sewn from an inexpensive wool-and-cotton blend
called satinette that simulated the look of broadcloth.
Cleaver, former chief justice of Angelina County,
Texas, served in New Mexico and far western Texas.
He was killed in a skirmish while foraging with his
company near El Paso in July 1862.

PREWAR PORTRAIT OF T. OTIS BAKER AND HIS WIFE

A Soldier's Bequest

Second Lieutenant T. Otis Baker, who fought with the 10th Mississippi Infantry under General Braxton Bragg, proudly preserved his uniforms, shown here. Baker served the Confederacy until the end of the War, earning a citation for "conspicuous bravery" at Chickamauga.

Baker's nonregulation single-breasted frock coat and pants *(right)* were made of butternut homespun wool. Although gray was the regulation color of Confederate uniforms, manufacturers increasingly resorted to using a dye made of copperas and walnut hulls, which produced the color known as butternut. Identifying true butternut uniforms poses a problem since vegetable-dyed gray oxidizes over time and takes on a tan cast.

EARLY WAR FROCK COAT WITH 2D LIEUTENANT'S SLEEVE BRAID

WOOL FELT SLOUCH HAT

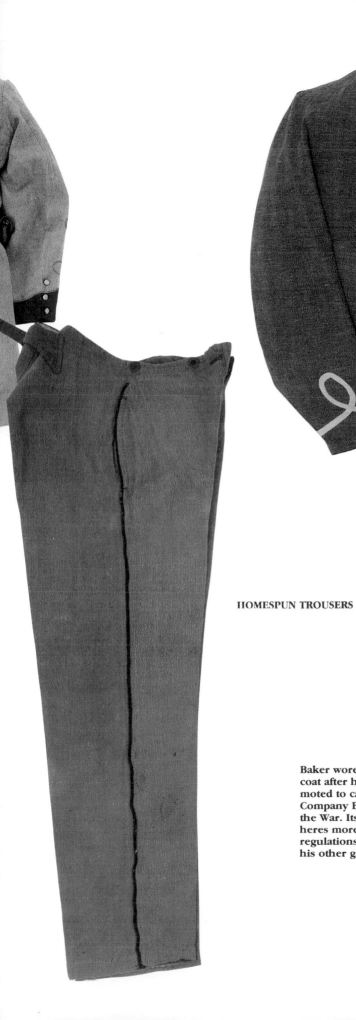

Militia-style false button-holes, like those on the collar of Baker's cotton captain's jacket, first appeared on military uniforms during the War of 1812.

HOMESPUN TROUSERS

Baker wore this frock coat after he was promoted to captain of Company B later in the War. Its style adheres more closely to regulations than do his other garments.

Washington Artillery

PVT. M. PAGE LAPHAM

Fashioned from fine wool kersey, Lapham's red-piped jacket, vest, and trousers typify those worn by the Washington Artillery of New Orleans. Lapham was one of many Virginians the Artillery recruited to replace its own men lost in battle. Fatally wounded at Drewry's Bluff less than a year after he enlisted, 18-year-old Lapham died in May 1864. His captain, J. B. Richardson, lamented the death of one of the Confederacy's "noblest and bravest defenders."

Well-to-do members of the Washington Artillery, shown here at their mustering-in camp, provided their own uniforms, which were subject to approval by the company's inspection committee. "In organization and equipment the Washington Artillery was not excelled by any command North or South, and the finest material in the state of Louisiana filled its ranks," claimed its commander, William Owen.

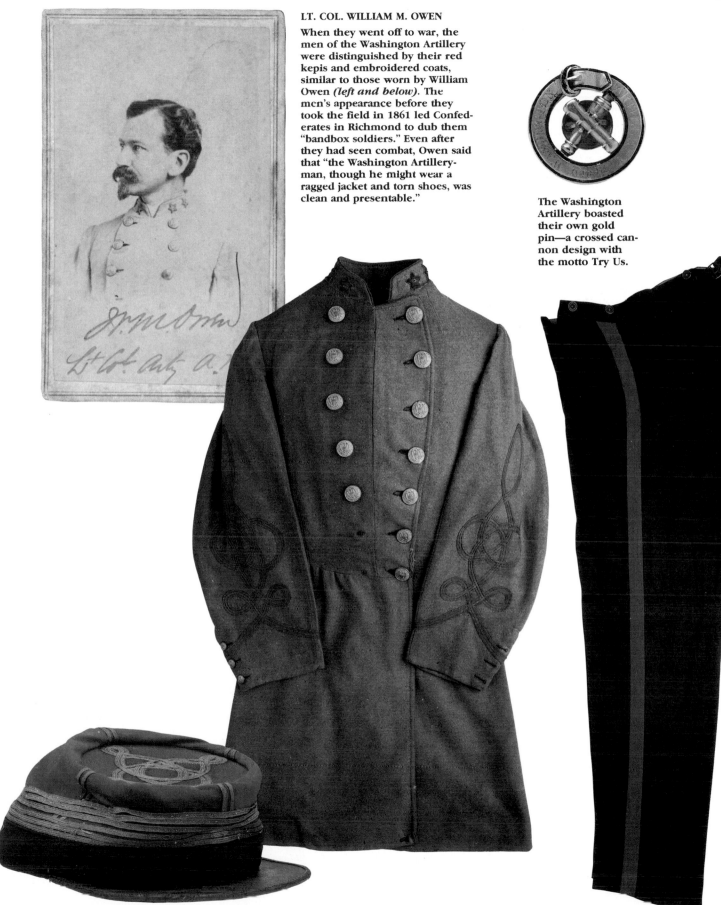

LT. COL. WILLIAM M. OWEN

When they went off to war, the men of the Washington Artillery were distinguished by their red kepis and embroidered coats, similar to those worn by William Owen *(left and below)*. The men's appearance before they took the field in 1861 led Confederates in Richmond to dub them "bandbox soldiers." Even after they had seen combat, Owen said that "the Washington Artilleryman, though he might wear a ragged jacket and torn shoes, was clean and presentable."

The Washington Artillery boasted their own gold pin—a crossed cannon design with the motto Try Us.

The Cloth-Saving Jacket

Almost as soon as Confederate officials formally issued dress regulations, "a short-waisted and single-breasted jacket usurped the place of the long-tailed coat, and became universal," observed one officer who served with the Army of Northern Virginia.

These jackets proved less expensive and easier to order than the frock coat since they required less cloth and every tailor knew how to make them. Confederate officers and enlisted men alike chose jackets as their standard upper garment, a fact that led the enemy to christen the Rebels "Gray Jackets."

Confederate officers held prisoner at Fort Delaware on Pea Patch Island in the Delaware River attend a prayer service. The officer standing in the middle of the back row wears the jacket in which he was captured.

**1ST LT. JOSEPH V. BIDGOOD
32D VIRGINIA INFANTRY**

The olive drab of Bidgood's late-War jacket illustrates the variety of fabrics used in making uniforms. A native of Williamsburg, Virginia, Bidgood gave up his studies at the College of William and Mary in April 1861 to join the Confederate army.

**CAPT. EDWARD S. MARSH
4TH NORTH CAROLINA INFANTRY**

Captain Marsh (whose jacket appears at right) led Company I of the 4th North Carolina into battle at Chancellorsville on May 3, 1863. As the 4th attacked the Federal center, Marsh was shot, the bullet passing through his lung. Despite the severity of his injury, he partially recovered and was promoted to major on May 19, 1863. Complications from the wound forced his resignation in February 1865.

INFANTRY AND RIFLEMAN BUTTONS

HAMMOND, TURNER & BATES, MANCHESTER

P. TAIT LIMERICK

S. ISAACS, CAMPBELL LONDON

E. M. LEWIS RICHMOND (LOCAL)

BLANK (LOCAL)

BLANK (LOCAL)

HAMMOND, TURNER & BATES, MANCHESTER

HALFMANN & TAYLOR MONTGOMERY

BLANK (LOCAL)

**MAJ. BENJAMIN H. GREEN
GENERAL EWELL'S STAFF**

Green, whose uniform is shown above, was chief of subsistence under General Richard Ewell. He narrowly avoided death when a bullet tore through the right side of his jacket. Luckily, the watch in his inside pocket stopped the projectile, saving his life.

The Cavalryman's Flair

**GEN. JAMES EWELL BROWN STUART
VIRGINIA**

Jeb Stuart *(above, right)* preferred a double-breasted shell jacket that mimicked the officer's frock coat but was more comfortable for riding. Renowned for his panache, Stuart was described by one English officer as "the only leader of the army who understood how to combine the effects of fire and shock." According to General Lee, the Confederacy lost "the eyes of the army" in May 1864 when Stuart was killed at the battle at Yellow Tavern.

**COL. JOHN S. MOSBY
VIRGINIA**

Recognized by his trademark slouch hat *(below, right)*, Mosby *(right)* organized his infamous Partisan Rangers in early 1863. Often accused of daredeviltry, Mosby took care never to expose his men to danger needlessly. "His cool, quiet courage and the almost unvarying success of every enterprise which he personally conducted secured the perfect confidence of his men," averred one of Mosby's Rangers.

CAPT. JOHN W. BULLOCK
5TH VIRGINIA CAVALRY

Early in the War, many tailors added belt loops, like those on Bullock's jacket, to the jackets they produced. These loops disappeared quickly, however, proving to be a waste of material. Bullock's company mourned the loss of their "dashing young leader," who died behind enemy lines at Dumfries, Virginia, in January 1863.

CAVALRY BUTTONS

HAMMOND, TURNER & BATES, MANCHESTER	CHATWIN & SONS BIRMINGHAM, ENG.	HALFMANN & TAYLOR MONTGOMERY
S. ISAACS, CAMPBELL LONDON	T. MILLER HOUSTON (LOCAL)	BLANK (LOCAL)

Artillery Officer's Jackets

ARTILLERY BUTTONS

HAMMOND, TURNER
& BATES, MANCHESTER

CHATWIN & SONS
BIRMINGHAM, ENG.

HALFMANN & TAYLOR
MONTGOMERY

S. ISAACS, CAMPBELL
LONDON

E. M. LEWIS
RICHMOND (LOCAL)

BLANK
(LOCAL)

**CAPT. JOHN DONNELL SMITH
BEDFORD LIGHT ARTILLERY**

Smith commanded part of this Virginia battery, which served in every campaign of the Army of Northern Virginia. Originally a Marylander, Smith put his state buttons on his cadet gray wool jacket *(above)*. Lieutenant Colonel E. P. Alexander, in one of his reports, praised Smith's performance at Fredericksburg in December 1862, saying, "I was personally impressed with the bearing of J. Donnell Smith in the attack on the evening of the 13th."

**CAPT. G. GASTON OTEY
13TH VIRGINIA ARTILLERY**

Hailed by the commander of the Washington Artillery as "a noteworthy organization, composed of the best young men in Richmond and Virginia," Otey's battery participated in campaigns in western Virginia and Knoxville before joining the Army of Northern Virginia. Otey, whose kepi *(below, right)* bears the crossed cannon designated for his branch of service, died at Lynchburg in October 1862 wearing his fatigue jacket *(right)*.

The Charmed Life of an Artillerist

Major Richard Snowden Andrews, the 31-year-old commander of General Charles Winder's divisional artillery, was still nursing an injury received during the Seven Days' Battles when he led his batteries into action at Cedar Mountain, Virginia, on August 9, 1862. There, near the front, a Federal shell ripped a gaping hole in his stomach, nearly disemboweling him.

Clasping his intestines in one hand, Andrews slid from his horse and managed to roll to the ground on his back. There he lay for three hours until an ambulance took him to a field hospital.

The army surgeons, on seeing Andrews' condition, declared that there was no hope: Even if the wound were closed, a fatal infection would surely follow. Told that his chances were less than one in a hundred, Andrews replied, "Well, I am going to hold on to my one chance."

A surgeon then cut away Andrews' jacket, washed the wound, and sewed him up crudely with a needle and thread. Eight months later, wearing a protective metal plate over his wound, Andrews rejoined his unit—just in time to be wounded again on the way to Gettysburg. After a second convalescence, Andrews was discharged and assigned as an envoy to Europe.

Hailed by General William Pendleton as a "brilliant and thoroughly meritorious artillery officer," Andrews kept the jacket he wore at Cedar Mountain as a memento of his narrow escape. The right side of the garment was torn by a Federal shell; the left half was cut to make the coat easier to remove.

124

This portrait of the Branch brothers together, John, Hamilton, and Sanford *(left to right),* was taken before the War, from which the oldest, John, would not return.

Three Brothers for Georgia

When word of war breaking out reached the Branch family in Savannah in the spring of 1861, brothers John, 23, Sanford, 21, and Hamilton, 18, eagerly cast their lot with the 8th Georgia Infantry. In late July, the Branch boys were shipped east to join the forces holding Bull Run in Virginia. On July 21, General Bartow ordered the 8th Georgia to the front.

"We left Manassas Junction on Sunday morning about four o'clock," Sanford Branch later wrote to his mother. "We gained a small piece of woods when I left the company and advanced in front. I thought I would look behind me to see if any of my company had fallen. But, Mother, just think of my horror to see John reel and fall. I dropped my gun and ran to him. He died in my arms."

**1ST LT. HAMILTON BRANCH
54TH GEORGIA INFANTRY**

The youngest and handsomest of the Branch boys, Hamilton *(right)* was wounded three times during the War. He received his second and severest wound near Atlanta in June 1864, and spent the next three months at home recuperating. He rejoined his command and was wounded again in December. In April 1865 when he returned to his company, his commander pronounced him unfit for field duty and detailed him to collect absentees. A photograph of Hamilton wearing his uniform hat *(below, right)* served as the model for a bronze statue of a Confederate soldier erected in 1879 and still standing in a Savannah park.

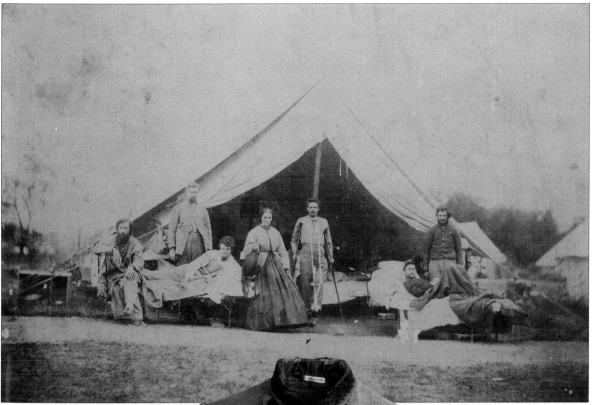

In a rare hospital photograph, Sanford Branch *(on cot at right)* recovers from a wound he received at Gettysburg. Left for dead on the field by his own men, Sanford was captured and treated by the Federals. He made a remarkable recovery and was exchanged in December 1864.

1ST LT. SANFORD BRANCH 8TH GEORGIA INFANTRY

The left sleeve of Sanford's frock coat *(right)* displays the mark of the bullet that penetrated his shoulder at Gettysburg; the coat's hem has burn marks probably caused by its wearer's huddling too close to a campfire. Sanford most likely covered the buttons and collar of his uniform coat in black velvet after the War in accordance with the Union order forbidding the display of any Confederate symbols.

Surgeons and Engineers

CONFEDERATE MAJOR FROM ALABAMA MEDICAL CORPS

Near the Dunker Church at Sharpsburg, Federal and Confederate Medical Corps officers shake hands during an improvised truce.

**LT. COL. SAMUEL M. BEMISS
SURGEON**

Samuel Bemiss served in
a hospital in Ringgold,
Georgia, that treated the
sick and wounded of
General Bragg's army.
Black cotton facings on
Bemiss' coat cuffs *(left)*
resembled those worn
by all Confederate sur-
geons. A friend once
said of Bemiss, "He was
so genial, so sympathetic,
so entirely en rapport
with everybody."

Enlisted men in the Ambulance Corps put
badges like these in their caps when working as stretcher-bearers behind the lines to
prove they were not shirking battle.

ENGINEER BUTTONS

S. ISAACS, CAMPBELL
LONDON

WILLIAM DOWLER
BIRMINGHAM, ENG.

CHARLES JENNENS
LONDON

E. M. LEWIS
RICHMOND (LOCAL)

**CAPT. CHARLES H.
DIMMOCK, ENGINEER**

Dimmock *(left)* super-
vised the design and
construction of the
outer line of Confeder-
ate fortifications ringing
Petersburg, Virginia. As
a railroad hub linking
Richmond with the
Deep South, Petersburg
was indispensable to the
defense of the Confeder-
ate capital and the sup-
ply of Lee's army.

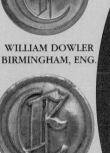

**MAJ. THOMAS M. R. TALCOTT
ENGINEER, LEE'S STAFF**

Talcott apparently had the insignia on his
kepi *(left)* custom-made in deference to
the regulations calling for the old English
letter *E* to be embroidered in gold on
the caps of chief engineers. Captured at
Roanoke Island, Virginia, in early February
1862, Talcott was exchanged a week later.

**1ST SGT. JOHN W. LESTER
10TH GEORGIA INFANTRY**

Of the 620,000 men who lost their lives in the Civil War, more than 60 percent perished from disease. John Lester was one of the latter: He died of typhoid fever. Lester's family made the vest, coat, and pants shown here and sent them to him at the front. Sadly, he died before they arrived.

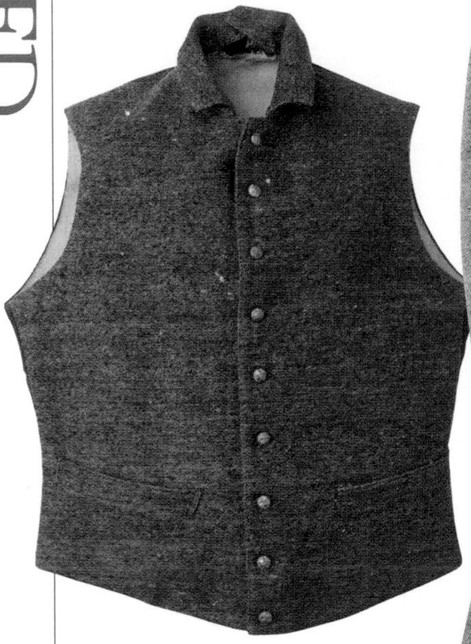

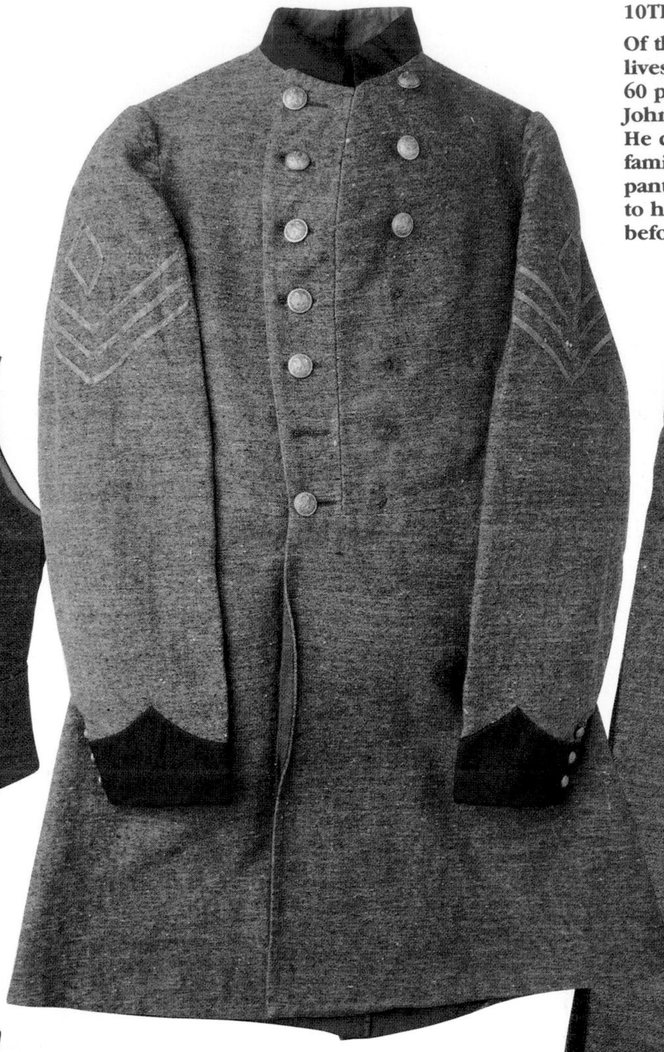

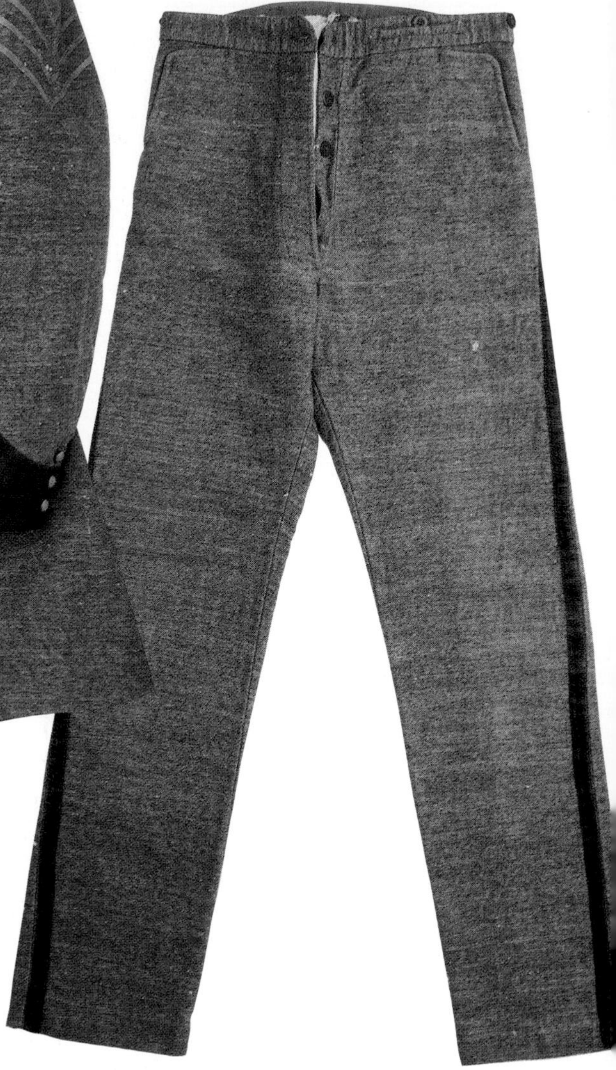

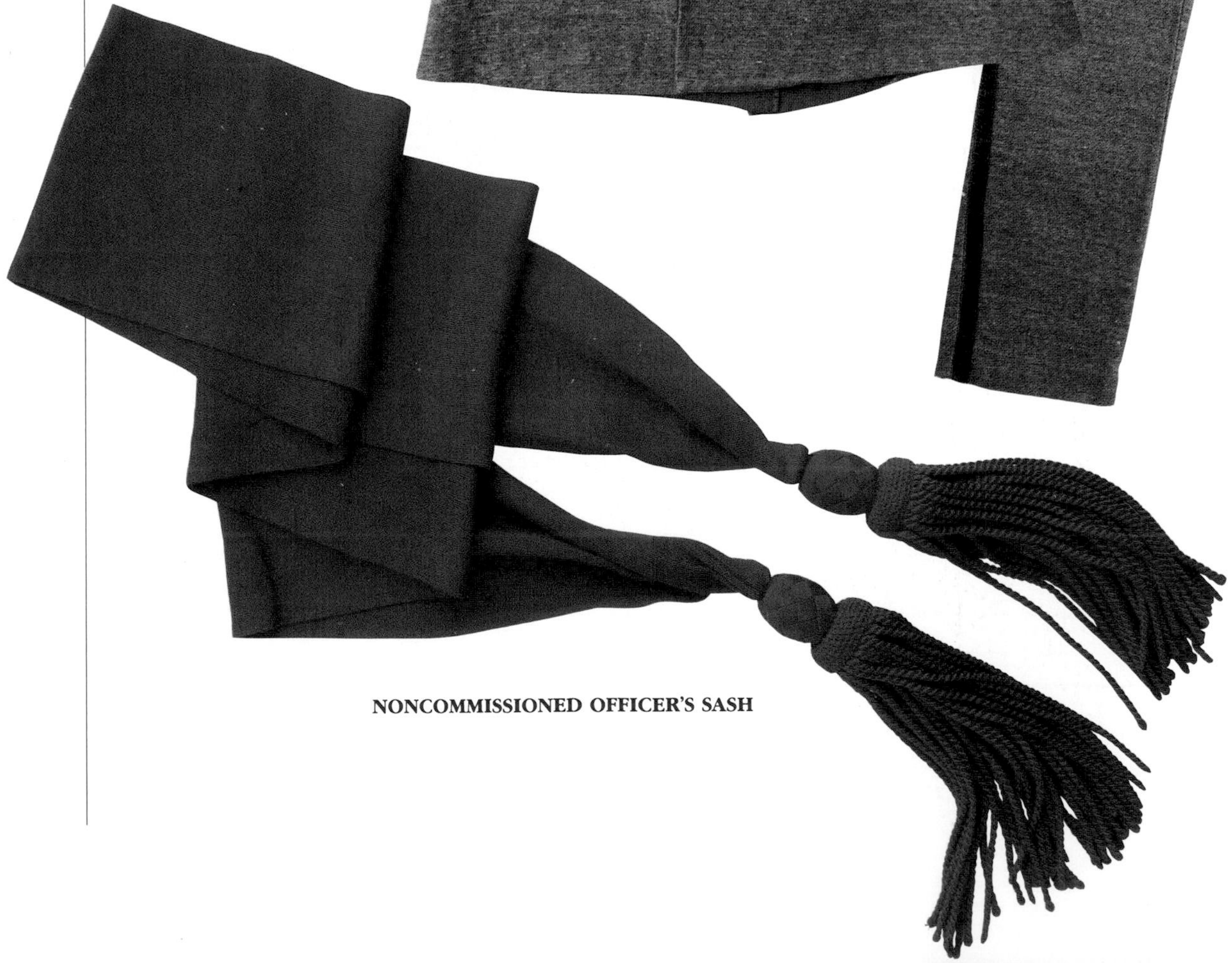

NONCOMMISSIONED OFFICER'S SASH

CONFEDERATE INFANTRYMEN

WILLIAM R. HODGE
14TH VIRGINIA CAVALRY

In December 1862, Yankees captured Hodge in Greenbrier County, Virginia, and took him to Camp Chase, Ohio. From there he was transported in an open boat to Vicksburg to be exchanged. For some reason, the exchange never took place, and the boat headed for an Illinois prison. Hodge never completed this voyage: He died en route, 30 miles from Vicksburg. A fellow prisoner returned Hodge's coat *(left)* to his family.

PVT. JOSEPH B. PHILLIPS
CRESCENT REGIMENT
LOUISIANA INFANTRY

The yellow piping on Phillips' coat did not, in this case, indicate his branch of service. Occasionally, individual regiments chose a specific color just because they liked it. Phillips, who enlisted in March 1862, fought with the Crescent Regiment in the Battle of Shiloh before he died of unknown causes three months later at Tupelo, Mississippi.

Coats for the Soldier

Loyal to their local men, Texas counties vied with each other to outfit and equip those who volunteered to serve the Confederacy—such as the men of the 1st Texas Infantry shown here in their frock coats at Camp Quantico, Virginia, in the winter of 1861.

LOUISIANA INFANTRYMAN

This coat, worn by a Louisiana infantryman, is probably one of the nine-button frocks issued by Louisiana. When called upon in 1861 to provide uniforms for its soldiers, the state first tried contracting with local firms. When that failed, they resorted to having jean-cloth uniforms manufactured at the state penitentiary.

1ST CORP. ROBERT A. BOMAR HAMPTON LEGION

Wade Hampton raised an entire regiment in South Carolina in the spring of 1861 and paid for each soldier's clothing out of his own pocket. Coats like Robert Bomar's were manufactured by local tailoring firms. Hit by three musket balls at First Manassas, Bomar was discharged in October 1861.

**PVT. B. N. G. SCHUMPERT
3D SOUTH CAROLINA INFANTRY**

No one knows the origin of Private Schumpert's odd ticking-striped frock coat and pants, but several such uniforms existed in the Western theater during the War. The 17-year-old Schumpert received a $50 bounty when he enlisted in the Confederate army in 1862. The bloodstains on the collar are from the mortal head wound he received at Chickamauga.

**PVT. JOHN E. JOHNSTON
29TH ALABAMA INFANTRY**

Johnston was wearing the jean-cloth coat below at the Battle of Peach Tree Creek in July 1864 when a Minié ball entered his chest just under the collarbone. His mother, on her way to bring her son additional homespun garments, discovered him dead on the battlefield.

**CORPORAL, 1ST
GEORGIA INFANTRY**

Shell Jackets

**PVT. JOHN Y. GILMORE
3D ALABAMA INFANTRY**

Dressed in this jacket of wool-and-cotton twill—in which he was also photographed *(above)*—Gilmore was wounded three times at Malvern Hill in July of 1862. Obtained under the commutation system—in which volunteer regiments provided their own clothing and were reimbursed by the government—Gilmore's coat is typical of the waist-length, single-breasted shell jackets worn by enlisted men in the early days of the War.

**PVT. JOHN DIMITRY
CRESCENT REGIMENT
LOUISIANA INFANTRY**

Private Dimitry was wounded at Shiloh in April of 1862 while wearing the shell jacket at right. Made under the commutation system, it was issued to him when he enlisted one month earlier. Because it was easily manufactured and required little cloth, the shell jacket was authorized early on by the Quartermaster's Department as the standard upper garment for enlisted men.

Uniformed in the regulation shell jacket of their unit, the enlisted men of the Sumter Light Guards stand at attention in Augusta, Georgia, in April of 1861. The officers and N.C.O.s wear frock coats.

Early Richmond Depot Jackets

Private William Moore and a youth believed to be his brother, both of Parker's Virginia Battery, posed in 1862 wearing jackets of the first style issued by the Richmond depot—a shell jacket trimmed with piping or tape.

**PVT. E. COURTNEY JENKINS
21ST VIRGINIA INFANTRY**

Kent, Paine & Company, a Richmond dry goods manufacturer, made Private Jenkins' jacket, which follows the basic pattern of the first Richmond depot jackets. None of the early jackets actually produced by the depot are believed to have survived the War.

The Merchant's Cotton Mill *(far right)* at Petersburg produced material used

**PVT. ANDREW E. DIGGS
5TH VIRGINIA CAVALRY**

Clad in the jacket at left, Diggs was killed at Malvern Hill in July of 1862. The garment is styled after the first Richmond depot jackets, which were being produced as early as February of 1862. Made from wool jean cloth with yellow cotton-tape piping, Diggs' jacket has an unusual brown-and-white plaid cotton flannel lining. A coarse cotton cloth known as osnaburg lined most enlisted men's jackets.

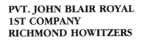

**PVT. JOHN BLAIR ROYAL
1ST COMPANY
RICHMOND HOWITZERS**

The left sleeve of Royal's jacket *(above)* bears the marks of the Federal shell that wounded him at Chancellorsville. An example of the second pattern of jacket issued by the depot, Royal's garment—which he apparently preserved as a souvenir of his close escape—displays the six-piece body, two-piece sleeves, nine-button front, plain cuffs, and belt loops that characterize the style.

PVT. GEORGE H. T. GREER

This gray wool jacket worn by Private Greer—who served as military secretary to General Jubal Early—is untrimmed, a feature that differentiates most of the second Richmond depot jackets from the first. Partially trimmed examples, however, do exist—such as Private Royal's *(above)*. The second-pattern jacket was produced from the spring of 1862 until mid-1864.

to line Richmond depot jackets.

Late Depot Jackets

**PVT. JOHN K. COLEMAN
6TH SOUTH CAROLINA INFANTRY**

Sometime after he was wounded
on October 1, 1864, Private Coleman received the third-pattern
Richmond depot jacket above,
which he wore at the surrender
at Appomattox. The South Carolina state seal buttons were
apparently added by Coleman;
Richmond depot jackets were
generally issued with standard
branch-of-service buttons.

Exhibited in 1866, this painting by Winslow Homer depicts his cousin, Colonel Francis Channing Barlow of the 61st New York Infantry, confronting three Confederate captives. The prisoners wear the third style of jacket issued by the Richmond depot.

THIRD-PATTERN RICHMOND DEPOT JACKETS

The Richmond depot issued the cadet gray wool kersey jackets at left and right to two brothers: Private Henry Redwood and Sergeant Major Allen C. Redwood. Except for the lack of shoulder straps and belt loops, the third style of jacket issued by the depot was identical to the second. The red tape on the jacket at right—believed to have been worn by Henry Redwood, who served with a local Virginia militia unit—was probably added at personal whim, since third-pattern jackets were issued untrimmed. Allen Redwood, a noted artist, served through the War with the Army of Northern Virginia.

Sack Coats for Enlisted Men

In addition to the shell jackets they produced for the army, the Confederate government depots sometimes issued sack coats, or fatigue blouses—loose, unfitted, middle-length coats with widely spaced buttons. The depots may have manufactured some of these plain coats themselves, but many of them were donated by state relief organizations and ladies' aid societies. Patterned after informal civilian coats worn since the 1840s, sack coats were popular for their comfort, simplicity of manufacture, and cheapness—they were often made from easily obtained inexpensive, loosely woven fabric.

CONFEDERATE SACK COAT

The sack coat at left was probably distributed to a soldier in the field through one of the official Confederate depots. The jacket is lined in the body and sleeves with osnaburg (a heavy, coarse cotton), the standard lining fabric used for enlisted men's garb.

Wearing a baggy sack coat and trousers, Private John T. Davis posed with his weapons for this wartime portrait. The bewhiskered private is believed to have served with an Alabama regiment.

**CORP. T. V. BROOKE
3D COMPANY
RICHMOND HOWITZERS**

Corporal Brooke wore this plain sack coat—which was issued to him through the Richmond depot—at the surrender of Lee's army at Appomattox. Of brown wool jean cloth with a black collar facing, the jacket has a horizontal-slit front pocket. The two-hole, recessed-center buttons down its front were of the type issued by the government for use on all sorts of garments.

A Bounty from Ireland

During the late days of the War, jackets manufactured by Peter Tait of Limerick, Ireland, were widely imported and issued to Confederate soldiers serving in Virginia and North Carolina. One of the largest ready-made clothing manufacturers in the world at the time, Tait not only contracted with the Confederacy for uniforms but delivered them in his own blockade runners. Tait jackets are characterized by a five-piece body, eight-button front, and a linen lining, which was usually stamped with size markings of the British army system. All surviving Tait jackets are made of the same cadet gray kersey used in the last pattern of Richmond depot jackets.

**PVT. HUGH LAWSON DUNCAN
39TH GEORGIA INFANTRY**

This Tait jacket owned by Private Duncan—who wore it at the surrender of the Army of Tennessee at the Bennett House in North Carolina—is believed to have been part of a blockade-run shipment that entered through Wilmington, North Carolina, sometime during the last two months of 1864. Duncan's jacket retains all of its original buttons, which are stamped "P. Tait, Limerick."

**PVT. GARRETT GOUGE
58TH NORTH CAROLINA**

In near-mint condition, Private Gouge's blue-trimmed Tait jacket was probably drawn just before he went home at the end of the War. Its markings read, "5 feet 10/39-34," which indicate that it was made for a man five feet 10 inches tall, with a chest of 39 inches and a waist of 34.

Western Depot Jackets

When commanders needed clothing for their troops, most of them had to request it from the quartermaster general in Richmond, who then decided which of the official depots could most efficiently fill the order. The Western clothing depots, for instance, usually supplied the Army of Tennessee, although products from the large depot in Columbus, Georgia, probably saw service in every theater of the War. In addition, a few depots operated independently of the quartermaster general and dealt directly with some commanders. The jackets produced by the Western depots were very similar; only through their histories have their origins been traced.

PVT. JOHN A. DOLAN AUSTIN'S BATTALION LOUISIANA SHARPSHOOTERS

Private Dolan's jacket is probably one of the thousands made especially for the survivors of the Army of Tennessee assigned to General Richard Taylor's Department of Alabama, Mississippi, and East Louisiana. Characterized by a five-button front and one exterior pocket, the wool jackets were manufactured in late 1864 or early 1865, most likely at an Alabama or a Mississippi depot. Written in ink on the lining of Dolan's jacket are the details of his service with the Confederate army, including the date of his enlistment in New Orleans—August 17, 1861—and the date of his surrender—May 12, 1865.

J. McDONALD, MISSOURI INFANTRY

Another example of the jacket made for General Taylor's Department of Alabama, Mississippi, and East Louisiana, the coat at left was reportedly worn by either Private John McDonald or Sergeant J. A. McDonald. Both men served with the 8th Missouri Infantry Regiment and were paroled at New Orleans in May 1865.

SHELL JACKET

Seven Confederate-issue wooden buttons fasten the unidentified jacket at right, which probably came from a Deep South depot—possibly the one in Mobile, Alabama.

PVT. THOMAS TAYLOR
8TH LOUISIANA INFANTRY

Private Taylor, pictured below, wore a jacket *(below, right)* that came from the Montgomery depot, but it is of finer fabric and cut than standard-issue jackets. Detailed to the Montgomery Quartermaster's Department, Taylor purchased his own material from the depot in November of 1863 and then had a tailor custom-make the garment.

Jackets from Georgia Shops

**PVT. JOHN C. ZEHRING
4TH TENNESSEE INFANTRY**

In early 1865, John Zehring, pictured above on his carte de visite, received this jacket in which he penned his name. Most likely a Georgia state issue, the jacket may have been made by the Milledgeville Manufacturing Company in Milledgeville, Georgia. Zehring was detailed in Milledgeville as a hospital steward in the C.S. Medical Department.

**1ST SGT. J. FULLER LYON
19TH SOUTH CAROLINA
INFANTRY**

Fashioned from a rough handloomed wool resembling salt-and-pepper burlap, Lyon's jacket *(left)* came from the Atlanta depot. The hole in the left arm was made by the bullet that wounded Lyon at Lovejoy's Station in Georgia.

**PVT. ELIJAH C. WOODWARD
9TH KENTUCKY INFANTRY**

This five-button wool jean jacket *(right)* worn by Private Woodward probably came from the depot in Columbus, Georgia. Designated as a Columbus Type I, the jacket has two interior pockets. Woodward enlisted in the Confederate army in September 1861; he deserted a year later.

Furnished by
North Carolina

Of all the Confederate states, North Carolina was the most successful at furnishing clothing for its troops throughout the War. This six-button sack coat *(above)* complies with early state regulations for enlisted men.

WILLIAM EDWARD TUCKER
Tucker wore this plain wool-and-cotton jacket *(right)* when he worked at the Confederate government shops at Charlotte, North Carolina. In 1865, Tucker helped guard the wagons containing the Confederacy's money at the time of Jefferson Davis' capture by the Federals.

Private Alfred Turner *(left)* of the 4th North Carolina State Troops is shown wearing an early state-issue sack coat. The black strip of cloth on the coat's shoulder marked him as an infantryman.

**PVT. HUGH L. DUNCAN
39TH GEORGIA INFANTRY**

When Duncan was surrendered near Greensboro in April 1865, he was wearing these military-style wool-and-cotton trousers.

**PVT. AMZI L. WILLIAMSON
53D NORTH CAROLINA INFANTRY**

North Carolina provided sack coats for its troops until early 1862, when it replaced them with gray jackets. Williamson's jacket *(above)*, which he was wearing when he was hit by musket fire at the Battle of Gettysburg, typifies North Carolina's longer-waisted version of the Confederate shell. His jean-cloth cap *(right)* closely copies the Federal army forage cap.

Trans-Mississippi Garb

**PVT. BURTON MARCHBANKS
30TH TEXAS CAVALRY**

After enlisting in the Confederate army on July 12, 1862, Burton Marchbanks *(inset, right)* went to war in this homespun butternut jacket and jean trousers stitched together by his wife. Only the metal buttons on the jacket were furnished by the Confederate government. On July 17, 1863, Private Marchbanks was seriously wounded and captured by the Federals at Honey Springs, Indian Territory. Paroled after the battle, he was allowed to go home to Johnson County, Texas, to die.

**LT. JOHN DUNCAN HOLIDAY
TAPPAN'S ARKANSAS BRIGADE**

An ordnance officer, Lieutenant Holiday wore this red-trimmed wool jacket in battles at Mansfield, Louisiana, and Jenkins' Farm, Arkansas. It features an unusual single-button closure at the neck and the gold-braid insignia of a first lieutenant on the collar. Lieutenant Holiday surrendered at Shreveport on June 8, 1865.

Colonel Richard M. Gano, commander of the 7th Kentucky Cavalry Regiment, posed for the camera *(left)* in a tasseled and plumed tricorne and a double-breasted frock coat. Gano won high praise for destroying a 250-wagon Federal supply train at Cabin Creek in the Indian Territory on September 19, 1864.

CAPT. WILLIAM H. CLEAVER 2D TEXAS MOUNTED RIFLES

The yellow cotton trim on the collar of this single-breasted, brown wool shell jacket worn by Captain Cleaver—who died in service in the New Mexico Territory in 1862—denotes his rank.

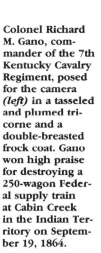

Captain Samuel Richardson of the 3d Texas went to war in jaguar-skin trousers with holsters to match—a striking example of the singular garb worn by some soldiers in the West, where little or no heed was paid to Confederate uniform regulations.

A silky scarf knotted in a bow around his collar adds a jaunty touch to the plain shirt and trousers worn by the soldier at left, an unknown private in the Texas cavalry.

PVT. CHARLES J. ANDERSON VIRGINIA MILITARY INSTITUTE

Buttons stamped with the VMI seal fasten this unlined butternut wool shell jacket worn by Private Anderson. He was one of more than 200 VMI cadets who joined the forces of Major General John C. Breckinridge in the Battle of New Market in May 1864. The cadets were assigned to Brigadier General John Echols' command; 10 of the youths died of wounds received in battle.

The VMI cadets Hardaway Dinwiddie, Gaylord Clark, Thomas Hayes, Richard Tunstall, and Edward Tutwiler *(clockwise from top left)* pose in their West Point-inspired dress uniforms. All five were mustered to counter the Federal thrust into the Shenandoah Valley.

Calling Up the Cadets

During the first years of the War, cadets from the many Southern military academies—a valued source of trained officers—were held in reserve. The primary contribution of Virginia Military Institute students, for instance, was to drill green troops at Richmond.

As the Confederacy's desperation deepened, however, some cadets were mobilized into fighting units. Many of the boys went off in government-issue fatigue-style uniforms, but as the War continued, the VMI cadet Corporal John S. Wise later wrote, "Our uniforms ceased to be uniforms; for as the difficulty of procuring cloth increased we were permitted to supply ourselves with whatever our parents could procure."

CADET CHARLES LOCKE BEARD

Now faded to light brown, Cadet Beard's cotton homespun shell jacket may originally have been gray. He wore it in 1865 when he was a 15-year-old student at the Florida Military Institute in Tallahassee. Similar jackets were issued to a number of Southern military schools by the Confederate government even before the cadets were mobilized.

**PVT. JOHN McNISH HAZLEHURST
GEORGIA MILITARY INSTITUTE**

John Hazlehurst was 17 when he posed for the picture below and then marched off with the Georgia Battalion of Cadets, which had been mobilized to join the home guard. He served from spring of 1864 until May 1865. Hazlehurst's matching jacket, vest, trousers, and kepi were probably provided by his family.

Overcoats

Lieutenant Colonel Harry W. Gilmor *(above)* rode with the 7th Virginia Cavalry. His overcoat follows the Federal pattern, which features a longer cape for mounted troops.

MAJ. GEN. JOHN B. HOOD ARMY OF NORTHERN VIRGINIA

Hood's double-breasted overcoat, with its red flannel lining, was undoubtedly warm. Speaking of Hood's Brigade, a distinguished U.S. congressman declared after the War, "I would rather have been able to say that I had been a worthy member of Hood's Texas Brigade than to have enjoyed all the honors which have been conferred upon me."

COL. ELLISON CAPERS 24TH SOUTH CAROLINA INFANTRY

Although the Confederacy prescribed overcoats only for its enlisted men, many of its officers, like Colonel Capers, had overcoats made to wear in foul weather. Capers' brown wool twill coat *(left)* exhibits no officer's insignia or sleeve braid, in accordance with official ordinance.

GEN. BRYAN GRIMES NORTH CAROLINA

Devoid of ornamentation except for buff-colored piping, Grimes' loose-fitting overcoat shows his penchant for plain clothing. His coat is not an official pattern; it may be an old civilian overcoat to which he added trim and military buttons.

Enlisted men Columbus C. Taylor, James D. Jackson, and James H. Porter *(left to right)* of the 3d Georgia posed in their overcoats when their regiment was camped near Richmond in the winter of 1861-62. Taylor and Jackson were killed at Malvern Hill.

**PVT. JAMES CURTIS
23D NORTH CAROLINA
INFANTRY**

Private Curtis enlisted in Company D (Pee Dee Guards), 23d North Carolina, on August 11, 1861. Curtis was issued the greatcoat at left before leaving for Virginia but never had the chance to wear it. He died of fever at Richmond's Chimborazo Hospital on January 25, 1862.

**PVT. J. O. McGEHEE
53D VIRGINIA INFANTRY**

McGehee wore this homespun overcoat during the winter campaign of 1864-65. He had it in early April 1865 when he was wounded at the Battle of Five Forks in Virginia.

Trousers

COTTON TROUSERS

Made from cotton jean cloth woven in Spartanburg, South Carolina, these light blue trousers were worn by a soldier named J. T. Moore. In the early days of the War, work-style trousers such as these were frequently issued to, or purchased by, soldiers in volunteer units.

RICHMOND DEPOT TROUSERS

Lined with light brown cotton and unbleached osnaburg, these blue wool trousers were probably issued to either Sergeant Major Allen C. Redwood or Private Henry Redwood by the Richmond depot. The buttons are of japanned tin.

CORP. T. V. BROOKE
3D COMPANY
RICHMOND HOWITZERS

The unusual gathered cuffs of these wool kersey trousers are equipped with hooks. The pants probably came from the Richmond depot and were later altered to Brooke's specifications.

153

**PVT. JESSE BRYANT BECK
25TH ALABAMA
INFANTRY**

A jagged tear and faded bloodstains mark Private Beck's trousers *(left)*, which he was wearing when he was wounded at the Battle of Atlanta on July 22, 1864. Of wool-and-cotton homespun cloth, the trousers are trimmed with bone buttons.

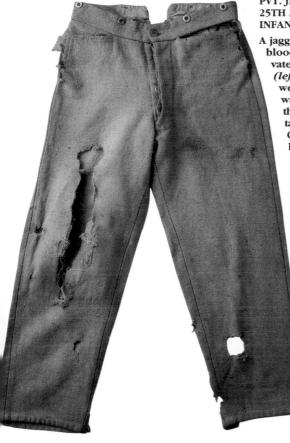

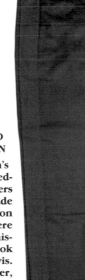

**LT. HAMILTON BRANCH
54TH GEORGIA INFANTRY**

The Georgia Relief and Hospital Association stamped its name in the lining of this pair of trousers, which it donated to the troops. Lieutenant Branch may have drawn them through the Richmond clothing depot.

**LT. SANFORD BRANCH
8TH GEORGIA INFANTRY**

Officer's trousers, such as the pair at left worn by Lieutenant Branch, were generally made to fit and were almost always of finer fabric than those worn by enlisted men.

**COL. EDWARD
ANDERSON**

Colonel Anderson's smartly tailored red-trimmed trousers *(right)* were made for him in London while he was there on a wartime mission he undertook for Jefferson Davis. An artillery officer, Anderson also supervised the Savannah defenses.

**CAVALRY OFFICER'S
TROUSERS**

The yellow piping down the trousers at left identifies them with the cavalry, in accordance with Confederate uniform regulations. Infantry officers' trousers were to be striped in dark blue, artillery officers' in red.

Shirts
Drab or Fancy

**PVT. JOHN BURGWYN MacRAE
STARR'S NORTH CAROLINA BATTERY**

Private MacRae's wool pullover shirt, which he wore at the Battle of Bentonville, was North Carolina state issue.

**PVT. ANDREW THOMAS BEAM
28TH SOUTH CAROLINA VOLUNTEERS**

White glass buttons fasten this cotton shirt worn by Private Beam, who was killed in action at Petersburg.

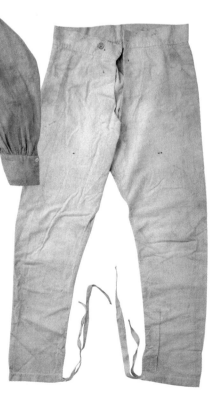

To keep them from riding up—and to keep out drafts—these long cotton drawers worn by R. I. Maury had ties at the cuffs.

IMPORTED SHIRT

Manufactured in England, this British army shirt was run through the Union blockade.

Casually attired, the men of Company A of the 5th Georgia Volunteers lounge about camp in this photograph taken at Augusta, Georgia, in 1861. The letters *CR* on the front of the wall tent stand for Clinch Rifles, the company's name.

PVT. M. PAGE LAPHAM WASHINGTON ARTILLERY OF NEW ORLEANS

A pleated front adorns this white cotton shirt worn by Private Lapham, who died on May 23, 1864, from wounds received at Drewry's Bluff on May 14.

BRIG. GEN. DAVID A. WEISIGER

General Weisiger's pullover shirt is patched where he was struck by a bullet during the Battle of the Crater on July 30, 1864. His actions there earned him an on-the-spot promotion to brigadier general.

Made from a wildly patterned wool tablecloth and trimmed with a black velvet collar and placket, this unique shirt was worn by an unidentified Confederate soldier captured at Vicksburg.

PVT. PETER S. HYDE

This blue-and-white plaid shirt worn by Private Hyde—whose regiment is unidentified—was reportedly made in camp by someone named Tom Buck out of a bedspread stolen from a Pennsylvania home.

HEADGEAR

ENLISTED MAN'S KEPI
Despite some difficulty in obtaining materials, Confederate quartermasters supplied kepis, the regulation headgear, throughout the War. This wool jean kepi, with an oilcloth brim, was probably issued by the Richmond clothing depot.

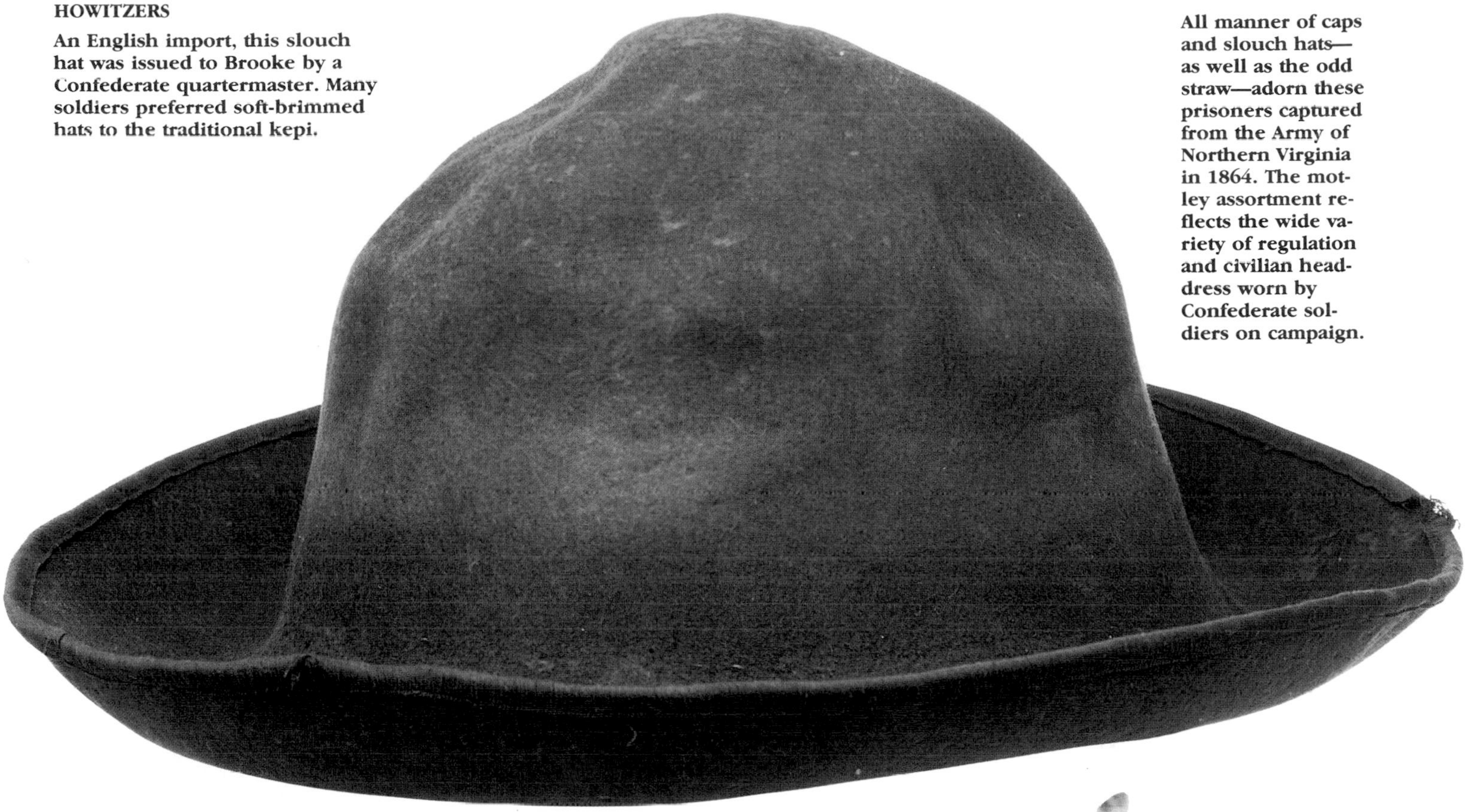

**CORP. T. V. BROOKE
3D COMPANY, RICHMOND
HOWITZERS**

An English import, this slouch hat was issued to Brooke by a Confederate quartermaster. Many soldiers preferred soft-brimmed hats to the traditional kepi.

All manner of caps and slouch hats—as well as the odd straw—adorn these prisoners captured from the Army of Northern Virginia in 1864. The motley assortment reflects the wide variety of regulation and civilian headdress worn by Confederate soldiers on campaign.

Volunteers' Headgear

GEN. THOMAS J. "STONEWALL" JACKSON

Jackson's cap was a relic of his faculty days at Virginia Military Institute.

**LT. W. R. MacBETH
12TH BATTALION
LOUISIANA INFANTRY**

MacBeth's unusual kepi was made from stiffened cloth.

HAVELOCK

Inspired by the cloth hat covers worn by British soldiers in India, the havelock was popular in the summer of 1861.

**CAPT. BENJAMIN CHASE
22D VIRGINIA INFANTRY**

A luxurious velvet band and top distinguish this low-crowned kepi worn by Captain Chase.

6TH BATTALION, TENNESSEE CAVALRY

The initials on the Mexican War-style hat above identified its owner as a member of the company known as the Hardeman Avengers.

**LT. J. KENT EWING
4TH VIRGINIA**

Ewing—mortally wounded at Gettysburg—sports an Italian-style fatigue cap cover intended for off-duty wear.

The cotton fatigue cap cover below was found in Captain O. J. Wise's haversack.

**CAPT. O. JENNINGS WISE
46TH VIRGINIA INFANTRY**

Wise, killed at Roanoke Island in early 1862, fought wearing this forage cap.

Officers' Kepis

**MAJ. G. B. LARTIGUE
1ST SOUTH CAROLINA**

Still bearing the label of its Charleston manufacturer, the kepi at far left was worn by Lartigue when he served as quartermaster under General Johnson Hagood. The number of strands of gold braid on an officer's kepi denoted rank: one for lieutenants, two for captains, three for field officers, and four for generals.

GEN. JOHN BANKHEAD MAGRUDER

Magruder's victory at Big Bethel, Virginia, on June 10, 1861, earned him the four stripes on his stylish, Paris-made kepi. Embroidered on its front are the initials "CSA."

GEN. FRANKLIN GARDNER

Gardner, who commanded a cavalry brigade at Shiloh, wore this kepi after being promoted to brigadier general on April 11, 1862.

ARTILLERY OFFICER'S KEPI

The kepi at right was made of red cloth to comply with regulations that called for a man's branch of service to be indicated by the color of his cap: red for artillery, dark blue for staff, sky blue for infantry, and yellow for cavalry. Many kepis, however, were gray because of dye and cloth shortages.

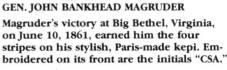

**MAJ. JOHN A. A. WEST
1ST REGULAR BATTERY
C.S. LIGHT ARTILLERY**

A pair of crossed cannons ornament the front of this red, gold, and gray kepi worn by West, a staff officer who saw action in the attack on Baton Rouge in August of 1862.

OFFICER'S KEPI

This low-crowned, flat-brimmed kepi with an embroidered "R" and crescent insignia on its front belonged to an officer who served with a Louisiana unit raised in New Orleans—possibly the Crescent Rifles.

LT. JOHN COLE

The holes on the side and top of this cap worn by Lieutenant Cole, an Alabaman, mark the path of the bullet that killed him near Petersburg, Virginia, on the day of the Battle of the Crater—July 30, 1864.

**COL. WILLIAM J. CLARKE
24TH NORTH CAROLINA INFANTRY**

Clarke's appointment to colonel in July 1861—the same month he organized his regiment—garnered him the three stripes trimming his regulation infantry kepi.

**CAPT. GEORGE J. PRATT
18TH VIRGINIA CAVALRY**

In the spring of 1864, Pratt fought in the battles of New Market and Piedmont wearing this regulation cavalry kepi. As an economy, its brim was made of inexpensive oilcloth instead of fine leather.

Enlisted Men's Caps

ENLISTED MAN'S INFANTRY KEPI

Made from inexpensive cotton jean cloth and finished with a polished blue cotton band, this high-crowned kepi came from a clothing depot in the Deep South.

PVT. CICERO BOWMAN

Although the red piping on his kepi identifies him as a member of the artillery, Bowman—who died of exposure in camp—reportedly belonged to a Georgia infantry regiment. It was not uncommon for troops to be issued whatever headgear the quartermaster had on hand, regardless of distinctions called for by regulations.

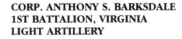

**CORP. ANTHONY S. BARKSDALE
1ST BATTALION, VIRGINIA
LIGHT ARTILLERY**

Barksdale's red kepi with a blue band was regulation issue for enlisted gunners.

**CAPT. DANIEL MORGAN
HART'S BATTERY
SOUTH CAROLINA**

Morgan, like many Confederate officers, wore an enlisted man's kepi despite his rank. This one probably came from the Richmond depot. Morgan's horse artillery battery fought with the Army of Northern Virginia.

**PVT. A. A. CREWS
29TH ALABAMA INFANTRY**

A brown leather visor and a cloth
chin strap finish Crews' kepi,
stained a butternut color by a dye
made of copperas and walnut
hulls. Southerners increasingly
relied on the locally produced
dye as the War drew on and the
Union blockade cut off imports.

ENLISTED MAN'S KEPI

This blue-banded kepi belonged to a
soldier attached to an unidentified Louisiana militia unit represented by the initials "C.G."—perhaps the Cannon Guards,
Clinton Guards, Continental Guards, or
Creole Guards, to name a few.

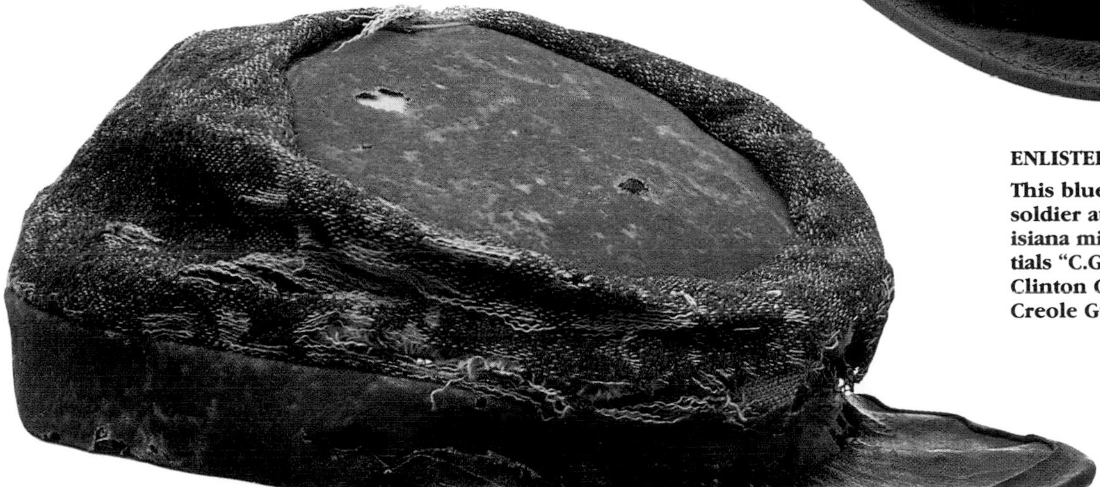

**PVT. ROBERT ROYALL
1ST COMPANY
RICHMOND HOWITZERS**

Private Royall's two-toned
artillery kepi probably came
from the Richmond depot.

Forage Caps

**INFANTRY OFFICER
ARMY OF NORTHERN VIRGINIA**

OFFICER'S FORAGE CAP

Instead of the regulation kepi, some Confederates wore caps patterned after the Regular Army's 1858 forage cap, such as the one above owned by a Captain Wallace of Gordonsville, Virginia. In general, forage caps are distinguished from kepis by their high crowns and flat tops.

**CAPT. WILL HARDIN
47TH GEORGIA INFANTRY**

With its soft sides and forward-sloping top, Hardin's forage cap is typical of the style worn in the early days of the War.

GEN. THOMAS J. "STONEWALL" JACKSON

Before the Battle of Fredericksburg, Jackson inspected his troops wearing a new gold-braided uniform and the gold-banded forage cap above—a splendid improvement over his customary thread-bare attire, which reportedly drew cat-calls and irreverent jests from his men.

CAPT. ROBERT H. ALEXANDER 30TII VIRGINIA INFANTRY

Captain Alexander—who commanded the company known as the Gordon Rifles until April of 1862, when he failed to be re-elected to rank—faced battle in the plain gray forage cap below.

COL. GEORGE WYTHE RANDOLPH 1ST VIRGINIA ARTILLERY

Randolph, who fought at Big Bethel in June of 1861, owned this forage cap with a sharply sloping top. He was later promoted to brigadier general and served as secretary of war for eight months in 1862.

2D LIEUTENANT, STONEWALL BRIGADE

The All-American Slouch Hat

**2D LT. JOHN T. PURVES
7TH LOUISIANA INFANTRY**

Made from beaver fur and lined with purple silk, Purves' slouch hat was folded up as a tricorne—the state-regulation hat style for Mississippi, which was widely copied in neighboring Louisiana.

NORTH CAROLINA SLOUCH HAT

Unlike the European-inspired kepis and forage caps, full-brimmed hats like that above were one of the few native American articles of clothing used during the Civil War. Cords on officers' hats traditionally had acorn ends; enlisted men's had tassels.

**CAPT.
PAUL HAMILTON
1ST SOUTH CAROLINA
LIGHT ARTILLERY**

A palmetto palm, the state badge of South Carolina, trims the upturned brim of Hamilton's hat, a model authorized by the Regular Army in 1858.

**LT. JOHN SELDON
1ST VIRGINIA ARTILLERY**

An ordnance officer with Cutshaw's Battalion, Seldon wore this soft-brimmed, beehive-style slouch hat on duty.

SLOUCH HAT

Lost by an unknown Confederate soldier on the battlefield at Gettysburg, this plain felt slouch hat shows evidence of once having been treated with some type of waterproof coating.

PVT. JAMES H. WILLIFORD 10TH GEORGIA INFANTRY

Private Williford lost his hat—which is adorned with the state seal of Georgia—in the Peach Orchard at Gettysburg, but escaped with his life. Williford fought with General Lafayette McLaws' division.

LT. W. JAMES KINCHELOE 49TH VIRGINIA INFANTRY

Kincheloe posed for this portrait wearing the blue-tasseled hat below—the same hat he had on when he was killed at Gettysburg.

PVT. JAMES W. POAGUE 1ST VIRGINIA CAVALRY

Poague ornamented the upturned brim of his hat with an elaborate leather star.

Hats of the Army of Tennessee

PVT. CLEMENT BASSETT
8TH TEXAS CAVALRY

Bassett's broad-brimmed hat bears the Lone Star insignia of the 8th Texas Cavalry, better known as Terry's Texas Rangers. Bassett got the hat from a fellow soldier in 1862 and wore it until the end of the War.

W. H. TENNISON
ARMY OF TENNESSEE

Tennison, a native son of Monticello, Mississippi, wore this beehive-style slouch hat while serving as a member of General Leonidas Polk's Escort Guard. He later died a prisoner in Camp Chase, Ohio.

SLOUCH HAT

A stitched leather band and trim ornament this otherwise plain felt slouch hat worn by an unknown soldier in the Army of Tennessee. A Virginian partial to such hats once wrote that "a man who has never been a soldier does not know the amount of comfort there is in a good soft hat."

MAJ. WILLIAMS J. CROOK
13TH TENNESSEE INFANTRY

The button on the side of Major Crook's slouch hat made it possible for him to tie up its brim.

MEMBERS OF THE 7TH TENNESSEE CAVALRY AND THEIR SLAVES

PALMETTO STRAW HAT
Working at home, Mrs. J. M. Bonney of Satartia, Mississippi, made this beribboned straw hat for the army. War relief organizations also provided similar headgear for the troops.

SGT. T. J. DUCKETT 3D SOUTH CAROLINA
Duckett's high-crowned, beehive-style slouch hat took the bullets meant for his head at the Battle of Chickamauga in 1863. The hand-lettered sign on the hat was made by Duckett himself, the better to show off his battle-scarred headdress at veterans' reunions after the War.

These bullet holes were received in the Battle of Chicamauga Sept. 20, 1863. Sergt. T. J. Duckett. Co. I 3d S.C.

1ST LT. JAMES A. TILLMAN 24TH SOUTH CAROLINA INFANTRY
A bullet-ridden relic of his brush with death, Tillman's slouch hat bore the brunt of the shots aimed at his head when he fought during the Franklin campaign.

In a Personal Style

MAJ. DAVID G. McINTOSH 1ST SOUTH CAROLINA

McIntosh, who served as chief of artillery for the II Corps of the Army of Northern Virginia at the end of the War, wore this oilcloth cover over the crown of his regulation kepi *(far left)* in inclement weather.

LT. RICHARD L. DOBIE 13TH VIRGINIA CAVALRY

This oilcloth rain hat protected Dobie, who rode with the Sussex Light Dragoons, far better than the cap cover specified by regulations.

ARTILLERY OFFICER'S KEPI

Worn by a North Carolina artillery officer, this oilcloth kepi was painted red to indicate its owner's branch of service.

GEN. PIERRE BEAUREGARD

The wearing of casual hats, such as this dapper straw model owned by Beauregard, during leisure time around camp became something of a fad among Confederate soldiers.

SGT. W. M. HUGHES 18TH MISSISSIPPI CAVALRY BATTALION

Hughes' camp hat has a Confederate flag embroidered on its top and the motto Try Again Boys on its back.

1ST LT. WILLIAM H. S. BURGWYN
35TH NORTH CAROLINA

Burgwyn's warm corduroy cap was made for him by a Miss May Galt while he was convalescing from a wound received at Cold Harbor on June 1, 1864.

BALACLAVA

A trenchbound South Carolina soldier wore this woolen hood, called a balaclava, during cold winter nights. The hand-knit hat was patterned and named after the headgear British troops used in Russia during the Crimean War.

1ST LT. J. A. CHARLARON
WASHINGTON ARTILLERY
OF NEW ORLEANS

Charlaron fought with the Army of Tennessee wearing this unusual black cotton cap in place of the scarlet kepi with dark blue band adopted by his unit in 1860.

PVT. LANDON CHEEK
1ST MISSISSIPPI CAVALRY

Private Cheek, who was wounded in three battles before he was 15, wore this ventilated hat made of wool jean material in seven battles altogether. After the War, he became a doctor in Canton, Mississippi.

GEN. ROBERT E. LEE

Lee received the stitched cotton hat at right as a gift but reportedly never wore it. He instead gave it to Beverly Randolph Codwise, a courier on his staff, who saved it as a memento.

**CAPT. G. GASTON OTEY
13TH VIRGINIA ARTILLERY**

Otey drew artillery pieces and figures on the palms of his gloves *(left)*. Mostly worn by mounted officers and cavalrymen, gloves were "worse than useless" to the enlisted man.

**LT. CHISWELL DABNEY
JEB STUART'S STAFF**

These cavalry gloves *(above)* belonged to Lieutenant Dabney, Jeb Stuart's aide-de-camp.

GEN. ROBERT E. LEE

It is believed that Lee was wearing these gauntlets *(above)* when he surrendered to General Grant at Appomattox.

**CAST BRASS SPUR
NASHVILLE PLOW WORKS**

COPPER SPUR, METAL SALVAGED FROM *MERRIMAC*

C.S. GENERAL'S SPUR

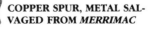

MAJ. GEORGE McKENDREE
GEN. JOHN ECHOLS' STAFF

McKendree, a former artilleryman, purchased his gloves *(left)* from the firm of H. W. Donnally of Lewisburg, Virginia.

PVT. ALEXANDER G. DIMITRY, JR.

One of Mosby's Rangers, Dimitry was buried in his cavalry boots *(right)* after he was killed in action in 1863. The boots were removed when Dimitry's body was exhumed in 1867.

This rakish member of Jeb Stuart's cavalry *(above)* adopted his commander's jaunty way of tucking his pant legs inside his boots. Mounted men more commonly wore their trousers outside their boots.

GEN. ROBERT E. LEE

Riding boots like Lee's *(left)*, made of supple leather rising well above the knee, were favored by officers.

GEN. BRAXTON BRAGG

These gold-plated spurs were given to Bragg by the staff of the *Atlanta Register*.

**CONFEDERATE SHOES BROUGHT
HOME BY A FEDERAL SOLDIER**

**SHOES RECOVERED FROM A
DEAD REBEL AT SHARPSBURG**

IMPORTED ENGLISH SHOES

English craftsmen fabricated this square-toed version of brogan-style shoes *(below)* from fine English leather, adding hobnail pegs in the soles. The pair at right are imported brogans also, but have been manufactured with a buckle closure instead of with the customary laces.

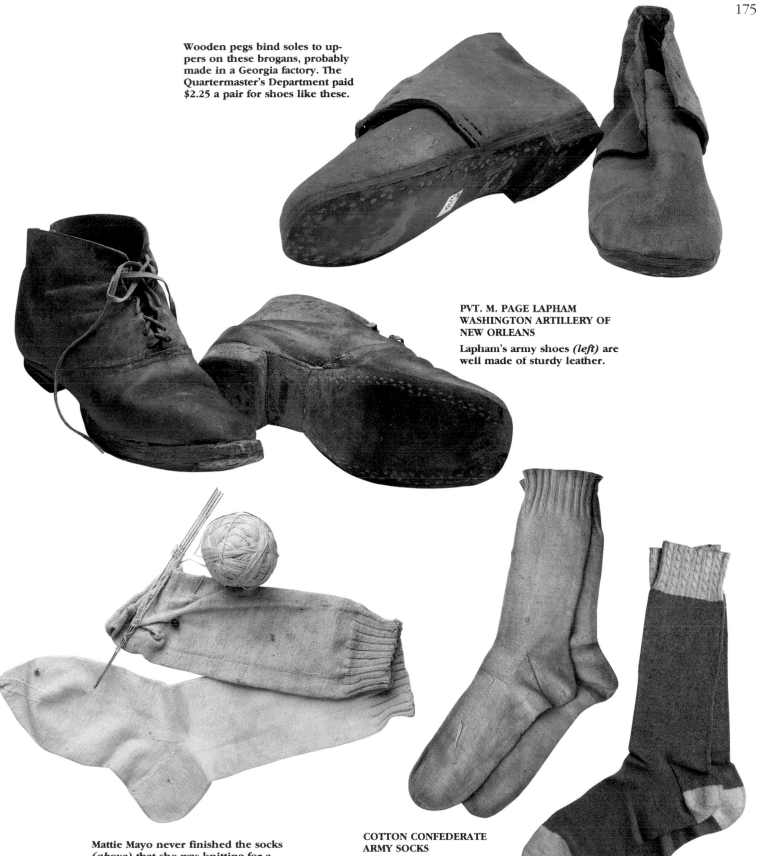

Wooden pegs bind soles to up-
pers on these brogans, probably
made in a Georgia factory. The
Quartermaster's Department paid
$2.25 a pair for shoes like these.

PVT. M. PAGE LAPHAM
WASHINGTON ARTILLERY OF
NEW ORLEANS

Lapham's army shoes *(left)* are
well made of sturdy leather.

Mattie Mayo never finished the socks
(above) that she was knitting for a
Confederate soldier. During the War,
Miss Mayo volunteered her services as
a nurse's aide in a Richmond hospital.

COTTON CONFEDERATE
ARMY SOCKS

HAND-KNITTED SOCKS
FOR A REBEL SOLDIER

C.S.N. CAP INSIGNIA

C.S.N. MASTER'S INSIGNIA

LT. ROBERT D. MINOR

The first uniforms worn by Confederate naval officers were blue, like the one belonging to Lieutenant Minor *(above)*. Minor, who served aboard the C.S.S. *Virginia,* was wounded by fire from the U.S.S. *Congress* in the Battle of Hampton Roads in March 1862.

A. LEE

Midshipman Lee's variant navy cap displays the remnants of the patent leather visor stipulated by C.S.N. regulations.

CAPT. RAPHAEL SEMMES

At anchor off Cape Town, South Africa, Captain Semmes *(foreground)* and his executive officer, Lieutenant John McIntosh Kell, lounge on the deck of the *Alabama*. The insignia on Semmes' navy cap *(below)* originally bore three stars above the anchor, designating his captain's rank. Semmes captured or destroyed a total of 69 Federal ships.

LT. ROBERT D. MINOR

Minor's double-breasted wool coat *(left)* adheres to navy regulations specifying a steel-gray frock coat with a rolling collar. Many officers balked at donning the compulsory gray. As one midshipman expressed it, "Who had ever seen a gray sailor, no matter what nationality he served?"

VEST, LT. MINOR, C.S.N.

NAVAL AND MARINE BUTTONS

FIRMIN & SONS LONDON	COURTNEY & TENNENT, CHARLESTON	COURTNEY & TENNENT, CHARLESTON
BLANK (LOCAL)	E. M. LEWIS RICHMOND (LOCAL)	HAMMOND, TURNER & BATES, MANCHESTER

178

**LT. DAVID G. RANEY, JR.
C.S. MARINE CORPS**

W. S. THOMPSON
CHIEF ENGINEER, C.S.N.

Lined with gray-brown sateen,
Thompson's frock coat *(below)*
was manufactured in England.

NAVAL OFFICER'S SWORD AND SCABBARD

C.S.N. BOARDING AX

C.S.N. CUTLASS

C.S.N. CUTLASS

C.S.N. CUTLASS

NAVAL OFFICER'S
SWORD BELT

C.S.N. ENLISTED MAN'S CAP

EQUIPMENT

In May 1861, the quartermasters of the new Confederate army faced an unenviable challenge—equipping 150,000 men for war. What the new recruits lacked was almost everything essential for fighting and living in the field. "There were on hand no infantry accouterments, no cavalry arms or equipment, no artillery, and above all, no ammunition," recalled Josiah Gorgas, Confederate chief of ordnance, when he sat down to write about the critical situation long after the war was lost. "There was nothing save small arms, and these almost wholly smooth-bore, altered from flint to percussion." Yet Gorgas' doleful assessment did not begin to cover the full range of the Confederacy's needs:

Rebel infantry lacked not only muskets, but also cartridge boxes, cap pouches, and bayonet scabbards; the cavalry required saber belts, revolver holsters, carbine slings, and all the various bits of saddlery.

Artillery units needed a host of specialized equipment to move and work the guns. Hospital stewards had to be equipped with knapsacks for medical supplies, and attendants needed litters.

Musicians could not play without drums and fifes. Everyone needed haversacks to carry rations, knapsacks for clothing and personal items, blankets, waterproof oilcloths, tents, cooking utensils, canteens, and cups.

As Gorgas noted, the supply of such equipment in the captured Federal posts and arsenals was almost nonexistent. The prewar militia companies in the South were at least partially equipped, but for most Confederate soldiers, basic military necessities were missing in the first weeks of the War. As late as First Manassas, the first major engagement, some Confederates went into battle with their cartridges in their pants pockets.

Within a short time, however, Southern industry began to respond. In Nashville, Richmond, New Orleans, and numerous other cities, firms large and small, mostly inexperienced and used to peacetime endeavors that were only marginally related to military equipment, moved rapidly and enthusiastically to fill the army's needs.

Among the most prolific of the Confederacy's early accouterment suppliers was the New Orleans firm of Horter, Magee & George. In the first year of the War, the company produced more than 50,000 sets of infantry accouterments—cartridge boxes, cap pouches, belts, buckles, and the like—and hundreds of knapsacks for the states of Louisiana and Mississippi and the Confederate central government, setting patterns for a number of later manufacturers.

Although the fall of New Orleans and Nashville in the spring of 1862 put a crimp in these initial activities, some manufacturers in the captured cities relocated to unoccupied territory and set up shop again, and a host of smaller private contractors, as well as the Confederate arsenals themselves, added to the flow of supplies. What could not be produced in the South was captured from the enemy or ordered from abroad and run through the Federal blockade. By the end of the War, the Richmond Arsenal alone had issued 375,510 sets of infantry and cavalry accouterments, 180,181 knapsacks, 328,977 canteens and straps, 115,087 gun and carbine slings, 69,418 cavalry saddles, 85,139 bridles, 75,611 halters, 59,624 pairs of spurs, 42,285 horse brushes, and 56,903 currycombs.

Given the difficulties under which the Confederacy operated—the lack of heavy industry, the shortage of raw materials, and the dearth of skilled workmen—the contrast between the grim picture of 1861 and the subsequent production levels attained is astounding. What was achieved came not only through sheer, stubborn effort and the use of vast amounts of captured material, but also by husbanding, repairing, simplifying, and substituting whenever possible—characteristics that are evident and striking in many surviving Confederate-produced items.

Confederate suppliers improvised constantly, on items large and small—even the lowly belt buckle. Some suppliers initially turned out solid or lead-filled brass belt plates, oval or rectangular and stamped with state seals or the letters "CS," "CSA." But these rather fancy and heavy fasteners were few and far between. To save material, weight, and production time, makers turned to plain iron or brass buckles.

This trend was set early in the War. The belt buckles produced by Horter, Magee & George for the state of Mississippi in 1861 were the first of many that were to come. Instead of a state seal, Mississippi requested wide, rectangular brass frames with forked tongues. Copied by later contractors, these "wishbone" buckles were the first of two distinctive types of Confederate belt fasteners. The other, the "Georgia frame," was a smaller buckle with integral cast hooks that fit into two holes in the belt. They were produced throughout the Confederacy, but the only contractor that marked its products was the firm of McElroy & Hunt of Macon, Georgia; hence the name *Georgia frame*. These two plates, the wishbone and the Georgia frame, far more widely used than the CS or CSA plates, were products that demonstrated ingenuity at a minimum of cost.

The same stress on simplicity and husbanding of resources is evident in other Confederate pieces. Leather cartridge boxes are obviously handsewn rather than finely crafted like their Union counterparts. They generally have hand-forged buckles, and often they have lead stud fasteners instead of brass ones. In 1864 the Confederates standardized their boxes in the .69-caliber size, the largest then made. This decision came at a time when Lee's army was overwhelmingly armed with .58-caliber weapons, but the one-size-fits-all concept was intended to apply to all Southern armies, many of whom were still struggling with a variety of weapons.

In addition, the Confederates simplified the tin liners for their cartridge boxes, producing a single tin instead of two as in the Union boxes. Later in the War, the Richmond Arsenal's shops, operating at Clarksville, Virginia, saved time and material by dropping the implement pouch from the outside of their boxes. By 1863 the Confederate arsenals were producing cartridge boxes, waist belts, and other items of painted cotton cloth stitched together in three or four thicknesses as a substitute for leather.

Leather, sorely needed and the material of choice for shoes, saddles, and bridles, became increasingly precious as the war wore on. General Gorgas wrote of the value of shoe leather with succinct irony: "An ardent admirer of the South came over from Washington to offer his patent for making soldiers' shoes with no leather except the soles. The shoes were approved by all except those who wore them. The soldiers exchanged them with the first prostrate enemy who no longer needed his leathern articles."

To save brass for more important uses, Confederate bayonet scabbards were often made with tin or lead tips. Eventually, many soldiers had to be satisfied with accouterments that were fastened with wooden studs.

Haversacks, simple cloth bags slung over one shoulder and intended for carrying rations, were usually made of unpainted cotton cloth, although a few arsenals produced painted ones, mainly for sale to officers. The unpainted haversacks were traditional and offered the advantage of being easily washed.

"The haversack held its own to the last, and was found practical and useful," wrote Carlton McCarthy, a private in the Army of

Northern Virginia, after the War. "It very seldom, however, contained rations, but was used to carry all the articles generally carried in the knapsack; of course the stock was small. Somehow or other, many men managed to do without the haversack, and carried absolutely nothing but what they wore and had in their pockets."

Knapsacks were of simple design, many patterned on those that had been standard in the U.S. Army for many years before the adoption in 1855 of the model that would be used by the Federals in the War. From the outset, the knapsack was a decidedly unpopular piece of equipment with Rebel soldiers. Loaded with a change of clothing and other gear, it caused aches, irritations, and fatigue, and most soldiers preferred to discard them, change of clothes and all. Eventually, when it became obvious that the troops would not use knapsacks, the Confederate ordnance department ceased making them altogether.

"The knapsack vanished early in the struggle," wrote Private McCarthy. "It was inconvenient to 'change' underwear too often, and the disposition not to change grew, as the knapsack was found to gall the back and shoulders, and weary the man before half the march was accomplished. The better way was to dress out and out, and wear that outfit until the enemy's knapsacks, or the folks at home, supplied a change. Certainly it did not pay to carry around clean clothes while waiting for the time to use them.

"Very little washing was done, as a matter of course. Clothes once given up were parted with forever."

The Confederate canteen was another model of simplicity. Confederate industry did not have the stamping dies required to make the Federal type of oblate-spheroid canteen. Instead, tinsmiths in the South produced canteens in a drum or cylindrical style, a familiar shape that had been in use since before the American Revolution. Also, the wooden canteen, a standard item of U.S. Army issue until the Mexican War, made its reappearance in the Confederate army. Most of the Rebels' wooden canteens were made in the pattern devised by F. J. Gardner, who worked at the Richmond Arsenal. (Gardner also devised the two-ring Gardner bullet.) His improved design modernized the wooden canteen and became the standard Confederate issue, produced by numerous arsenals and contractors. Other types of wooden canteens were also used, as were glass flasks converted for rugged use. In addition, there were a variety of compartmentalized canteens that purported to filter stagnant water from one side of the container to the other, through charcoal or felt, and make it potable.

Confederate cavalrymen rode to war in their own civilian saddles, but in time the arsenals began to produce a saddle designed by Lieutenant Walter H. Jenifer, a Maryland-born Confederate officer. The Jenifer, a light, flat-seated saddle, worked well as long as the horses remained well fed. But as inadequate feed began to show its effects, the Jenifer proved to be extremely painful to the bony withers of half-starved Confederate horses. It was phased out in 1863 and replaced by the McClellan saddle, a more contoured make that was easier on the horses. Both types of saddle were often adorned by painted canvas skirts, and Confederate bridles also were often made of the same canvas that was used in belts and cartridge boxes.

Home-produced items amounted to only a portion of Confederate army equipment; captured equipment served a major function in Confederate service. A Union soldier, speaking of prisoners being sent to the rear at Gettysburg, noted that the captives relinquished "several thousand of our own Springfield rifled muskets with full suits of accouterments, even to the belt plates with 'U.S.' on them. As they threw down their arms and accouterments they would say, 'There's what we got from you'uns at Harpers Ferry. We'uns have had 'em long enough.'"

The Northern soldier's maladroit rendering of the Southern vernacular notwithstanding, his observation is generally accurate. From shoes to rifles, in the last year of the War the Confederate soldier's main supply house was often the Union army.

Confederates often bashed in the faces of captured Union belt plates to obliterate the "U.S." markings, or wore the plates upside down. Sometimes they melted the lead out of the plates in their campfires and salvaged only the hooks.

Federal knapsacks, haversacks, rubber blankets, shelter halves, and numerous other items seemed nearly as common in the Confederate army as in the Union. After Chancellorsville, Confederate General Robert Rodes said, "The enemy abandoned such a large number of knapsacks that when this division began its homeward march in the rain it was thoroughly equipped with oilcloths and shelter tents of the best quality."

Edward A. Moore, an artilleryman who served with Lee, wrote, "Any soldier carrying a Confederate canteen was at once recognized as a new recruit, as it required but a short time to secure one of superior quality from a dead foeman on a battlefield." Indeed, many surviving Confederate wooden canteens were traded by their Rebel owners to Union pickets, often in exchange for the Yankee article.

Items imported through the blockade were another important source of supply. English furnishings, particularly cartridge boxes, waist belts and buckles, bayonet scabbards, knapsacks, and mess tins were common items in the Confederate army. English military saddles were imported in quantity and sold to Confederate officers, generally as sets consisting of a saddle, a bridle, and a cloth saddle blanket.

Items from earlier wars and prewar militia service also saw use, though in decreasing amounts over time. Many Confederate officers went to war carrying old militia swords, and members of their companies often wore state or company belt plates and other insignia left over from prewar musters.

Confederate officers had to buy their own equipment, and it varied widely in quality and price. A number of firms specialized in officers' swords, among them Boyle & Gamble of Richmond; Leech & Rigdon of Memphis; and Thomas, Griswold & Company of New Orleans. Most of them also produced sword belts and plates to go with their products. Knapsacks, haversacks, and canteens were also purchased from private firms, but in many cases Confederate officers bought their equipment from the same arsenals that supplied their men.

The exigencies of life in the field and on the march soon taught the Confederate soldier to regard his equipment with a keen eye toward simplicity. In time, he learned to lighten his burden by discarding everything that was not absolutely essential.

"Reduced to the minimum," observed Private McCarthy, "the private soldier consisted of one man, one hat, one jacket, one shirt, one pair of pants, one pair of drawers, one pair of shoes, and one pair of socks. His baggage was one blanket, one rubber blanket, and one haversack. The haversack generally contained smoking tobacco and a pipe, and a small piece of soap, with temporary additions of apples, persimmons, blackberries, and such other commodities as he could pick up on the march."

As another Confederate soldier later put it, "The road to glory cannot be followed with too much baggage."

ACCOUTERMENTS

Three of the some 2,500 Confederates taken prisoner at Gettysburg pose beside the logs of a breastwork for one of Mathew Brady's photographers on July 15, 1863. The captives wear knapsacks as well as blanket rolls, possibly in preparation for a lengthy captivity.

GENERAL SERVICE BELT PLATE, WESTERN ARMIES

PREWAR WOODEN CANTEEN

carried by a member of the Fayetteville (N.C.) Light Artillery.

CONFEDERATE CARTRIDGE BOX
PVT. W. F. A. DICKERSON

Private Dickerson served in the 38th Georgia and carried this single-tin cartridge box, a pattern introduced in 1864, suspended from a painted cloth sling.

CAP POUCH

A container for metal percussion caps used to fire small arms, this pouch was made of multiple layers of painted cotton cloth.

Sword Belts and Plates

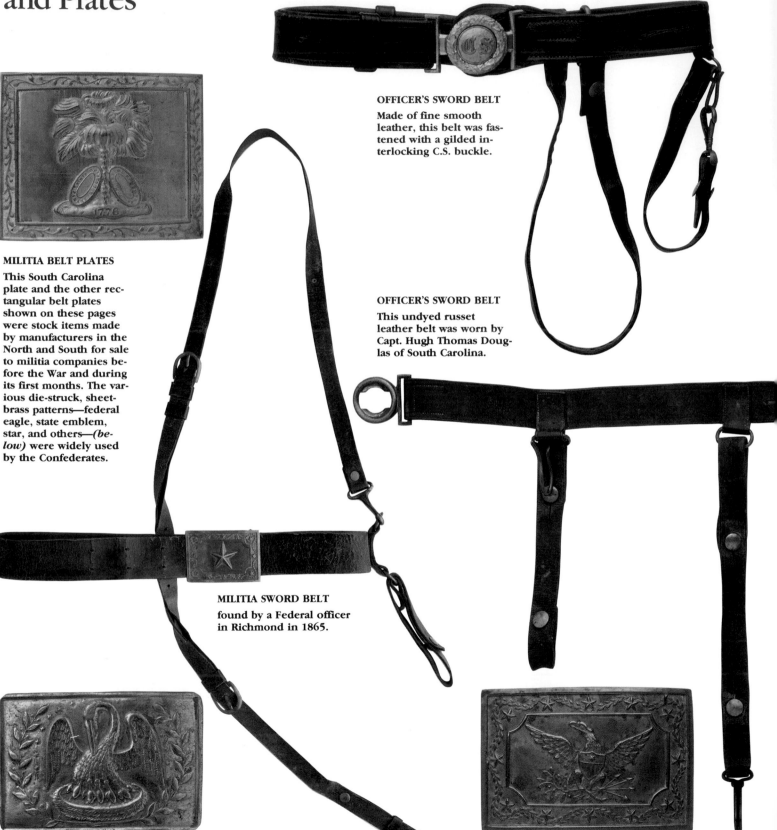

OFFICER'S SWORD BELT
Made of fine smooth leather, this belt was fastened with a gilded interlocking C.S. buckle.

OFFICER'S SWORD BELT
This undyed russet leather belt was worn by Capt. Hugh Thomas Douglas of South Carolina.

MILITIA BELT PLATES
This South Carolina plate and the other rectangular belt plates shown on these pages were stock items made by manufacturers in the North and South for sale to militia companies before the War and during its first months. The various die-struck, sheet-brass patterns—federal eagle, state emblem, star, and others—*(below)* were widely used by the Confederates.

MILITIA SWORD BELT
found by a Federal officer in Richmond in 1865.

LOUISIANA PELICAN PLATE

FEDERAL EAGLE MILITIA PLATE

COL. ARTHUR HERBERT, 17TH VIRGINIA INFANTRY REGIMENT

OFFICER'S SWORD BELT
The gilt buckle on this belt was probably made by a local jeweler.

OFFICER'S SWORD BELT
Colonel E. A. Spotswood, assistant adjutant general to Gen. Nathan B. Forrest, wore the belt above.

SOUTH CAROLINA PLATE, 1840s

LOUISIANA MILITIA BELT PLATE, 1840s

For Officers

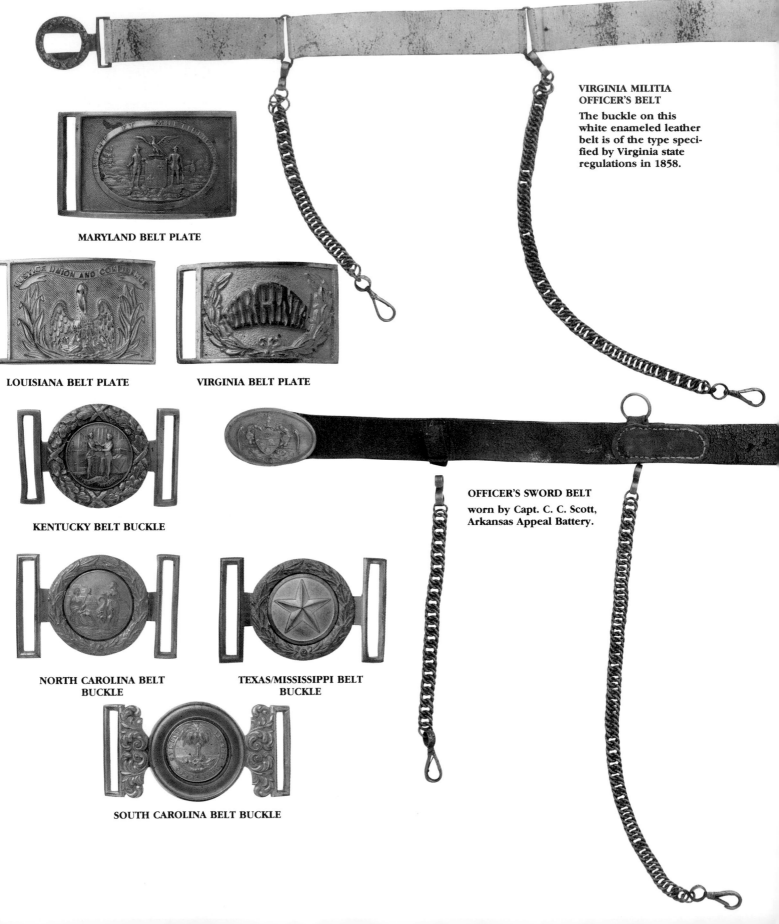

MARYLAND BELT PLATE

LOUISIANA BELT PLATE

VIRGINIA BELT PLATE

KENTUCKY BELT BUCKLE

NORTH CAROLINA BELT BUCKLE

TEXAS/MISSISSIPPI BELT BUCKLE

SOUTH CAROLINA BELT BUCKLE

VIRGINIA MILITIA OFFICER'S BELT

The buckle on this white enameled leather belt is of the type specified by Virginia state regulations in 1858.

OFFICER'S SWORD BELT worn by Capt. C. C. Scott, Arkansas Appeal Battery.

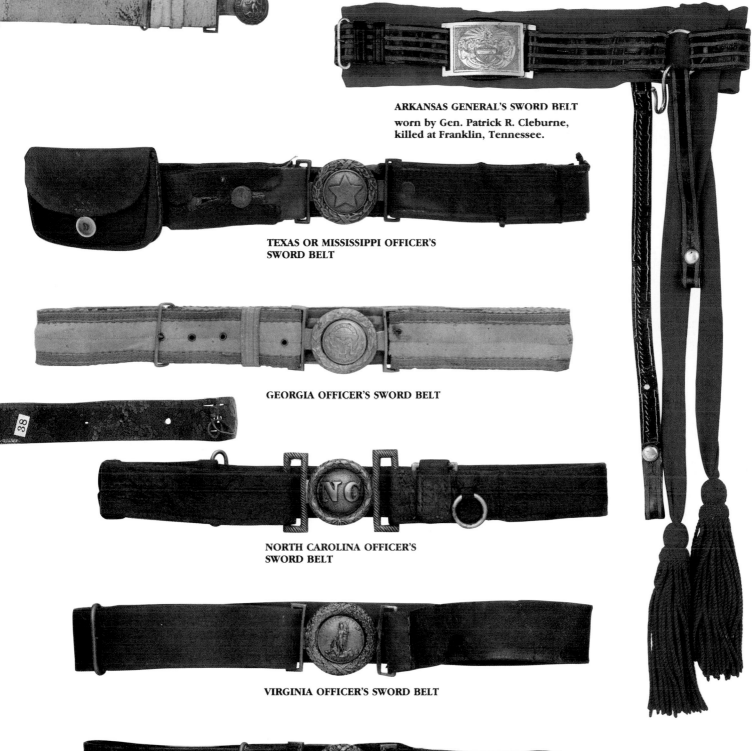

189

ARKANSAS GENERAL'S SWORD BELT
worn by Gen. Patrick R. Cleburne,
killed at Franklin, Tennessee.

**TEXAS OR MISSISSIPPI OFFICER'S
SWORD BELT**

GEORGIA OFFICER'S SWORD BELT

**NORTH CAROLINA OFFICER'S
SWORD BELT**

VIRGINIA OFFICER'S SWORD BELT

**SOUTH CAROLINA OFFICER'S
SWORD BELT**

For Enlisted Men

**GENERAL SERVICE BELT PLATE
WORN BY TENNESSEE REGIMENTS**

**GENERAL SERVICE BELT PLATE
WESTERN CONFEDERATE ARMIES**

**STOCK MILITIA BELT PLATE
WORN BY TEXAS/MISSISSIPPI TROOPS**

**NORTH CAROLINA STATE
BELT PLATE**

**6TH NORTH CAROLINA INFANTRY
MANUFACTURED IN 1861**

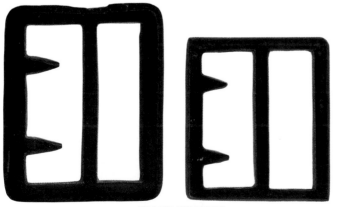

FRAME BUCKLES

**GEORGIA BELT PLATE
AMES/GAYLORD, CONTRACT 1860**

ALABAMA BELT PLATE
AMES/GAYLORD, CONTRACT 1860

ARKANSAS BELT PLATE
AMES/GAYLORD, CONTRACT 1860

GENERAL SERVICE BELT BUCKLE
MODIFIED, 1840 U.S. N.C.O. BUCKLE

GENERAL SERVICE
ENLISTED MAN'S BELT BUCKLE

GENERAL SERVICE CAST-BRASS
ENLISTED MAN'S BELT PLATE

GENERAL SERVICE BELT
PLATE, WESTERN ARMIES

MARYLAND BELT PLATE
PREWAR MANUFACTURE

GENERAL SERVICE BELT
PLATE, WESTERN ARMIES

Cavalry Gear

**SHARPS CARBINE
CARTRIDGE BOX**

**CONFEDERATE CAVALRY
TROOPER FROM KENTUCKY**

**REVOLVER AMMUNITION
BOX WITH TIN AND
ACCESSORY POUCH**

**N.C.O.'S ACCOUTERMENTS, GOVERNOR'S
GUARD OF VIRGINIA, 1860 STATE PURCHASE**

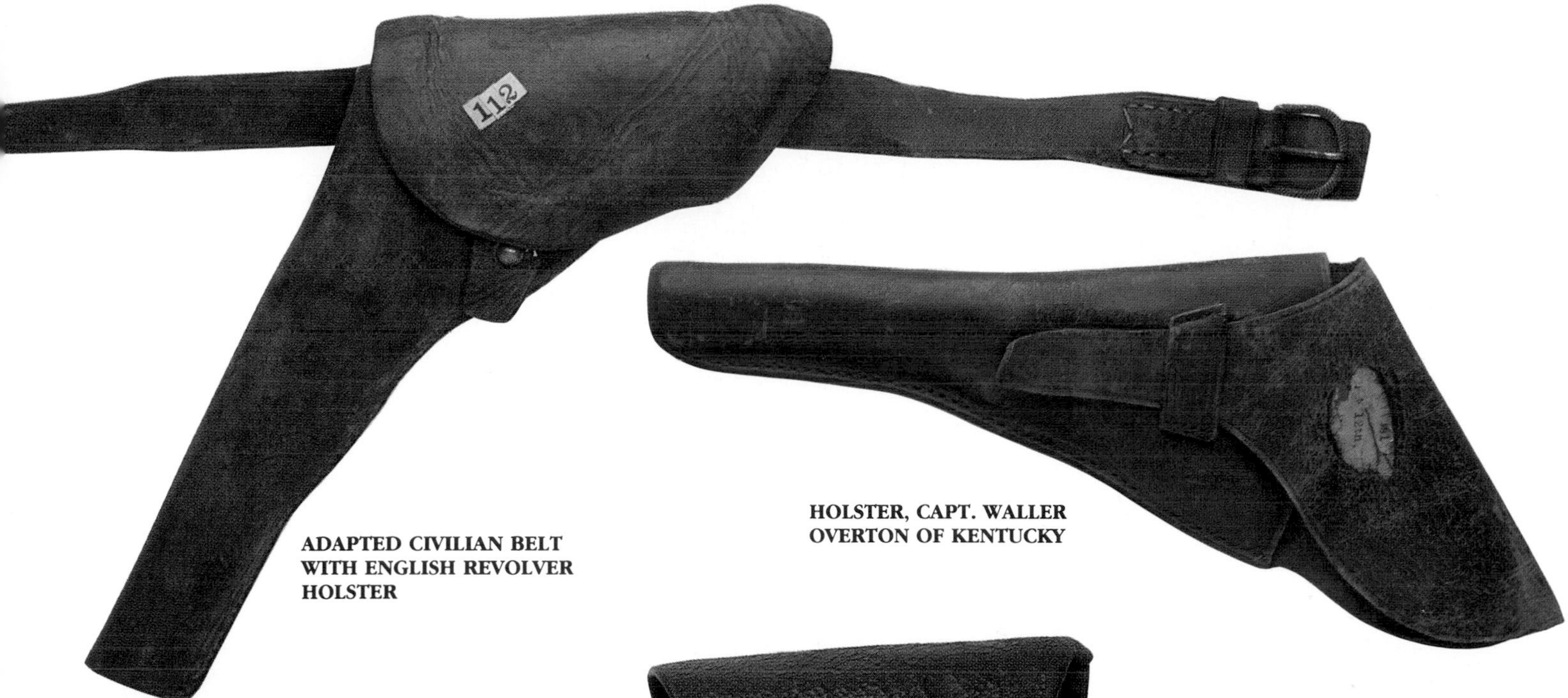

ADAPTED CIVILIAN BELT
WITH ENGLISH REVOLVER
HOLSTER

HOLSTER, CAPT. WALLER
OVERTON OF KENTUCKY

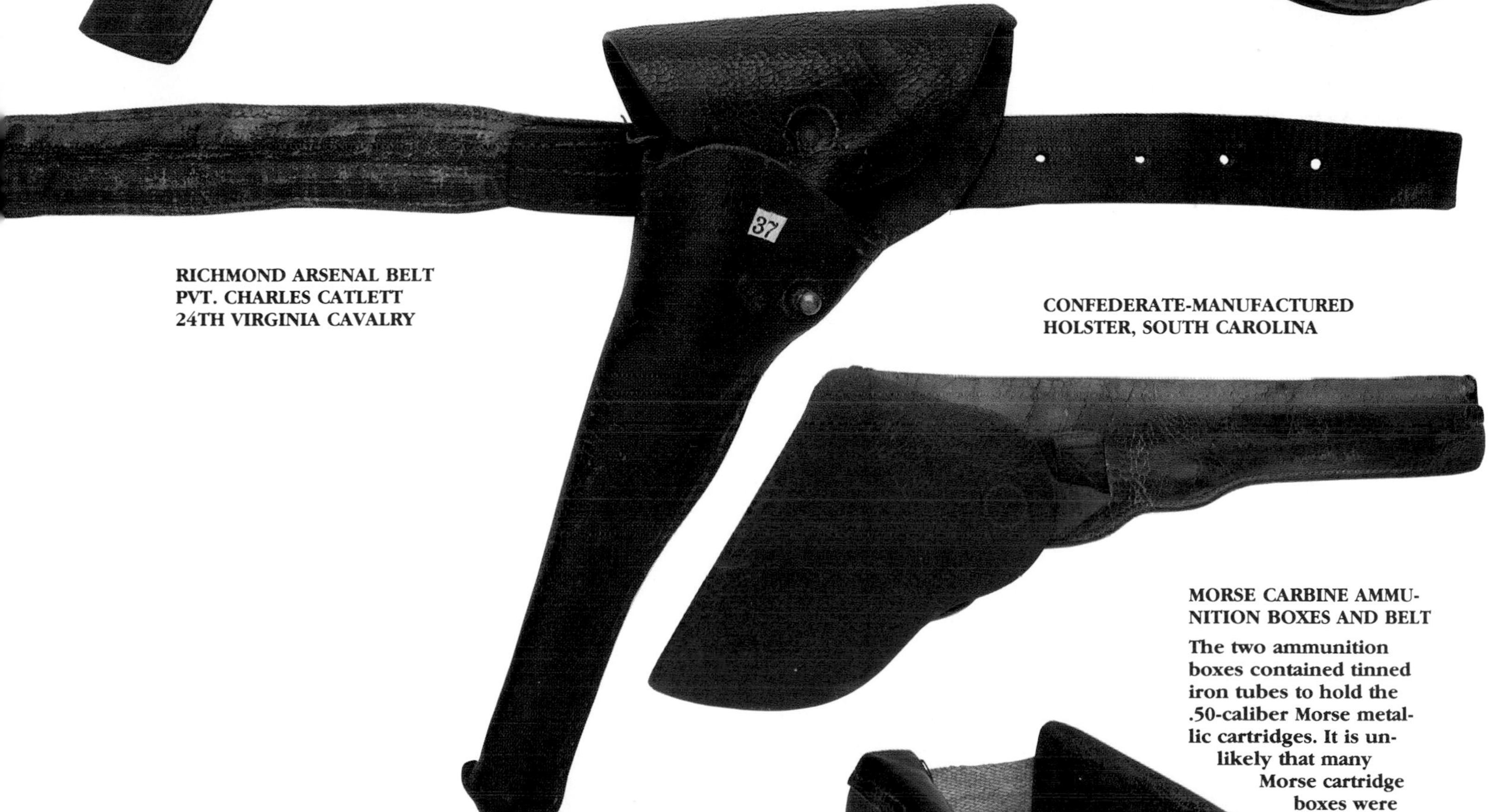

RICHMOND ARSENAL BELT
PVT. CHARLES CATLETT
24TH VIRGINIA CAVALRY

CONFEDERATE-MANUFACTURED
HOLSTER, SOUTH CAROLINA

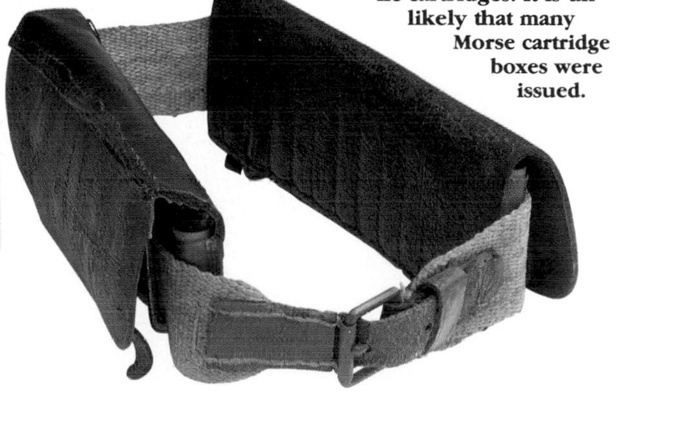

MORSE CARBINE AMMU-
NITION BOXES AND BELT

The two ammunition
boxes contained tinned
iron tubes to hold the
.50-caliber Morse metal-
lic cartridges. It is un-
likely that many
Morse cartridge
boxes were
issued.

Infantry Equipment

This cartridge box, bearing the mark of a bullet, was carried by Virginia soldier C. A. Fornerdon when he was wounded at First Manassas. It has been modified with straps to fit on a waist belt.

INFANTRYMAN WITH .69-CAL. MUSKET ACCOUTERMENTS

CARTRIDGE BOX PVT. C. A. FORNERDON

CONFEDERATE-MANUFACTURED CARTRIDGE BOX AND SLING

CAP POUCH AND PERCUSSION CAPS

CONFEDERATE INFANTRY WAIST BELT
Atlanta Arsenal-type cast plate.

INFANTRY WAIST BELT WITH FRAME BUCKLE
made by McElroy & Hunt, Macon, Georgia.

BUFF LEATHER INFANTRY WAIST BELT
with carrier for a sword bayonet.

CONFEDERATE-MANUFACTURED PER-CUSSION CAP POUCH

CONFEDERATE-MANUFACTURED PERCUSSION CAP POUCH

CONFEDERATE-MANUFACTURED PERCUSSION CAP POUCH

BAYONET SCABBARD, RICHMOND ARSENAL HARNESS SHOPS, CLARKSVILLE, VIRGINIA

Soldiers' Gear

Private Ruben Nations of the 12th Louisiana wears accouterments probably manufactured by the New Orleans firm of Horter, Magee & George. Nations was severely wounded at Decatur, Alabama, on October 28, 1864, losing his legs to shellfire.

CAP POUCH MADE BY OLIVER WELLBORN DALTON, GEORGIA

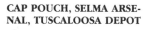

CAP POUCH, SELMA ARSENAL, TUSCALOOSA DEPOT

HORTER, MAGEE & GEORGE BELT PLATE

HORTER, MAGEE & GEORGE INFANTRY BELT WITH UNIDENTIFIED CAP POUCH

HORTER, MAGEE & GEORGE INFANTRY BELT AND PLATE

HORTER, MAGEE & GEORGE BELT WITH J. R. SICKLES (ST. LOUIS) CAP POUCH

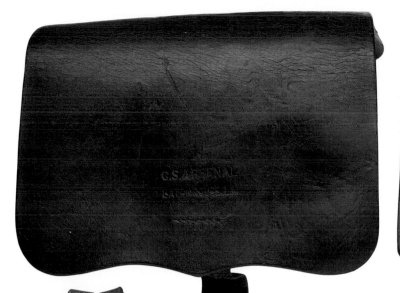

**.577-CAL. CARTRIDGE BOX
BATON ROUGE ARSENAL**

CARTRIDGE BOX, HOUSTON ORDNANCE DEPOT

**CAP POUCH, BATON
ROUGE ARSENAL**

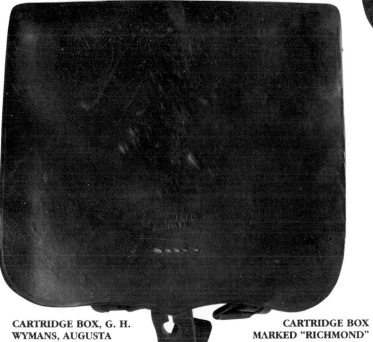

CARTRIDGE BOX, M. H. RICHMOND & SONS

**CARTRIDGE BOX, G. H.
WYMANS, AUGUSTA**

**CARTRIDGE BOX
MARKED "RICHMOND"**

Improvising with Cloth

PAINTED CLOTH INFANTRY BELT

Painted cotton or linen belting could be cut up in standard widths and made into waist belts or cartridge-box slings.

PAINTED CLOTH INFANTRY BELT

The cast-brass, round-cornered C.S. belt plate is of a pattern common in the Western Confederate armies.

PAINTED CLOTH CARTRIDGE BOX

probably made by either William Brands & Co. or N. Crown & Co. in Columbus, Georgia.

PAINTED CLOTH CAP POUCH WILLIAM BRANDS & CO. COLUMBUS, GEORGIA

PAINTED CLOTH CAP POUCH COLUMBUS, GEORGIA

PAINTED CLOTH CAP POUCH

CARTRIDGE BOX WITH CANVAS SLING

The sling was contracted by Hughes, Pendergrass & Snow of Monroe, Georgia.

CARTRIDGE BOX FROM NORTH CAROLINA

The sling is reinforced with a figure eight stitched along its length.

LEATHER-REINFORCED LINEN RIFLE SLING

Haversacks

OFFICER'S HAVERSACK
Captain C. Netherland of the Virginia Home Guard bought this haversack from the Richmond Arsenal in 1864.

OFFICER'S HAVERSACK
owned by Gen. William Nelson Pendleton, chief of artillery of the Army of Northern Virginia.

OFFICER'S HAVERSACK
used by Lt. William A. B. Branch, an aide to Gen. Robert Hoke.

This fully accoutered sergeant of the Louisiana Crescent Regiment wears a typical, if somewhat oversize, Confederate cloth haversack. The utilitarian haversacks could be easily produced by tailors or amateur sewing groups.

CONFEDERATE HAVERSACK

This haversack is made of striped ticking material from the state of Georgia.

HAVERSACK

carried by Sgt. A. H. Bayley of Company D (Peyton Artillery), 18th Virginia Artillery Battalion.

CANVAS HAVERSACK

owned by Lt. Hamilton Branch, 54th Georgia Infantry Regiment.

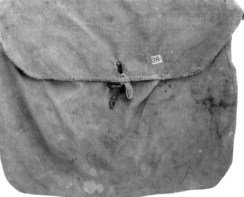

CANVAS HAVERSACK

A soldier from Virginia carried the homemade haversack above.

Knapsacks and Blankets

SOFT KNAPSACK
25TH SOUTH CAROLINA INFANTRY

Captured by a Federal soldier at the Battle of Weldon Railroad near Petersburg in 1864.

SOFT KNAPSACK
PVT. JAMES A. KIBBLER

Kibbler served in Company F, 10th Virginia Infantry. His knapsack was copied from a U.S. Army, Mexican War design.

**SOFT KNAPSACK, PVT.
MARION C. PRITCHARD**

A member of the 7th
Virginia, Pritchard was
killed at the Battle of
Williamsburg in 1862.

**PVT. KENNEDY PALMER
13TH VIRGINIA INFANTRY**

**ISSUE BLANKET OF
CORP. T. V. BROOKE
RICHMOND HOWITZERS**

**CHARLOTTE QUARTERMASTER'S
DEPARTMENT BLANKET**

owned by Capt. John S. R. Miller, 1st North Carolina, killed in action at Winchester, June 14, 1863.

MILITIA BOX KNAPSACK
PVT. JOHN H. WEST

**Private West served in the artillery
company of the 1st Virginia Regiment.**

**CONFEDERATE INFANTRYMAN
WITH A SOFT KNAPSACK**

**BOX KNAPSACK
PVT. GEORGE T. STOVALL**

**Private Stovall was killed at First Manassas
serving in Company A of the 8th Georgia
Infantry Regiment, the Rome Light Guards.**

**BOX KNAPSACK
PVT. CHARLES A. PACE**

**Pace was a member of the Dan-
ville Blues, Company A, 18th
Virginia Infantry Regiment.**

RUSSET LEATHER BELT
taken from the body of a Rebel at Gettysburg by Capt. W. H. Warner of the 40th New York.

CAVALRY SABER BELT
This white buff leather saber belt was of the type worn by British cavalry regiments.

The Confederate cavalryman at left wears the standard "snake" buckle provided with British belts. Snake buckles were chosen for export because they bore no national or regimental device.

ENFIELD CAP POUCH
The angled belt loop was intended to fit on the cartridge box shoulder strap.

Goods from Overseas

The shortage of domestically manufactured accouterments forced the Confederacy to turn to Great Britain as a source. The equipment purchased by Confederate agents through companies such as S. Isaac, Campbell & Company and Fraser Trenholm & Company generally conformed to British-army regulation gear for the 1853 Enfield rifle.

ENFIELD .577-CAL. CARTRIDGE BOX
The single tin of this sturdy box could hold 50 cartridges.

BUFF LEATHER BELT

delivered in sets that included an Enfield cartridge box, cap pouch, and bayonet.

LE MAT REVOLVER HOLSTER GEN. JEB STUART

REVOLVER HOLSTER

BRUNSWICK RIFLE POUCH

marked S. Isaac, Campbell & Co., of a type issued to C.S. marines.

ENFIELD-PATTERN KNAPSACK

This painted canvas soft pack bearing the label of S. Isaac, Campbell & Co. was owned by a soldier from South Carolina. It was carried with the flap against the wearer's back.

The Essential Canteen

CONVERTED FEDERAL CANTEENS

In need of a cork, Corp. T. V. Brooke of the Richmond Howitzers carved a cedarwood replacement *(above)*. The Federal canteen at right is slung from a Hughes, Pendergrass & Snow canvas sling.

SHAPED WOOD CANTEEN

Private W. D. Smith of the 47th North Carolina owned this canteen patented by Nathaniel Nuckolls of Alabama.

GARDNER-PATTERN CANTEEN

carried by an unknown artilleryman in Pegram's Artillery Battalion, Army of Northern Virginia.

GARDNER-PATTERN CANTEEN

carried by Pvt. I. H. Reynolds of the 2d Arkansas Infantry Regiment, Army of Tennessee.

This unidentified private of the Sussex Light Dragoons, Company C, 5th Virginia Cavalry Regiment, carries a commercial double-spout filter canteen. Such canteens could filter mud or debris from drinking water but did little to prevent disease.

TIN DRUM CANTEEN

The owner, an unidentified South Carolinian, modified his cotton-webbing sling with a trouser buckle.

FILTER CANTEEN

This canteen, carried by Capt. William A. Wright of the 55th Virginia Infantry, was struck by the Federal bullet shown resting near the entry hole.

TIN DRUM CANTEEN

This "C.S."-embossed canteen may have been made in New Orleans for issue to Louisiana troops.

TIN DRUM CANTEEN
This canteen was recovered from the battlefield at Chickamauga, Georgia.

MILITIA-STYLE CANTEENS
These simple canteens *(above and lower left)* were patterned after pre-Civil War designs.

PERSONAL EFFECTS

Men of the Palmetto Light Artillery of South Carolina gather around campfire and card game in this photo taken near Charleston in 1863. Soldiers bought small comforts and necessities—razors and toothbrushes, tobacco, playing cards, and the like—from local merchants or received them from home.

PIPES, TOBACCO, AND MATCHES

TOBACCO POUCHES

IMPORTED CARDS

SOLDIERS' WALLETS

carried by Virginia soldier Joseph B. Webb *(right)* and Pvt. William Crosby, 3d Virginia Militia *(below).*

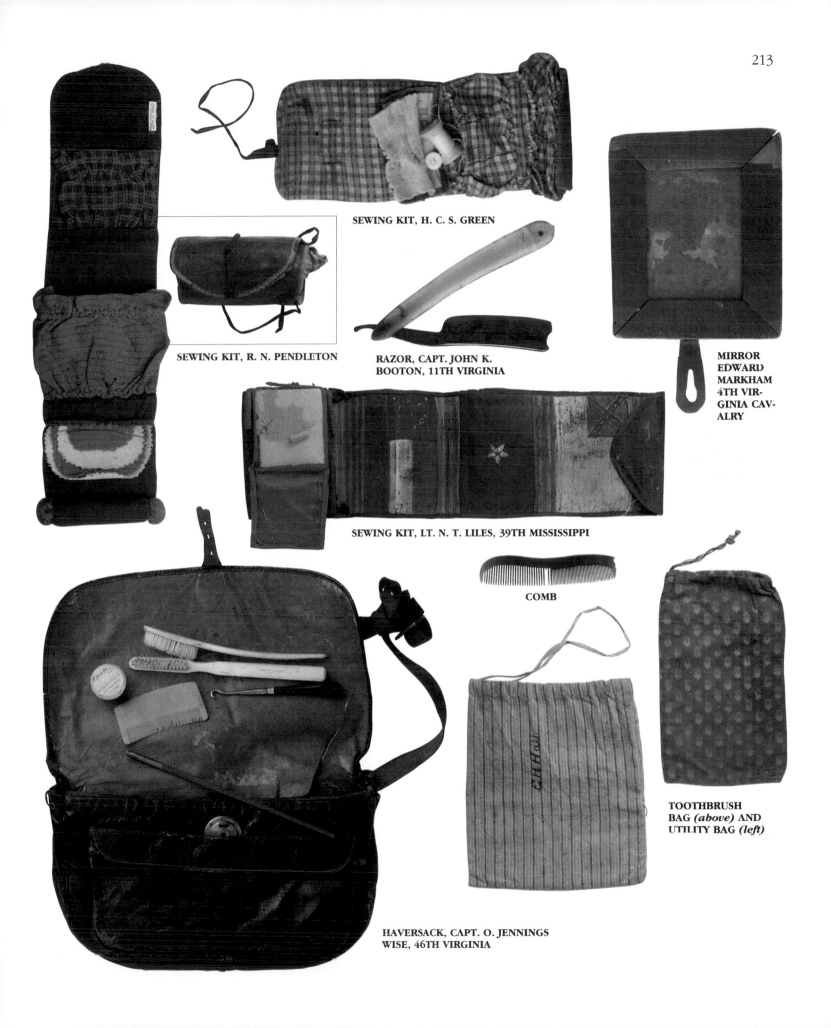

SEWING KIT, H. C. S. GREEN

SEWING KIT, R. N. PENDLETON

RAZOR, CAPT. JOHN K.
BOOTON, 11TH VIRGINIA

MIRROR
EDWARD
MARKHAM
4TH VIR-
GINIA CAV-
ALRY

SEWING KIT, LT. N. T. LILES, 39TH MISSISSIPPI

COMB

TOOTHBRUSH
BAG *(above)* AND
UTILITY BAG *(left)*

HAVERSACK, CAPT. O. JENNINGS
WISE, 46TH VIRGINIA

MESS EQUIPMENT

KNIFE AND SPOON
PVT. G. CAPERSON, 7TH VIRGINIA
FOUND AT FIRST MANASSAS

CUP, T. V. BROOKE
RICHMOND HOWITZERS

GOVERNMENT FLOUR BAG

CUP, FRANK D. REYNOLDS
WASHINGTON ARTILLERY

COVERED CUP
GEN. JOHN PEGRAM

TIN PLATE, GEN. ROBERT E. LEE

WROUGHT-IRON FRYING PAN

MESS CHEST, MAJ. J. ARTHUR
JOHNSTON, Q.M. MAHONE'S STAFF
ARMY OF NORTHERN VIRGINIA

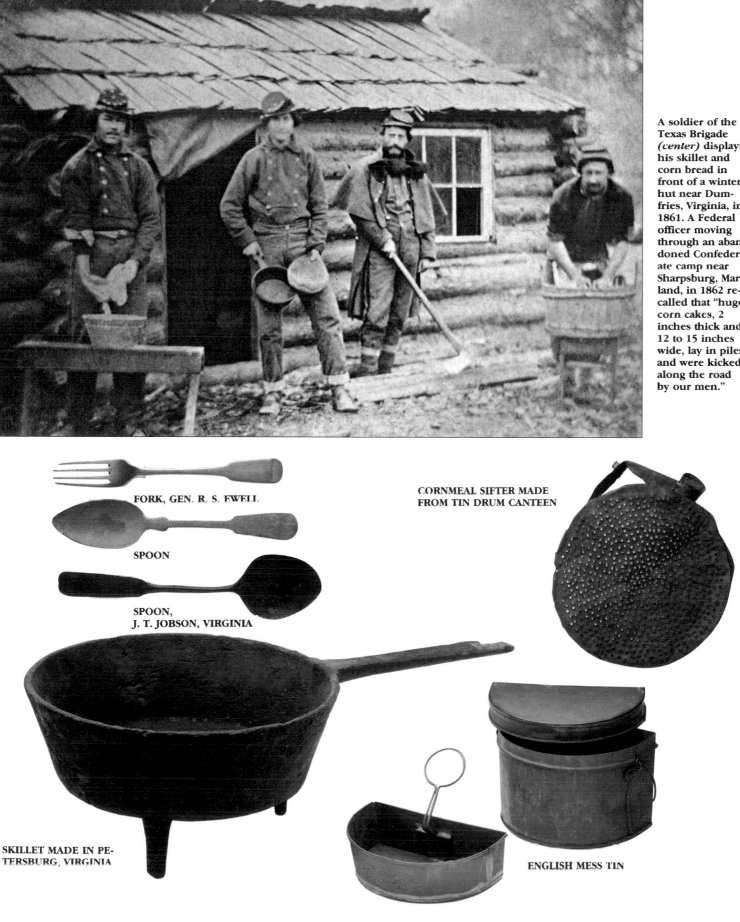

A soldier of the Texas Brigade *(center)* displays his skillet and corn bread in front of a winter hut near Dumfries, Virginia, in 1861. A Federal officer moving through an abandoned Confederate camp near Sharpsburg, Maryland, in 1862 recalled that "huge corn cakes, 2 inches thick and 12 to 15 inches wide, lay in piles and were kicked along the road by our men."

FORK, GEN. R. S. EWELL.

SPOON

SPOON, J. T. JOBSON, VIRGINIA

CORNMEAL SIFTER MADE FROM TIN DRUM CANTEEN

SKILLET MADE IN PETERSBURG, VIRGINIA

ENGLISH MESS TIN

SADDLERY

JENIFER SADDLE
This high-combed saddle with a rawhide seat was manufactured by the firm of C. A. Farwell, located in Mobile, Alabama.

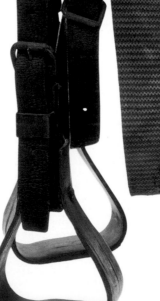

SADDLEBAGS
Property of Capt. E. M. Hudson, aide to Maj. Gen. Arnold Elzey, chief of artillery of the Army of Tennessee.

Major John W. Woodfin of the 2d North Carolina Cavalry sits astride his horse, Prince Hal, on a Hope, or Texas-type, saddle. These Spanish-pattern saddles had been made popular by U.S. Army officers serving in the Florida or Mexican wars.

CONFEDERATE McCLELLAN SADDLE

This saddle was used by Capt. W. Stuart Symington of Virginia, an aide to Gen. George Pickett.

SADDLEBAGS

captured by Federal officer Charles F. Bowers at Sayler's Creek, Virginia, in April 1865, and returned to their owner, W. N. Jones, after the War.

MUSIC

During the sultry July evenings after the Battle of Kennesaw Mountain in 1864, Confederates and Yankees encamped in breastworks near Atlanta engaged in an odd sort of musical repartee. James Cooper Nisbet, a 24-year-old colonel with the 66th Georgia, described the tuneful exchanges in his memoirs: "The officers and most of the men of Shoaff's Battalion were from Savannah. They had a splendid brass band; their cornet player was the best I have ever heard. In the evening after supper he would come to our salient and play solos. Sometimes when the firing was brisk he wouldn't come. Then the Yanks would call out, 'Oh, Johnnie, we want to hear that cornet player.' We would answer, 'He would play, but he's afraid you will spoil his horn!' "

The Yanks would then cease their sniping and the cornet player would perform a medley of favorite airs. "How the Yanks would applaud!" remembered Nisbet. "They had a good cornet player who would alternate with our man." And so the opposing armies, amassed to kill each other by day, regaled each other with concerts by night.

From the long perspective of 130 years such goings-on seem strange indeed; but to the soldiers of the Civil War, music and bullets were natural consorts. From sunup to moonrise, music dictated the rhythms of camp life and inspired the battle charge. General Robert E. Lee summed up the importance of music to his troops in 1864 when, after listening to the stirring tunes of a brass band, he commented, "I don't believe we can have an army without music."

Like the Federal government, the Confederacy established regulations in 1861 allowing for the formation of regimental bands, each having "16 privates to act as musicians."

Such provisions aside, Confederate bands numbered far fewer than their Federal counterparts owing to the scarcity of instruments and the pressing need for full-time line soldiers. Even so, a British army officer visiting Confederate army headquarters in 1863 reported that "almost every regiment had a small band with brass instruments."

Confederate regulations also authorized the assignment of two field musicians. Usually, a fifer and a drummer were assigned to each infantry company. Buglers were most often assigned to cavalry and artillery units. Infantry-company musicians were in turn part of a larger regimental drum corps consisting of up to 10 fifers and 10 drummers under the direction of a drum major. Once assembled, drums thundering and shrill fifes piping, the field musicians roused a powerful esprit de corps in the Rebel ranks.

Whether garrisoned, on the march, or in the line of fire, Confederates timed their workday to the roll of the drum and the blast of the bugle. In camp, field musicians drummed and tooted Johnny out of bed around 5:45 a.m., and marshaled him through housekeeping, assembly, sick call, meals, drill rehearsal, and tattoo—the last roll call of the day—finally serenading him to sleep with taps around 10:30 p.m.

Camp routine also called for daily dress parades in which the drum corps joined the brass band in leading regimental troops through a half-hour of maneuvers. Less common was the formal review—the massed exhibition of as many as 100 regiments, all marching in step to such tunes as "Dixie" and "The Southern Soldier Boy." Julius Leinbach, cornet player with the renowned 26th North Carolina Band, recalled one particularly impressive review in which General Ambrose Hill's entire III Corps paraded for General Lee: "Twenty-five or thirty thousand men were collected in one body all under the eye of one. There were 17 bands in the field. The troops were formed in three parallel lines, four men deep. If in one, it would have extended two miles or more. It took us two hours to pass in review. It was certainly a grand sight."

While encamped, Rebel bands were also given to impromptu concerts, or serenades. Stonewall Jackson is said to have enticed his wife, Mary Anna, to visit him for a fortnight at his Virginia headquarters in August 1861 by writing to her of the "sweet music" of the 5th Virginia Band.

Confederate bands did not limit their performances to peaceful interludes between battles. Mindful of the tonic effect music had upon frightened and demoralized recruits, field commanders often dispatched orders to strike up the band during combat—sometimes with peculiar effect. British Lieutenant Colonel Arthur J. L. Fremantle, traveling with the Confederate army during the Battle of Gettysburg, wrote of hearing a Rebel band from Lee's headquarters atop Seminary Ridge: "When the cannonade was at its height, a Confederate band of music between the cemetery and ourselves began to play polkas and waltzes, which sounded very curious, accompanied by the hissing and bursting of the shells."

Even more than the brass band, Confederate commanders relied upon the field musicians to inspire and direct their troops in battle. During First Manassas, Colonel James Preston of the Stonewall Brigade ordered Private David Scantlon to "beat the rally" to reassemble his fragmented regiment. Scantlon reportedly did so—but only after turning his back to the fray. Puzzled, Preston asked the drummer why he had turned around. "So you suppose I wanted the Yankees to shoot a hole through my bass drum!" answered the surly musician.

Band members and field musicians alike were called upon to exchange their instruments for muskets, particularly in the Confederate ranks where combat-ready recruits were in desperately short supply. More frequently still, musicians were expected to double as ambulance crews and surgeon's assistants. Bandsman Julius Leinbach commented upon his three years of medical duty with the 26th North Carolina in his diary: "We had considerable experience in giving first aid to the wounded, and I, for one, got myself to believe that I could amputate a man's leg as well as some of the doctors."

Despite their regular and often selfless service as medics, the musicians of the Confederacy were most revered and best remembered for the music they made—music with the power to transport heartsore soldiers beyond the privations and terrors that daily plagued them. Wrote one Confederate camped in the Wilderness in 1864: "There is a brass band and they are playing 'Shells of Ocean,' and as the familiar notes of this sweet air are gently wafted in delightful cadences over the woody hills and dewy fields, numberless visions of home in happier hours and sweet reminiscences of the past crowd thick and fast upon my soul."

BANDS

THE 26TH NORTH CAROLINA INFANTRY REGIMENT BAND

BASS SAXHORN TUBA

Band member Julius Leinbach *(second from left, top)* played an over-the-shoulder horn identical to the one pictured above—an instrument that contributed a throaty, mellow bass line to the group's melodic strains.

To the frightful accompaniment of bursting shells, regimental bandleader Samuel Mickey trumpeted such Confederate favorites as "The Bonnie Blue Flag" on his E-flat cornet *(right)*, inspiring the 26th North Carolina throughout three years of battle. The band, composed of eight members of the renowned Moravian Salem Brass Band, was recruited in March 1862 to serve with the regiment. At the War's end, Union forces captured the group in Virginia at the Battle of Five Forks and confiscated the instruments—all except for Mickey's silver cornet, which he secreted in his haversack.

BANDLEADER SAMUEL MICKEY AND CORNET

Resplendent in his bearskin shako and gold-tasseled frock coat, drum major C. M. Pohlé directed the 1st Virginia's corps of drummers. At the onset of battle, such royal regalia was soon exchanged for more practical fatigues.

Alexander Grove. A. J. Turner. J. W. Alby. Dalias.

D. M. Drake. Wm. A. Burnet. John B. Koye.

J. Harvey Bumbaer. D. S. Strasburg. J. A. Armentrout.

H. A. McClanahard. S. C. Bashins. J. S. Ast. B. M. Cushing.

The Stonewall Brigade Band, perhaps the most famous of the Confederate regimental bands, mustered eight of its members in 1861 from the Mountain Saxhorn Band *(above)* of Staunton, Virginia. Brigadier General Stonewall Jackson reportedly had a great fondness for the brigade band, although he confessed privately that he could not distinguish one song from another, regardless of who played it. To the band's great dismay, it was denied furlough to play at Jackson's funeral in Lexington, Virginia. The band members' services as surgical assistants—a secondary role assigned to many regimental musicians—were urgently needed at Chancellorsville in the aftermath of the battle in which Jackson was mortally wounded by his own men.

This upright B-flat saxhorn, played by a member of the 30th Virginia Infantry Band, sounded the dirge that accompanied General Stonewall Jackson to his final resting place. According to one onlooker, "The mournful cortege moved on in silence, broken by the solemn strains of music and the discharge of artillery. Hundreds wept as though mourning a brother."

Solemnly clutching their over-the-shoulder saxhorns, four members of Smith's Armory Band of Richmond, Virginia, were immortalized in this circa 1860 photograph. The band, which served with the Virginia Light Infantry Public Guard prior to the War, went on to become the 1st Virginia Regimental Band in April 1860. It was the favorite musical ensemble of Jefferson Davis, president of the Confederacy.

FIELD MUSIC

CONFEDERATE DRUMMER'S COAT
Captured at the Battle of New Bern, North Carolina, in March 1862, this drummer boy's tunic once belonged to a young member of the Gaston Light Guard Unit.

Charles F. Mosby was 13 when he enlisted in 1861 as a drummer with the "Elliott Grays," a company of the 6th Virginia Infantry. Mosby survived his four years of service; many others, some as young as 10, died in battle and were eulogized in such ballads as "The Dying Drummer Boy," by Mary Lathbury and E. C. Howe.

REBEL SNARE DRUM

A rare Confederate copy of the Federal eagle drum, this snare drum lacks the United States motto, *E Pluribus Unum,* or "Out of Many, One," on its banner. It was carried into battle by the 1st Florida Infantry in 1861.

13TH VIRGINIA INFANTRY DRUM

This rope-tension drum was captured by the Union Worcester Continentals on a battlefield near Winchester, Virginia. As was true of most such instruments of the era, the drum's shell was made of wood and its heads were of calfskin or sheepskin.

Confederate fifers and drummers—like the unidentified "straw-blower" and "sheepskin fiddler" pictured here—controlled troop maneuvers instrumentally.

GERMAN SILVER FIFE, 44TH TENNESSEE

WOODEN FIFE OF LEWIS CREBS EVERLY, 33D VIRGINIA

32D NORTH CAROLINA REGIMENTAL DRUM

Retrieved from the battlefield at Spotsylvania Courthouse on May 11, 1864, this snare drum belonged to J. W. Brunet, who was killed in action. The drum's tack design helped secure the overlapping glued seam of the shell.

CONFEDERATE CAVALRY BUGLE

Fifteen-year-old Noel Davenport of Mobile, Alabama, shucked his studies at Spring Hill College in 1862 to play this cavalry bugle for the 23d Tennessee Regiment, with which he served till 1865.

ARTILLERY BUGLE, RICHMOND HOWITZERS

This bugle fell into the hands of the Rebel soldier Reuben Pleasants of the Richmond Howitzers in June 1863 during a skirmish in Winchester, Virginia. Some nine years after the War, Pleasants' fellow artilleryman John Jones formally dedicated the bugle to the veteran battery.

At first light, a Confederate bugler stirs his regiment with a round of reveille in this painting by W. L. Sheppard. The wake-up call was an electric tonic to drowsing troops, who associated its clarion tones with the crash and rumble of battle.

INFANTRY BUGLE, 2D KENTUCKY

Battered and tarnished from long years of rough use, this bugle once summoned the foot soldiers of the 2d Kentucky to roll call, assembly, and other regimental drills. Chief Bugler John Washington Payne captured the instrument from Union forces at Hartsville, Tennessee, in December 1862.

FLAGS

A reporter for the New Orleans *Daily Crescent* caught the mystique of Confederate flags at a presentation ceremony in April 1861. Miss Idelea Collens, the reporter wrote, presented new colors to the DeSoto Rifles of Louisiana and threw them a heartfelt challenge: "Receive then, from your mothers and sisters, from those whose affections greet you, these colors woven by our feeble but reliant hands; and when this bright flag shall float before you on the battlefield, let it not only inspire you with the brave and patriotic ambition of a soldier aspiring to his own and his country's honor and glory, but also may it be a sign that cherished ones appeal to you to save them from a fanatical and heartless foe."

Then the color sergeant took the flag from Miss Collens' hands and made a speech of equal fervor, concluding: "May the god of battles look down upon us as we register a soldier's vow that no stain shall ever be found upon thy sacred folds, save the blood of those who attack thee or those who fall in thy defense.

"Comrades, you have heard the pledge, may it ever guide and guard you on the tented field. In the smoke, glare, and din of battle, amidst carnage and death, there let its bright folds inspire you with new strength, nerve your arms and steel your hearts to deeds of strength and valor."

Flags, war, and the Confederate States of America were inextricably bonded in the idealism, vanity, and ultimate disaster of the Southern cause. Since the Confederacy was at war through all but the first few months of its brief and violent existence, almost from birth most of its flags served military purposes. Beyond mere symbolism, regimental flags had a concrete purpose: They were the chief means of recognition in the hellfire confusion of a 19th-century battlefield.

Before the Confederacy was born in February 1861, six slave states of the South had dissolved their ties to the Union and resumed their status as independent republics. To assert this independence, many adopted distinctive flags to symbolize their nationality. The flags designed for this purpose both before and after the establishment of the Confederate national government fell into three broad categories.

States with strong colonial traditions often chose to display symbols (usually a coat of arms) on a blue field. The flags officially adopted by South Carolina and Virginia and those used unofficially by Georgia and Maryland secessionists in early 1861 exemplify that trend. States such as Alabama, with less attachment to colonial symbols, heralded their secession by taking the single star that had represented them in the United States flag and placing it upon a blue field—the famous Bonnie Blue Flag.

The flags adopted by North Carolina, Mississippi, and Texas symbolized secession by displaying a single star as the prominent device. The official Louisiana flag followed this trend. The flag consisted of a field of 13 alternating red, white, and blue stripes with a single yellow star in its red canton. Florida had adopted a similar flag, but one that resembled the United States flag even more; it substituted a single star for the 33 that then graced the canton of the Stars and Stripes, but later changed to a design more like the Stars and Bars, the new national flag of the Confederate States of America.

During its four years, the Confederate Congress successively adopted three designs to symbolize its national existence. Like some of the early state flags, the first national flag (adopted March 4, 1861) looked a lot like the Stars and Stripes; hence its nickname, the

Stars and Bars. Its design, offered to a congressional committee by Nicola Marschall of Alabama, consisted of a field of three equal horizontal bars: red-white-red. Its blue canton extended two-thirds the height of the flag and bore a circle of stars equal to the number of states in the Confederacy. When it was first adopted, the stars numbered 7; by July of 1861, with the secession of Virginia, Arkansas, North Carolina, and Tennessee, there were 11. By the end of the year, Kentucky and Missouri were admitted to the Confederacy, bringing the total of stars to 13.

These stars were usually five-pointed and white. The maker of the flag would sometimes choose to arrange the stars in some pattern other than a pure circle. In flags of this design made for presentation, other devices such as coats of arms and mottoes were often added for extra distinction.

The inadequacy of the Stars and Bars soon became apparent. The flag was simply too similar to the Stars and Stripes to be distinguished at a distance or through smoke, fog, or rain. After two years of debate over substitutes, the Confederate Congress finally resolved in May 1863 to change its national flag.

The new flag was nicknamed the Stainless Banner because of its plain white field. Its red canton was crisscrossed by a white-edged, dark blue saltire (Saint Andrew's Cross) emblazoned with 13 white stars. The canton conformed to the battle flag that had been used since 1861 by the Confederate armies fighting east of the Appalachians. Unfortunately, in calm weather it hung so limply that it could be mistaken for a flag of truce. After almost two years, in March 1865, the Congress changed its proportions and added a wide red vertical bar to its fly edge. However, only a few such flags were made before surrender made the issue of a distinctive Confederate flag irrelevant.

As early as the fall of 1861, it became apparent to the Confederate armies both east and west of the Appalachians that a battle flag distinctly different from the Confederate national flag should be adopted to avoid the disastrous mistakes of identity on the battlefield caused by the similarity of the Stars and Bars to the Stars and Stripes. In the Eastern theater the idea of a new battle flag was championed by General P. G. T. Beauregard, commander of the Confederate Army of the Potomac. In September 1861 he proposed that a design that William Porcher Miles had submitted to Congress as a national flag be adopted as a battle flag.

Miles' design was a rectangular red field traversed by a blue saltire bearing white stars equal in number to the seven states then represented in the Confederate Congress. After Beauregard discussed the matter with the departmental commander, General Joseph E. Johnston, the design was adopted (but only after making it square to save cloth). To limit wear, the battle flags were protected by borders of various colors.

Constance Cary Harrison of Richmond speaks in her diary of the spontaneity of Confederate flag design. She writes: "Another incident of note, during the autumn of '61, was that to my cousins, Hetty and Jennie Cary, and to me was entrusted the making of the first three battle flags of the Confederacy. They were jaunty squares of scarlet crossed with dark blue edged with white, the cross bearing stars to indicate the number of the seceded States. We set our best stitches upon them, edged them with golden fringes, and, when they were finished, dispatched one to Johnston, another to Beauregard, and the third to Earl Van Dorn, then commanding infantry at Manassas. The banners were received with all possible enthusiasm; we were toasted, feted, and cheered abundantly. After two years, when Van Dorn had been killed in

Tennessee, mine came back to me, tattered and storm-stained from long and honorable service in the field."

After a few battle flags of this design had been made for presentation, the Confederate quartermaster ordered 120 for the Army of Northern Virginia. They were made of dress silk purchased on the open market. Red silk was scarce, so various shades of pink were usually substituted. The flags were produced by volunteer sewing circles in Richmond. These 12-star, yellow-bordered battle flags were distributed to the troops at the close of 1861. Second Lieutenant Colin McRae Selph, a quartermaster in the Army of Northern Virginia, reported that he had "exhausted the supply of silk in Richmond" and "the ladies will have to do without silk dresses, as I have bought all the material."

As the Confederate army grew in size, especially during the spring of 1862, more battle flags were needed. Having run out of silk, the quartermaster turned to wool bunting, first from the stock available at the captured U.S. navy yard at Norfolk, Virginia, and later by import from England. The new flags were manufactured at the quartermaster's clothing depot in Richmond.

From 1862 through 1865, the Richmond depot produced seven subvarieties of the bunting battle flag, each with minor changes. The most prominent distinctions involved the sizes of the components, although the first two subvarieties had yellow-orange borders and the other five all had white borders. Changes in the width of the saltire generally reflected the availability of blue bunting. Star size and spacing seemed to be a matter of the patternmaker's taste, and this kept changing.

By 1863, the quartermaster's department had become so proficient that entire divisions of the Army of Northern Virginia were supplied with flags simultaneously. As the War progressed, the pattern was copied by

the Staunton, Virginia, clothing depot to furnish the Army of the Valley and by the Charleston clothing depot to supply units in South Carolina, Georgia, and Florida.

Oddly enough, the Confederate War Department never approved for general use the battle flag adopted for the field in the Eastern theater. It was, strictly speaking, a matter left to the discretion of unit commanders. The transmittal of the Eastern armies' battle flag to other theaters of the War did not, therefore, descend the chain of command from the War Department, but occurred laterally as the two main proponents of a new Confederate battle flag, Generals Beauregard and Johnston, were transferred to commands outside Virginia. Hence, the battle flag used in the East was introduced to the main Confederate army in the West, then called the Army of the Mississippi, when Beauregard was sent to become its second in command in early 1862.

Beauregard, however, was only partly successful in transmitting the Eastern armies' design to the West in 1862. The concept of a distinctive battle flag had preceded him. General Van Dorn, a recipient of one of the first Army of Northern Virginia battle flags, had been sent to take command of forces in the Trans-Mississippi Confederacy before Beauregard arrived. Van Dorn had designed his own battle flag—a red field bordered in yellow with a white crescent in the upper staff corner, the rest of the field studded with 13 white stars—for his Army of the West. When this force moved to reinforce Beauregard's Army of the Mississippi after Shiloh, it took along its flag, which continued in service through 1862.

When Beauregard arrived in the West, he found that the two main elements holding the Kentucky line had also chosen their own battle flags. Polk's troops on the Mississippi had adopted a blue flag traversed by a red

Saint George's Cross bearing white stars, and the Army of Central Kentucky under General William J. Hardee had adopted a blue field bordered in white, with a white disk in its center. Only General Braxton Bragg's forces from the Gulf Coast arrived without battle flags, and only they were issued the battle flags patterned after the Virginia design that Beauregard had ordered.

When Johnston took control of the Army of Tennessee (formerly the Army of the Mississippi) during the winter of 1863-64, he called for the adoption of his version of the Army of Northern Virginia battle flag—rectangular and borderless. When a new corps was added to that Western army in the spring of 1864, its units carried a variant of the same flag, made by James Cameron of Mobile. However, when Johnston insisted on his design for the entire army, the men of Cleburne's Division (who had always carried the blue flag of Hardee's Corps) so objected to the change that they were allowed to keep their old design.

National flags were important when dust, thick smoke from cannon and muskets, and the early similarity of Union and Confederate uniforms necessitated some way to distinguish friend from foe. But the individual unit flags also served an important tactical function. Despite major advances in weaponry, the first years of the Civil War were fought according to the rigid discipline of linear deployment. This system demanded precise alignment when a unit was in battle formation. A unit's flags were often the soldier's only guide, his only way of knowing if he was where he was supposed to be.

To explain why his regiment's worn-out battle flag was retired in January of 1865, a North Carolina officer recollected: "So much of the old flag had been shot away that it could not be distinctly seen by other regiments during brigade drills, and as the 44th was always made the central regiment, upon which the others of the brigade dressed in line of battle, as well as on parade, a new flag had become a necessity."

Alignment was not the only battlefield function of the unit colors. Where the colors went, the men followed, their flag guiding the unit forward during an assault or serving as the focus for a rally after a retreat.

Although unit colors were identical when issued, they soon took on characteristics that permitted soldiers to recognize their own colors instantly. In units where capable hands and materials were available, an abbreviated unit designation was added to the flag, either directly upon the field or on a strip of cloth sewn to it. Other distinctions came from higher echelons of the command system. On July 23, 1862, the Confederate War Department authorized army commanders to "cause to be entered in some conspicuous place on the standards the names of the several battles in which their regiments, battalions, and separate squadrons have been actually engaged."

In issuing this order, the War Department was merely approving actions already taken by field commanders. In the Western theater, Hardee had authorized some units to inscribe "Shiloh" on their banners. And in the East, Longstreet, commanding the Right Wing of the Virginia army in June 1862, had authorized strips of cloth imprinted with "Seven Pines!" to be sewn on the battle flags of his units that had honorably fought there. (At Seven Pines, 10 members of the color guard of the Palmetto South Carolina Sharpshooters were killed or wounded. It was reported that four of them in succession passed their flag along as they fell without letting it touch the ground.)

Although a few regiments under other commands sought to continue this practice by attaching their own battle-honor strips,

234

the strips so encumbered the flags as to be impractical. As an alternative, several regiments applied battle honors directly to the fields of their battle flags. Cutting and sewing separate letters worked for this purpose, but this was a tedious process that few units could accomplish. In the Western armies, some units turned once again to the contractor James Cameron, who could embellish their flags for them—for a fee.

Another means of adding honors involved painting them directly on the field. Again, the task was too much for individual units, so their commanders occasionally employed outside contractors to paint authorized battle honors on their flags. Associated units would seize the opportunity to have honors painted on their flags at the same time.

Paint posed another problem. Not only did it weigh down the fabric, but it often bled through the loosely woven bunting to the opposite side, especially when large letters were applied. In Virginia, the problem was solved when the Richmond quartermaster's depot started applying honors in small dark blue or black letters to the fields of newly issued battle flags. The flags also bore the regimental number over the center star and an abbreviated title in yellow under it.

A few units received special recognition through other additions to the colors. The 1st Maryland Infantry was granted the honor of appending a "bucktail" (the symbol of the 13th Pennsylvania Reserve Regiment) to its flagstaff for having defeated the Pennsylvanians at Harrisonburg, Virginia, on June 6, 1862. The 18th Georgia Infantry adopted a similar trophy after decimating the 5th New York Zouaves at Second Manassas on August 30, 1862: A tuft of hair from the head of a slain Zouave was sewn to its battle flag.

For noble conduct in the Battle of Frayser's Farm on June 30, 1862, the 60th Virginia Infantry Regiment was honored with a flag bearing a device of crossed bayonets. The crossed bayonets award was unique to the 60th Virginia but similar to the inverted crossed cannon awards authorized for units of the Army of Tennessee that had captured enemy artillery in battle.

In the Western theater, General Bragg authorized a number of units of the Army of Tennessee to inscribe their banners with "Perryville" after they had fought there. He also allowed units that had captured enemy artillery pieces to place inverted crossed cannons on their colors.

One other factor distinguished Confederate battle flags, but it did not come from regimental initiative or higher authority. Enemy fire often reduced a flag to tatters. Officers of the 28th Tennessee Infantry Regiment who fought at Chickamauga wrote that their flag was "riddled with balls, being pierced not less than 30 times." And the flag of Hilliard's Alabama Legion bore "the marks of over 80 bullets," while its bearer was "thrice wounded and the flagstaff thrice shot away," recalled Brigadier General Archibald Gracie. In some cases, bullet- or shell-riddled flagstaffs were carefully repaired so as to retain visible evidence of the damage.

The heroic endeavors of the color bearers and the color guards to keep their flags aloft under withering fire were often cited by regimental commanders after a battle. The melee around the colors of the 21st Virginia Infantry at the Battle of Cedar Mountain, Virginia, in August 1862 typifies the fate of many a color party: "Our color bearer knocked down a Yankee with his flagstaff, and was shot to death at once," wrote Private John H. Worsham. "One of the color guard took the flag, and he also was killed; another, Roswell S. Lindsay of F Company, bayoneted a Yankee, and was immediately riddled with balls, three going through him. Four color bearers were killed with the colors in their hands, the

235

fifth man flung the riddled flag to the breeze, and went through the terrible battle unhurt."

Many color bearers would yield their flags only with their lives. A few others, seeing no hope of saving their flags from capture, endeavored to hide or destroy them. In the assault on Fort Harrison, Virginia, in September 1864, Color Sergeant J. R. Barnhardt of the 8th North Carolina State Troops ripped his flag to pieces rather than see it taken. Others tried to pull flags from their staffs and conceal them.

When capture seemed imminent at Murfreesboro, Tennessee, in December 1862, Sergeant William N. Cameron of the 25th Tennessee Infantry tore his regiment's flag from its staff and stuffed it under his coat. He kept it concealed throughout his subsequent captivity. At Spotsylvania Courthouse, Virginia, in May 1864, the color sergeant of the 4th Virginia Infantry Regiment also tried to hide his battle flag in his jacket. His ruse failed, however, and the flag became a trophy of the victorious Union forces.

On the night after the 7th Louisiana Infantry was captured at Rappahannock Station, Virginia, the color bearer revealed to his comrades that he had hidden their battle flag when they were overwhelmed. He burned it in the campfire that night so it would not become a Union prize. A like desperation overtook Color Sergeant George Barbee of the 44th North Carolina as his regiment retreated from Petersburg, Virginia. Upon crossing the Appomattox River, Barbee took the battle flag from its staff, wrapped it around a stone, and threw it into the river, declaring, "No enemy can ever have a flag of the 44th North Carolina Regiment."

In the 21st Virginia Infantry, when it was known positively that General Lee was going to surrender, the response was emotional and dramatic. The gallant color bearer, Ensign John H. Cumbia, who had carried the colors for so long a time, tore them from the staff. He cut the flag into small pieces and gave them to his comrades. On April 12, 1865, survivors of the Army of Northern Virginia silently marched to Appomattox Courthouse, stacked their muskets and accouterments, and then furled their cherished battle flags and laid them on the stacks. The Confederacy surrendered 71 unit flags that day; many others were never surrendered.

The Stars and Bars

On the morning of April 18, 1861, four days after Federal Major Robert Anderson had been forced to lower the Stars and Stripes to surrender Fort Sumter, the batteries surrounding Charleston Harbor thundered in salute of the Western Hemisphere's newest flag. As the sound of cannon echoed across the water, Captain Robert Fergusson of South Carolina's state navy raised the Stars and Bars of the Confederate States of America to the top of a 15-foot-high staff lashed to one of the guns on Sumter's eastern rampart, facing Charleston. On a pole next to it, two members of Governor Francis Pickens' executive staff, Colonels Edward Carroll and Franklin J. Moses, raised the palmetto ensign of South Carolina.

Variations on a Theme

Confederate national flags were manufactured in various sizes for display over public buildings or over military fortifications, garrisons, camps, and headquarters. The standard garrison-size flag made at the Richmond clothing depot measured 16 feet by 24 feet. Such large flags were expensive, so smaller flags (8 feet by 12 feet and 10 feet by 15 feet) were provided for daily use. Since flags flying over public buildings and garrisons were exposed to the elements daily, they were fashioned of durable materials such as cotton or wool bunting.

Tattered by months of Federal bombardment, Fort Sumter's garrison flag flies defiantly from a jury-rigged flagpole atop the fort's parapet in 1863.

SECOND NATIONAL FLAG

General Hoke's headquarters flag *(left)* conforms to the length-to-width proportion of one to two mandated by Congress. Military-issue flags were longer.

FIRST NATIONAL FLAG

This garrison flag flew over Fort Norfolk, situated at the mouth of the Elizabeth River's eastern branch. The fort was evacuated by the Confederates after the fall of Yorktown in 1862.

THIRD NATIONAL FLAG

Only a few large third-national-pattern garrison flags and naval ensigns were made before the end of the War. This postwar example was made for Virginia's last Confederate governor.

Gifts from a Grateful People

In the spring and summer of 1861, volunteer companies all over the South received bright new banners presented with all the pomp and ceremony that a romantically inclined society could muster.

Groups of patriotic women assembled to stitch and embroider flags for local units. On occasion, businessmen, such as the Richmond "clothing and trimming merchant" George Ruskell, who produced several painted flags including that of the 2d Virginia Volunteers *(opposite page, lower left),* received orders for company and regimental banners. So many companies were determined to carry their own flags that some newly formed regiments marched off to war with as many as 10 different flags.

PRINCESS ANNE CAVALRY, 14TH VIRGINIA CAVALRY BATTALION

The company's gold silk flag, with its painted seated liberty device, was made by the ladies' aid society of the London Bridge Baptist Church of Princess Anne County. On April 20, 1861, the company mustered under Captain E. W. Capps to seize the Gosport Navy Yard.

1ST SOUTH CAROLINA INFANTRY REGIMENT

The regiment's silk flag was embroidered by the nuns of the Carmelite order in Charleston. At Gaines' Mill in 1862, Colonel D. H. Hamilton recalled that the enemy "opened a deadly fire upon my regiment, killing a large number of my officers and men."

Designers of volunteer colors such as these often derived their inspiration from the national flag, simply adding a motto or crest. Others copied state crests or adopted heraldic designs such as the Marion Artillery's palmetto palm and the swamp fox of Revolutionary War hero Francis Marion *(top left)*.

MARION ARTILLERY, SOUTH CAROLINA

FORSYTH RIFLES, NORTH CAROLINA INFANTRY

1ST LOUISIANA INFANTRY BATTALION

FLORIDA INDEPENDENT BLUES, COMPANY E, 3D FLORIDA INFANTRY

2D VIRGINIA INFANTRY

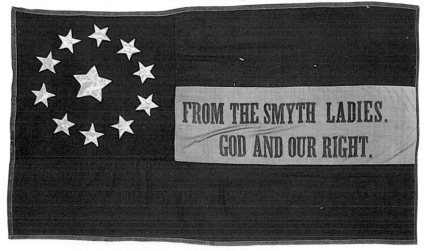

SMYTH DRAGOONS, 8TH VIRGINIA CAVALRY

242

Flags for the Virginia Army

Over the winter of 1861, the Cary cousins and patriotic sewing groups in Richmond produced silk flags for special presentation to selected regiments and senior general officers. In October 1861, Confederate Quartermaster Colin M. Selph tasked Mrs. James Alfred Jones' sewing circle and two other Richmond sewing groups with making 120 silk battle flags *(below and opposite page, top right)* to be issued to the army at Centreville, Virginia.

At a presentation ceremony, Colonel W. D. Smith of the 20th Georgia Infantry voiced his concern to General Beauregard that his banner's pale color might be mistaken for a token of surrender. The peppery general tersely replied, "Dye it red, sir! Dye it with blood, sir!"

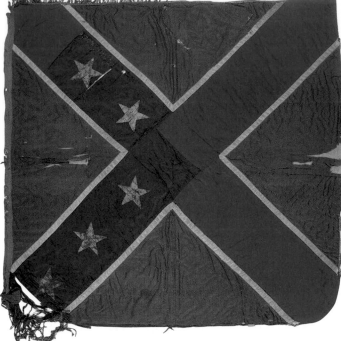

VAN DORN'S BATTLE FLAG

General Earl Van Dorn used Constance Cary's gift as his personal flag at the battles of Elkhorn Tavern, Corinth, and Holly Springs. When he was assassinated in May 1863, the flag was returned to Miss Cary by one of his aides. It bears the name "Constance" on the reverse side.

4TH NORTH CAROLINA INFANTRY REGIMENT

"Yelling and firing as they advanced," the 4th charged a Federal battery at Seven Pines on May 31, 1862. The color bearer, James Bonner, was killed, and Major Bryan Grimes, unhorsed just moments earlier, seized the flag. The Carolinians went on to capture six Federal guns.

GEN. JOHNSTON'S BATTLE FLAG

When the Cary cousins made this and two other battle flags for Generals Johnston, Beauregard, and Van Dorn, they chose gold instead of white stars, and enlisted the aid of a chemist to affix gold leaf to the silk. Other presentation flags also bore gold stars and fringe.

16TH MISSISSIPPI INFANTRY REGIMENT

At Gaines' Mill on June 27, 1862, the 16th Mississippi's flag was pierced 11 times and the color sergeant was killed. The flag's upper quadrant bears a handwritten inscription: "Through God we shall do valiantly, for He is that shall tread down our enemies."

6TH SOUTH CAROLINA INFANTRY REGIMENT

The regiment, part of General David R. Jones' brigade, received its flag on November 28, 1861, in a ceremony that one soldier recalled as "the grandest time we ever had. We were drawn up in a hollow square and several speeches were made. The noise of the men was deafening."

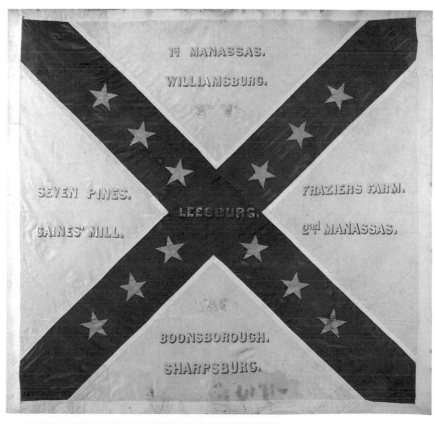

8TH VIRGINIA INFANTRY REGIMENT

General P. G. T. Beauregard presented the regiment this silk battle flag to honor the men for their courageous performance at Ball's Bluff, Virginia, on October 21, 1861, an occasion marked by the "Leesburg" battle honor at the center of the cross. The other battle names were probably painted on later, when the flag was retired after Sharpsburg.

Headquarters Flags

In the Army of Northern Virginia, generals' stationary headquarters and the headquarters of tactical commands such as divisions and brigades might be distinguished by a large national flag or, less commonly, by the personal device of a commanding officer. No armywide system of flags to designate headquarters was ever ordered.

National-pattern headquarters flags were generally flown over campsites and were not displayed on the battlefield. Smaller devices, however, such as General Bradley Johnson's swallowtail guidon *(lower right),* might be carried in battle by an enlisted aide.

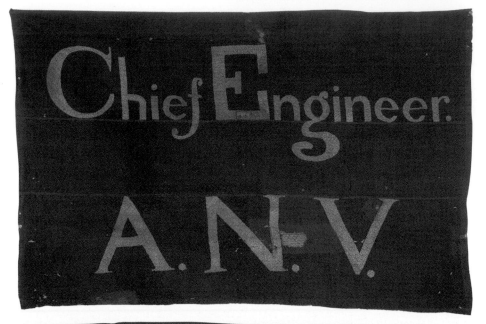

CHIEF ENGINEER'S HEADQUARTERS FLAG
This homemade wool bunting flag marked the headquarters of the chief engineer of the Army of Northern Virginia. The flag was captured during the Appomattox campaign by William J. Bremer, a scout on Sheridan's staff.

HEADQUARTERS FLAG, LT. GEN. JAMES EWELL BROWN STUART

Jeb Stuart's 4′ x 6′ headquarters flag was manufactured at the Richmond clothing depot sometime after the autumn of 1863. The inscription was placed on the flag after the War by Major H. B. McClellan, Stuart's assistant adjutant general.

Head Quarters Cavalry Corps, A.N.V.
GEN. J.E.B.STUART'S FLAG,
Presented to the
Richmond Library, by
H. B. McCLELLAN, MAJOR, & A.A.G.

GEN. ROBERT E. LEE'S HEADQUARTERS FLAG

The cotton and wool bunting national flag at left was used by Robert E. Lee as a headquarters flag during the early part of the War. It flew only over stationary camps, not on the battlefield. At the end of the War the flag was found stored with the Confederate War Department's records, packed among captured Federal colors. It is possible that the flag, or at least its odd star arrangement, was produced by the general's wife.

PERSONAL GUIDON OF MAJ. GEN. BRADLEY JOHNSON

Johnson's Maryland Brigade guidon, a forked-pattern flag usually carried by smaller units of cavalry and light artillery, bore the Calvert cross from the state arms. This device was worn as a pin by many Maryland soldiers serving in the Army of Northern Virginia.

REGIMENTAL BATTLE FLAG, JOHN M. JONES' BRIGADE

When men of the 60th New York Infantry advanced from their entrenchments on Culp's Hill after the bloody repulse of Johnson's Confederate Division on July 2, 1863, they found seven officers and the color guard dead around the cotton flag above. "The effects of our fire were so terrible," recalled a Federal chaplain, "that the flags were abandoned and the prisoners were afraid to either advance or retreat."

Richmond's First Bunting Issue

When his supply of silk ran out, Chief Quartermaster William L. Cabell substituted battle flags made of cotton. These were first issued to Elzey's and Steuart's brigades in May 1862, and to portions of General Whiting's division, including Hood's Texas Brigade.

By the spring of 1862 new flags were required for the expanding Virginia army, and stocks of wool bunting from the Gosport Navy Yard were made into battle flags at the Richmond clothing depot. They were bordered in yellow wool flannel left over from the manufacture of army wing badges. Presentation of the bunting flags began with General Longstreet's Right Wing, Army of Northern Virginia, in May and June of 1862.

UNIDENTIFIED BATTLE FLAG, CAPTURED AT THE WILDERNESS

All of the cotton battle flags bore 12 stars on an eight-inch-wide, poorly dyed blue cross that lacked the customary white edging. Instead of a border, the edges of the cotton flags were bound with orange tape.

18TH GEORGIA INFANTRY

It is said that the lock of hair attached to the top edge of this flag was taken from a soldier of the 5th New York Zouaves who tried to seize the colors at Second Manassas. The color sergeant was killed while advancing on a second battery.

1ST OR 3D NORTH CAROLINA INFANTRY

For most of the War, the 1st and 3d North Carolina fought as a single unit. At Sharpsburg, under this flag, survivors of the morning's fight in the Cornfield held the fence line of the Hagerstown Pike with "only one man to every panel of fence."

14TH NORTH CAROLINA INFANTRY

The two battle honors, printed on strips of polished cotton at Longstreet's headquarters, were awarded to any regiment of his command "that goes through the battle creditably." The honors were presented on June 12, 1862.

3D ALABAMA INFANTRY

On July 1, 1862, at Malvern Hill, the 3d's commander, Major Robert M. Sands, reported the loss of his colors and color guard: "There were six men shot while carrying the colors forward." The colors were retrieved by members of the 83d Pennsylvania.

14TH LOUISIANA INFANTRY

As part of the Louisiana Tiger Brigade, the 14th Louisiana carried this flag into the fight for the Cornfield at Sharpsburg, sending an entire Federal brigade streaming back into the East Woods.

Second Bunting Issue

In the spring of 1862, a new pattern of wool bunting battle flags was produced at the Richmond clothing depot. Similar in size and design to the first bunting issue, the pattern reduced the width of the blue saltire from eight to five inches to conserve depleted stocks of blue cloth. Nevertheless, the depot soon used up all of the red and blue bunting captured at the Gosport Navy Yard and the last of its stock of yellow wool border material.

These new flags were first issued to General John B. Magruder's Army of the Peninsula and then generally to all regiments of the Right Wing of the Army of Northern Virginia. ("Wing" was the early Confederate designation for *corps.*) This included new elements of Longstreet's command and the divisions of D. H. Hill and A. P. Hill.

An unidentified Virginia ensign poses with his regiment's flag. The rank of ensign authorized the recipient "to bear the colors of the regiment, but without the right to command in the field."

38TH NORTH CAROLINA INFANTRY REGIMENT

At Mechanicsville on June 26, 1862, the 38th advanced to outflank entrenched Federal artillery and infantry, losing nearly one-third of its number. The wounded color bearer remained at the regiment's head and brought the colors to safety.

11TH ALABAMA INFANTRY REGIMENT

At Gaines' Mill, the 11th Alabama led Cadmus M. Wilcox's brigade in the forefront of Longstreet's attack on the Federal left. Carrying this flag, the regiment rushed over a log breastwork, fighting hand to hand to capture a battery of Napoleon guns.

60TH VIRGINIA INFANTRY REGIMENT

Crossed bayonets commemorate the action at Frayser's Farm where, according to brigade commander Charles Field, "bayonets were really crossed, several of the enemy being killed with that weapon and several of the 60th now bearing bayonet wounds."

5TH VIRGINIA INFANTRY REGIMENT

This flag was issued to the 5th Virginia, part of the Stonewall Brigade of Jackson's Army of the Valley, when it joined the Army of Northern Virginia in June 1862. Before this, Jackson's brigades carried various designs of presentation colors.

17TH MISSISSIPPI INFANTRY REGIMENT

The 17th was organized at Corinth, Mississippi, in 1861 and transferred to Virginia. It received a silk Army of Northern Virginia battle flag at Leesburg in December 1861 and seems to have retired it in favor of this second bunting, issued later in 1862.

3D ARKANSAS INFANTRY REGIMENT

This three-foot-square artillery flag may have been issued by mistake to the 3d Arkansas Infantry, the only Arkansas regiment serving in the Army of Northern Virginia, when a quartermaster misread *Artillery* for *Arkansas*.

15TH LOUISIANA INFANTRY REGIMENT

At Second Manassas, the 15th Louisiana held part of the railroad cut against repeated Federal assaults. "It was at this point," recalled their commander, "that the ammunition of the brigade gave out. The men fought with rocks and held their position."

28TH VIRGINIA INFANTRY REGIMENT

The 28th Virginia's flag was part of a group presented to Virginia regiments at Centreville on October 30, 1861, by Governor John Letcher. More flags of this pattern, with a center device painted by H. P. Keane, were manufactured at Richmond in December by the firm of J. R. Thompson.

State Battle Flags

Despite Confederate army orders after the Seven Days' Battles prohibiting commands that fell under the control of the Army of Northern Virginia from carrying flags of designs other than that of the Virginia army, two states issued their own distinctive battle flags—Virginia and North Carolina. These flags were generally brought out on special occasions.

Virginia and North Carolina commands that did not fall under the control of Lee's army, such as General John C. Breckinridge's Army of Southwestern Virginia and the forces on the North Carolina coast, were not issued Virginia-pattern battle flags but carried state colors instead. In addition, the designs of some early regimental flags from other states were an attempt to conform to state regulations or a state seal.

36TH VIRGINIA INFANTRY REGIMENT

This flag was part of a batch manufactured in early December 1863 and issued to regiments in the Army of Southwestern Virginia. Eleven flags were made for infantry and cavalry. They were sewn by Rosaline Hunter, and the devices were painted by John Varni for $500. The 36th Virginia's flag bore battle honors from theaters of war in western Virginia and Tennessee. On September 19, 1864, harried by Federal cavalry during the retreat after the Battle of Winchester, the regiment lost its colors to Sergeant P. H. McEnroe of the 6th New York Cavalry.

38TH NORTH CAROLINA INFANTRY REGIMENT

The 38th enlisted in January 1862 and was deployed for local defense. In April it was reorganized for war and received this state battle flag, made at the Raleigh clothing depot. Such flags, bearing the dates of independence and secession, were issued to all North Carolina regiments upon formation. The 38th North Carolina reported to Virginia in time to see its first action at Fredericksburg in May 1862. The regiment fought in most of the battles of the Army of Northern Virginia and retained its state flag until the end of the War.

47TH NORTH CAROLINA INFANTRY REGIMENT

The 47th North Carolina arrived in time to participate in Pickett's and Pettigrew's disastrous charge on July 3, 1863, at Gettysburg. The regiment lost its Army of Northern Virginia battle flag within the Federal lines. When the replacement flag was lost at Hatcher's Run in 1864, the 47th carried its state flag while awaiting another new flag from the Richmond depot.

GEORGIA STATE REGIMENTAL FLAG

This hand-painted silk flag is typical of flags presented to Georgia regiments in 1861. Originally, the state arms, consisting of an arch labeled "Constitution" and supported by the three pillars of Justice, Wisdom, and Moderation, were to be displayed on a white field, but few flags conformed to that pattern. On most Georgia military flags the seal was placed on blue. One Georgia flag used a red field. The state never issued a regulation design.

KING WILLIAM ARTILLERY BATTERY VIRGINIA

In common with most artillery batteries of the Army of Northern Virginia, the King William Artillery was issued an infantry-size (4 feet by 4 feet) battle flag.

Third Bunting Issue

In July 1862, the Richmond depot began production of the third and largest issue of Army of Northern Virginia battle flags. These white-bordered colors were made until May of 1864, in quantities that allowed issue to entire divisions at a time. D. H. Hill's division received new colors after Fredericksburg, A. P. Hill's division after Chancellorsville, and several commands that had lost heavily in colors were given replacements after Gettysburg. New flags were provided to regiments regardless of the condition of their old flags, and most units chose to carry the new colors, which had the most battle honors.

At first some brigade commanders paid to have distinctive battle honors painted on their flags. After April 1863, all honors were applied in blue paint, on one side of the flag only.

11TH MISSISSIPPI INFANTRY REGIMENT

Flags with yellow battle honors in this style were presented to General Whiting's former brigade after Sharpsburg. At Gettysburg, the 11th Mississippi advanced in the first line of Pettigrew's Division in the assault of July 3. Under an artillery bombardment that "fairly melted away" their brigade, survivors of the 11th reached the stone wall that marked the Federal line before being forced back. Their flag was captured by the 39th New York.

28TH NORTH CAROLINA INFANTRY REGIMENT

As part of Branch's Brigade, the 28th probably received this battle flag while encamped near Fredericksburg in the winter of 1862-63. It was carried in Jackson's flank attack at Chancellorsville in May 1863 and on the left of the line in Pickett's Charge at Gettysburg. There the flag was captured by the 126th New York.

42D VIRGINIA INFANTRY REGIMENT

The regiment's colors, issued sometime after the Battle of Gettysburg, bear battle honors recalling honorable service during Stonewall Jackson's Valley campaign and the Army of Northern Virginia's greatest battles. Honors were not awarded exclusively for Confederate victories; hence the inclusion of Gettysburg. The flag was captured at Spotsylvania in 1864.

18TH MISSISSIPPI INFANTRY REGIMENT

Speaking of the 18th Mississippi's defense of the Sunken Lane at Second Fredericksburg, General William Barksdale stated: "A more heroic struggle was never made by a mere handful of men against overwhelming odds. According to the enemy's own accounts, many of this noble little band resisted to the death with clubbed guns even after his vast hordes had swept over and around the walls." The 18th Mississippi suffered 58 casualties, some of whom still lay in the lane when Federal photographer Andrew J. Russell took the picture at right on May 4, 1863. The regiment's battle flag was claimed by the 77th New York Infantry.

12TH VIRGINIA INFANTRY REGIMENT

Holding aloft his shattered flag-pole in the epic painting at right, Color Sergeant William Smith of the 12th Virginia leads his comrades in the decisive charge against Federals holding the mine crater at Petersburg on July 30, 1864. After the battle, Smith *(below)* found the flag, pierced by more than 75 bullets, beyond repair, and the late-pattern Richmond depot flag at near right was requisitioned as a replacement.

General Beauregard's Mandate

Although the Army of Northern Virginia adopted standard battle flags, other armies scattered throughout the Eastern theater took no such step. When General Beauregard assumed command of the Confederate forces at Charleston in 1862, he found a variety of colors in use. In an attempt to impose order, he abolished them and directed the Charleston clothing depot to begin production of a single Virginia-pattern flag as a replacement.

Late in 1863, the Richmond depot began to issue the second pattern of the national flag as a battle flag. Many of these went to regiments that joined the Army of Northern Virginia from other commands. The clothing depot at Staunton, Virginia, also began to turn out second national flags to supply commands in the Shenandoah Valley and southwestern Virginia.

SECOND NATIONAL REGIMENTAL BATTLE FLAG RICHMOND DEPOT

Many Army of Northern Virginia regiments, particularly the cavalry, requested replacement flags of the second national pattern. This tattered Richmond depot flag was reported captured at Farmville Crossroads on April 5, 1865, by Private G. W. Stewart of the 1st New Jersey Cavalry. His commanding officer suspected that it was "possibly taken from a wagon."

SECOND NATIONAL REGIMENTAL BATTLE FLAG, STAUNTON DEPOT

General John C. Breckinridge's Army of Southwestern Virginia had no tradition of a battle flag, and many units accepted second national flags as regimental colors. This Staunton depot flag was captured at the Battle of Winchester by Federal Commissary Sergeant Andrew J. Lorish on September 19, 1864. In the confusion of the Confederate retreat, many flags of the Valley Army were captured or abandoned.

27TH SOUTH CAROLINA INFANTRY

When Beauregard took command of the Charleston area, he found that flags in this unusual design had been adopted by at least four local garrison regiments. The flag was modeled on a proposed national color recommended by the *Charleston Mercury* in March 1862. The shield in the center bears the legend "Secessionville" in honor of the battle of June 16, 1862, and the initials of the regiment's old designation as the Charleston Light Infantry.

26TH SOUTH CAROLINA INFANTRY REGIMENT

In the spring of 1864, the regiment carried this Charleston depot battle flag to Virginia and into action at Bermuda Hundred and Petersburg. In the assault on Fort Steadman on March 25, 1865, the 26th's color bearer, Samuel J. Reid, was "knocked down by the explosion of a shell." Captain H. L. Buck retrieved the flag but was captured, along with many of his men.

REGIMENTAL BATTLE FLAG, HAGOOD'S SOUTH CAROLINA BRIGADE

This Charleston depot flag of an unidentified regiment in General Johnson Hagood's brigade was captured at the Battle of Weldon Railroad, near Petersburg, Virginia, by men of the Federal V Corps. Hagood's Brigade attacked echeloned Federal regiments and found itself surrounded, but nevertheless managed to break out.

REGIMENTAL BATTLE FLAG, STAUNTON DEPOT

Battle flags of this design, with white cotton flannel borders, were manufactured at the Staunton clothing depot late in 1864 to supply the needs of the Valley Army. This flag was captured at Waynesboro, Virginia, on March 2, 1865, by Private M. Crowley of the 22d New York Cavalry. The entire lower third of the flag was soaked in the blood of its bearer, which caused its eventual decay.

WESTERN BATTLE FLAGS

14TH MISSISSIPPI INFANTRY REGIMENT

On February 16, 1862, when Fort Donelson in Tennessee surrendered to the Federals, Andrew S. Payne, color bearer of the 14th Mississippi, cut this hand-painted shield—Lady Liberty with Jefferson Davis— from the center of the regimental flag and sewed it into the lining of his coat to keep it out of Yankee hands. When he and his comrades were paroled in October, Payne triumphantly returned the shield to his regiment.

8TH ARKANSAS INFANTRY REGIMENT

The women of Jacksonport, Arkansas, presented this flag to the 8th Arkansas Volunteers in the summer of 1862. Its gold-embroidered inscription reads, "March on! March on! All hearts are resolved on victory or death."

ARKANSAS VOLUNTEERS

This 12-star flag on the first national model was captured from an Arkansas unit by Michigan troops during the Confederate campaign of General Sterling Price in Missouri in 1862.

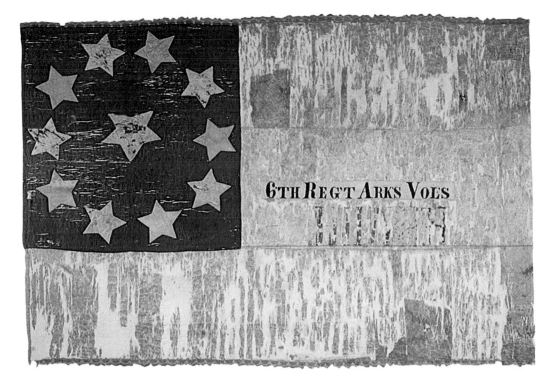

6TH ARKANSAS INFANTRY REGIMENT
This silk flag may have been carried briefly in the autumn of 1862 to replace the 6th Arkansas' worn-out battle flag based on the Hardee model. The flag bears the battle honor "Perryville" painted on the reverse side.

Modeled on the Stars and Bars

At the time of secession, most Confederate states had traditional flags of sovereignty that were modified for use as colors in the field by companies and regiments. Some states in the West, however, had no traditional state flags and did not authorize official state battle colors until after the outbreak of hostilities. With little regulation and guidance, soldiers from these states turned to the Confederate first national flag as a model for their regimental colors.

Such flags varied according to the taste and capabilities of the makers. The arrangement of the stars differed from flag to flag, and mottoes, inscriptions, unit crests, and state seals were added. Most of these flags were retired, but a few were carried until late in the War.

LOWRY RIFLES, 6TH MISSISSIPPI INFANTRY

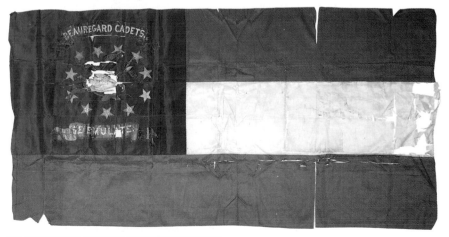

BEAUREGARD CADETS OF NEW ORLEANS

30TH ARKANSAS INFANTRY REGIMENT

On December 31, 1862, at Murfreesboro, Tennessee, the 30th Arkansas lost two color bearers and with them, this flag. A soldier recalled that one of the bearers was forced to abandon it in a cedar brake after his hand was shot off. The pattern had been adopted by General McCown's division in the Army of Kentucky.

Favorite Flags in the West

By 1861, senior army officers in the Western theater were well aware of the confusion resulting from the similarity between the Stars and Stripes and the Stars and Bars, and they attempted to establish a single distinctive battle flag for the forces under their command. They met with considerable resistance, however. Because the Confederate War Department never specified a pattern for a battle flag, the scattered commands in the West adopted their own versions. When these corps were combined to form first the Army of the Mississippi and later the Army of Tennessee, they had become deeply attached to their old standards and refused to give them up. By 1863, no fewer than eight different designs were being carried in the Army of Tennessee.

4TH MISSOURI INFANTRY REGIMENT

The 4th Missouri, which carried this flag, was organized in April 1862 in Springfield and left its home state to join Van Dorn's Army of the West in Tennessee. At Corinth, on October 3, 1862, the regiment suffered 129 casualties.

1ST (MANEY'S) TENNESSEE INFANTRY REGIMENT

This flag was lost at Perryville, Kentucky, on October 8, 1862, in fighting that cost the 1st Tennessee more than half its strength. Colors of this type were forwarded from New Orleans to General Leonidas Polk's corps shortly before the Battle of Shiloh on April 6, 1862.

VAN DORN BATTLE FLAG

Despite having received one of the first Army of Northern Virginia battle flags, General Earl Van Dorn chose this pattern for his Army of the West in February 1862. It was also carried by some of Van Dorn's old units in the Army of Mississippi and East Louisiana.

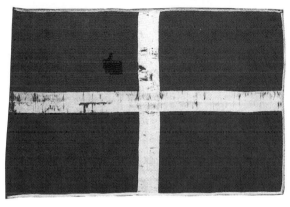

24TH ALABAMA INFANTRY REGIMENT

This flag, a variation of General Polk's corps standard, was lost at the Battle of Chickamauga after the color bearer, George B. Moody, was wounded.

NORTHWEST 15TH ARKANSAS INFANTRY REGIMENT

One of three Arkansas regiments designated the 15th, this small unit added the word "Northwest" to distinguish itself from the others. Its colors were captured in fierce fighting on May 1, 1863, at Port Gibson, Mississippi, by Private Amos Nagle of the 18th Illinois Infantry.

1ST FLORIDA INFANTRY BATTALION

The "Shiloh" citation, as shown on the 1st Florida Battalion's flag, was a hard-won honor. The commander of the brigade in which the 1st Florida served reported, "The desperation with which the troops fought brings new luster to the arms of the state they represented."

57TH GEORGIA INFANTRY REGIMENT

Forced to surrender at Vicksburg on July 4, 1863, the 57th Georgia was liberated months later in a prisoner exchange and was issued this battle flag. The unit then fought with the Army of Tennessee in all the engagements of the Atlanta campaign, during which it could barely muster 100 men.

An Inspiration from Virginia

In February 1862, General Beauregard placed an order through the departmental quartermaster in New Orleans for battle flags to equip Braxton Bragg's corps of the Army of the Mississippi. The flags were contracted with a local sailmaker, one H. Cassidy, whose inspiration for the design came from a silk standard that the 5th Company, Washington Artillery of New Orleans, received from its fellow companies serving in Virginia. His first flag was square, made of cotton, with 12 white silk, six-pointed stars and a pinkish serge border. A subsequent rectangular design by Cassidy was gradually issued throughout the Western armies.

CLACK'S CONFEDERATE RESPONSE BATTALION

5TH COMPANY, WASHINGTON ARTILLERY OF NEW ORLEANS

The 5th Company carried this flag from the time the unit was mustered, in February 1862, through the Battle of Perryville in October. The standard was then retired to Mobile.

9TH MISSISSIPPI INFANTRY REGIMENT

Organized in March 1861, the 9th Mississippi first served at Pensacola *(left)* and went on to fight in the Battle of Chickamauga in September 1863 where, re-counted Major T. H. Lyman, the regiment drove the Federals back about one mile. "In the onward move-ment our regimental battle line swept over three pieces of the enemy's cannon."

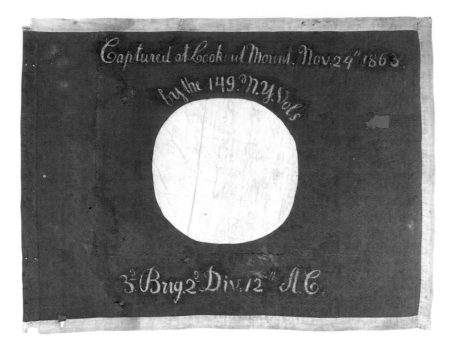

REGIMENTAL BATTLE FLAG, WALTHALL'S BRIGADE

This flag was captured from Walthall's Mississippi Brigade at the Battle of Lookout Mountain by Peter Kappesser of the 149th New York Infantry.

17TH TENNESSEE INFANTRY REGIMENT

At Murfreesboro on December 31, 1862, the 17th Tennessee advanced 500 yards under heavy fire to overrun a Federal battery. In the final charge, the color bearer, W. T. Jones, was killed, carrying the flag shown above "well to the front."

6TH AND 7TH ARKANSAS INFANTRY REGIMENT

The alteration to the regimental designation on this flag, as well as the late battle honors, were probably added to the standard after the 7th Arkansas was combined with the 6th Arkansas in December 1863.

8TH ARKANSAS INFANTRY REGIMENT

This large flag was probably an 1863 replacement for a Hardee flag. The regiment won the cannon insignia for capturing a battery at Chickamauga.

General Buckner's Distinctive Design

The distinctive battle flags shown here were inspired by a design created by General Simon Bolivar Buckner when he was in command of a division of the Army of Central Kentucky in November 1861. Buckner, determined that his regiments be easily identifiable in the field, devised a "flag which has no artistic taste about it, but which could not be mistaken" for other standards. Buckner's wife sewed the prototype, using cotton and wool bunting.

General William J. Hardee adopted the design for the corps that he organized in the Army of Tennessee in 1862. The colors issued to Hardee's regiments that year bore an eliptical "new moon," as some soldiers described it, while a later model distributed in 1863 featured "full moon" disks.

5TH COMPANY, WASHINGTON ARTILLERY OF NEW ORLEANS

The 5th Company replaced their flag of the Virginia-army design with this Hardee pattern late in 1863.

Entertained by a fiddler, men of the 5th Company, Washington Artillery, pose for a photographer in March 1862.

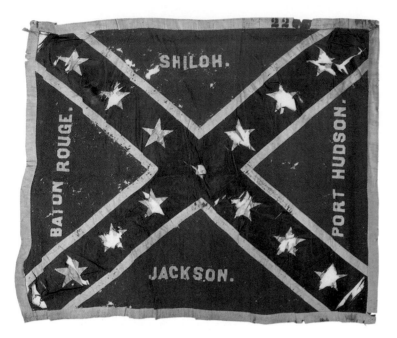

3D KENTUCKY MOUNTED INFANTRY

This Virginia-pattern flag, presented to the 3d Kentucky by its officers at Mobile in 1864, was taken by Federals at Richmond Creek, Tennessee, on December 16, 1864.

The Sign of the Cross

Flags bearing the Roman cross, a motif that associated Christian virtues with the Confederate cause, first gained prominence among the Missouri regiments of General Sterling Price's Army of the West and then spread to other units serving in the Department of Mississippi and East Louisiana. During the struggle for Vicksburg in 1863, such flags were flown in profusion—by the six Missouri regiments of Price's army and by units from other armies and states.

A few scattered regiments participating in the Vicksburg campaign favored battle flags of the Army of Northern Virginia style, most of which had been presented by various individuals or purchased by regimental officers.

3D KENTUCKY INFANTRY REGIMENT

The 3d Kentucky fought at Shiloh before being transferred to the Department of Mississippi and East Louisiana. The regiment carried the flag above in battle at Baton Rouge in August 1862, and at Jackson, Mississippi, in 1862.

9TH BATTALION (PINDALL'S) MISSOURI SHARPSHOOTERS

The five companies of the 9th Battalion were recruited from marksmen who were serving in various Missouri units; the battle flag shown here was issued in late 1863.

PERSONAL FLAG OF GEN. DABNEY H. MAURY

Major General Dabney H. Maury *(right),* a Virginian serving with the Western Confederate armies, chose this Missouri-style flag for the division he commanded at Vicksburg.

In a line to drape their colors across stacked rifles, the men of General J. S. Bowen's division surrender at Vicksburg on July 4, 1863.

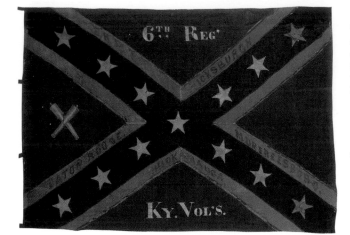

6TH KENTUCKY INFANTRY REGIMENT

On September 4, 1864, "ordered to mount this command using blankets if saddles could not be procured," the 6th Kentucky was converted to mounted infantry. Their flag was lost at Jonesboro, Georgia, that same month.

41ST GEORGIA INFANTRY REGIMENT

On March 22, 1864, near Dalton, Georgia, General Cheatham's Tennessee Division and Walker's Georgia Division squared off for a snowball fight. The 41st Georgia lost their colors (right) briefly to the Tennesseans.

Joe Johnston's Edict

"The lieutenant general commanding can well understand the pride many regiments of the corps feel in other flags which they have gloriously borne in battle," wrote General John B. Hood on March 11, 1864, "but the interests of the service are imperative. To avoid dangerous confusion in action, each regiment and battery will be required to bear the Confederate battle flag."

Thus did Hood's order to his corps relay the edict of the new commander of the Army of Tennessee, General Joseph E. Johnston, who instructed that the battle flag modeled on the Army of Northern Virginia's be issued to all divisions. The flags were made at the Atlanta clothing depot and issued to the army beginning in January 1864.

13TH LOUISIANA INFANTRY REGIMENT
The 13th Louisiana, devastated in fierce fighting at Nashville and Atlanta, carried this battle flag through both campaigns.

3D TENNESSEE INFANTRY REGIMENT
By December 21, 1864, although it had been combined with the 18th Tennessee, this regiment mustered only 17 men.

7TH MISSISSIPPI INFANTRY REGIMENT
The 7th Mississippi, decimated in the fighting at Jonesboro, lost its colors the next day during the Federal counterattack.

18TH TENNESSEE INFANTRY REGIMENT
This regiment, part of Major General John Brown's brigade, hired an artist to paint honors and unit designations on its colors.

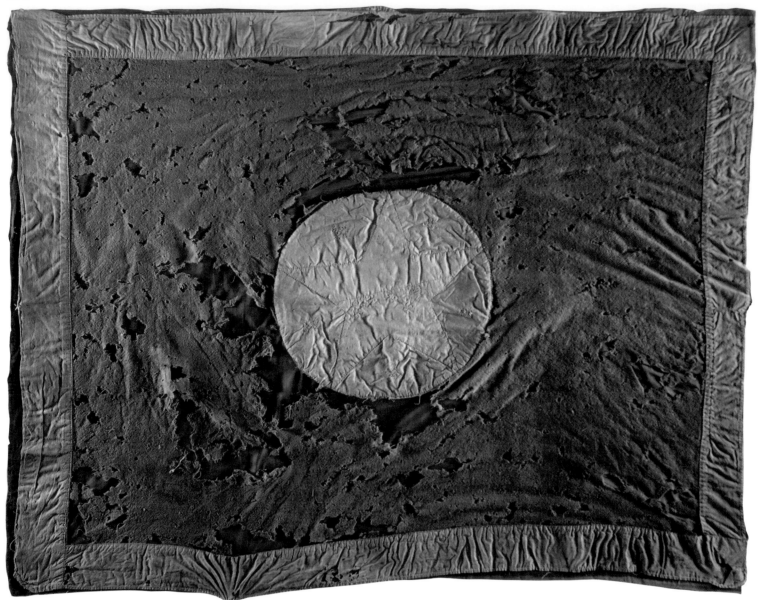

Patrick Cleburne's Dissent

Around the same time that General Joseph E. Johnston assumed command of the Army of Tennessee in the spring of 1864, three divisions from the Army of Mississippi, under Leonidas Polk, joined Johnston bearing the Virginia flags that the new commander favored and tried to make standard. Polk's flags had been tailored in March by the firm of James Cameron, the printer and flag maker from Mobile, who charged 12 Confederate dollars each for 25 new battle flags.

Cameron produced nearly identical colors for General Henry D. Clayton's brigade, whose regiments had lost or worn out their colors in fighting at Chickamauga and in the battles around Chattanooga. Cameron charged $2 a letter to sew on the battle honors.

Johnston's policy of replacing old colors with Virginia-type battle flags was fiercely resisted by General Patrick Cleburne, and his command was permitted to retain their Hardee pattern.

6TH AND 15TH TEXAS INFANTRY REGIMENT
The flag of the 6th and 15th, part of General Cleburne's division, bears the Texas star stitched into the central disk. It was issued after the siege of Atlanta and was carried in the disastrous campaign of Franklin and Nashville. At the War's end, Private Mark Kelton removed the flag from its staff and returned it to Texas.

271

22D LOUISIANA INFANTRY (CONSOLIDATED)

Following its exchange after the surrender of Vicksburg, the 22d Louisiana Infantry Regiment was assigned to the defenses of Mobile Bay.

38TH ALABAMA INFANTRY REGIMENT

At the Battle of Resaca, after the color sergeant was wounded, Colonel A. R. Lankford seized the banner and carried it into the enemy lines only to be captured, the Federals "deeming him too brave to be shot."

The replacement battle flags sent to General Patrick Cleburne's division were made of blue cotton flannel (now faded) in lieu of the more expensive wool. Late in the War, a Texas soldier proudly recalled, "The Yanks was all afraid of the blue flag division."

1ST AND 15TH ARKANSAS INFANTRY REGIMENT

16TH ALABAMA INFANTRY REGIMENT

33D ALABAMA INFANTRY REGIMENT

14TH MISSISSIPPI INFANTRY REGIMENT

12TH LOUISIANA INFANTRY REGIMENT

The Second National Pattern in the West

Throughout the War, a number of disparate units serving in the West chose to replace their worn-out colors with new standards based on the second national model. General Randall L. Gibson, a division commander in the Army of Tennessee, had his adjutant write to the quartermaster in Mobile on November 8, 1863, with a request for new colors: "The flags are so tattered and soiled as to no longer serve well for the purpose intended on the field." The prolific James Cameron of Mobile got the contract and produced a batch of second national flags for Gibson's regiments. Other units, such as the 1st Alabama, purchased second national flags privately from Cameron. Some Western commands who fancied replacements in the second national pattern bought cloth and made their own flags.

1ST ALABAMA INFANTRY REGIMENT

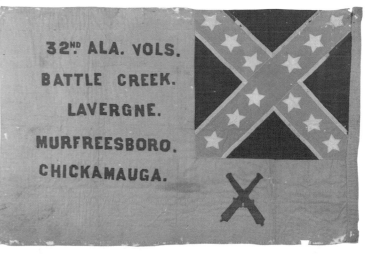

32D ALABAMA INFANTRY REGIMENT

32ND ALA. VOLS.
BATTLE CREEK.
LAVERGNE.
MURFREESBORO.
CHICKAMAUGA.

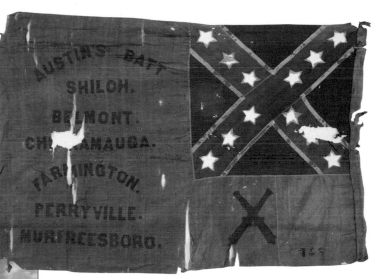

AUSTIN'S BATT
SHILOH.
BELMONT.
CHICKAMAUGA.
FARMINGTON.
PERRYVILLE.
MURFREESBORO.

AUSTIN'S BATTALION, LOUISIANA SHARPSHOOTERS

While other regiments in Randall L. Gibson's brigade adopted other flags, Austin's troops flew their "Stainless Banner" until it was captured at Columbus, Georgia, in April 1865. At the Battle of Atlanta, the Sharpshooters carried their flag into the fray to support the Confederate breakthrough *(left)* around the Pope House west of the city.

COMPANY A, CRESCENT REGIMENT, LOUISIANA

This unusual standard was carried in the Crescent Regiment (named for New Orleans, the "Crescent City"), a unit that was combined with two other battalions and sent to the Trans-Mississippi Department.

Styles from across the Mississippi

The Confederate armies serving across the Mississippi River on the far western flank of the Confederacy had no clothing depots, private contractors, or other facilities to produce battle flags. The lack of supply became more severe when the Federals captured Vicksburg and closed the Mississippi River in July 1863, isolating the forces in the far west.

Although a few flags from the Confederate Army of Mississippi or Army of Tennessee made their way across the river, most regiments in the Trans-Mississippi had to rely on flags that had been presented by citizens' groups or local dignitaries, or had to find cloth somehow and cobble up their own makeshift colors.

1ST CHEROKEE MOUNTED RIFLES

The flag at right was carried by the 1st Cherokee, a unit composed of Cherokee Indians mustered in the Indian Territory in July 1862. The 5 red stars within the ring of 11 white ones represent the 5 "Civilized Tribes"—Cherokee, Creek, Chickasaw, Choctaw, and Seminole—recognized by the Confederacy.

CHEROKEE BRAVES

3D LOUISIANA INFANTRY REGIMENT

This flag, made in Mobile (possibly by James Cameron), was presented to the 3d Louisiana on August 30, 1863, by General Dabncy Maury, to replace the flag captured at Vicksburg.

DOBBIN'S 1ST ARKANSAS CAVALRY REGIMENT

This flag is a variation based on the battle flags originated by Walker's Division of the Trans-Mississippi. Dobbin's regiment was raised in the spring of 1863 and served in Sterling Price's Missouri Expedition in September and October 1864.

KING'S 22D/20TH ARKANSAS INFANTRY REGIMENT

The makers of this variation of the Confederate second national flag added two horizontal red bars to the white field to make sure that the flag would not be mistaken for the all-white banner of surrender.

SPECIALTY FLAGS

MARKER/CAMP FLAG

The flag at left, of a type used to mark the area of an encampment or the flanks of a regiment in the field, was ordered by General Beauregard for the Department of South Carolina, Georgia, and Florida.

AMBULANCE AND HOSPITAL FLAG

Vitally important were the flags that helped stretcher-bearers and walking wounded to find the locations of ambulance depots and field hospitals. In the Eastern armies, such flags were usually red.

This Confederate field hospital tended the wounded during the battles around Petersburg in 1864.

Headquarters and Hospitals

Beginning in 1863, the U.S. Army maintained a complex system of specialty flags to designate larger commands, such as divisions, corps, and armies. The Confederate army, however, left it to individual generals and departments to devise their own system of flags for indicating higher commands. In February 1864, General Joseph Johnston proposed a system of such flags for the Army of Tennessee, but most Confederate commands simply chose to forgo so-called designating flags. A scattering of miscellaneous banners was produced to identify various field headquarters, encampments, and special units such as the ambulance and medical corps.

STOVALL'S HEADQUARTERS

This small silk flag, once bearing the stitched inscription "Stovall," identified the headquarters of General M. A. Stovall's Georgia Brigade, which lost a similar flag at the Battle of Nashville.

FRENCH'S DIVISION

The flag at left, which identified the headquarters of General Samuel G. French's division in the Army of Tennessee, was one of a unique set of marker flags that featured a Maltese cross.

Flags for the Rebel Navy

Warships and merchantmen of the Confederate states flew the Confederate national flag from the halyards and masts of their vessels, and kept several sizes and variations in their flag lockers. On special occasions, and to ensure identification by friendly vessels during action, a warship hoisted an oversize ensign that measured 12 feet long or longer. Because these huge flags were susceptible to wind and weather damage, the ship usually flew a smaller storm flag. Other ships' flags included a jack, flown from the bow or mast in port to identify the vessel as a commissioned warship, and boat flags, intended to be displayed on the sterns of a man-of-war's small boats. In addition, commerce raiders and blockade-runners might carry the flags of foreign countries as decoys or camouflage.

ENSIGN, C.S.S. *VIRGINIA*

The ironclad *Virginia* carried two ensigns of the first national design in her flag locker. This early 7-star flag was replaced by an 11-star version during the ship's epic battle with the U.S.S. *Monitor* in Hampton Roads, Virginia, on March 9, 1862.

STORM FLAG, C.S.S. *SHENANDOAH*

The Confederate sloop of war *Shenandoah (left)* circumnavigated the globe, destroying 38 Federal merchantmen and whalers between October 1864 and June 1865 and devastating the United States whaling industry. This storm flag and other colors were surrendered to British authorities in Liverpool on November 6, 1865, seven months after the Civil War had ended.

STORM FLAG, C.S.S. *FLORIDA*

During its seven-month cruise, the *Florida* took 23 Federal prizes. This flag and others were captured when the Federal steam sloop *Wachusett* rammed and boarded the *Florida* illegally in the harbor of Bahia, Brazil.

BOAT FLAG, C.S.S. *FLORIDA*

This small flag, found on the *Florida,* was originally fashioned with no stars on its saltire. It may have been sewn on board the ship, its maker copying the United States Navy practice of reducing or eliminating the number of stars used on boat flags.

HAMBURG MERCHANT FLAG

This German state merchant flag was ordered from the firm of G. T. von Lindeman of St. Thomas in the Virgin Islands by a certain Van Schwartz, captain of a blockade-runner. Confederate ships flew foreign flags as camouflage to confuse Federal blockading vessels.

The Fate of the Lost Flags

Confederate colors captured in battle or handed over in surrender were forwarded to the War Department in Washington, D.C. In 1868, the flags were identified and cataloged, and later, between 1874 and 1882, they were displayed in the Washington Ordnance Museum. Then the flags were placed in storage, and despite repeated requests for their return, it seemed that the Southern colors would forever remain in the North.

An effort by the Cleveland administration to return the flags in 1887 was blocked by vehement protest from the powerful Union veterans' associations. Finally, on February 28, 1905, a joint resolution of Congress authorized the secretary of war, William H. Taft, to begin returning captured flags to the former Confederate states. All unidentified colors went to the Confederate Memorial Literary Society in Richmond, Virginia.

At Appomattox on April 12, 1865, as Robert E. Lee surrendered his troops, the Union general Joshua Chamberlain recalled that the Rebel flags were "crowded so thick, by thinning out of men, that the whole column seemed crowned with red." As Chamberlain watched, each regiment stacked arms and "reluctantly, with agony of expression, they tenderly folded their flags, battle-worn and torn, bloodstained, heart-holding colors, and laid them down."

ARTILLERY

As the Confederate army embarked on war, its greatest weakness was its artillery corps. While Southern infantry proved the equal of its Yankee counterpart, and Rebel cavalry initially enjoyed clear superiority over the horse-shy Union mounted troops, Southern artillery was outtrained, outgunned, and outmaneuvered throughout most of the conflict—especially during the first two years.

A veteran artillery sergeant named Humphreys recounted after the War the tragicomic ineptitude of many Rebel artillery detachments: "I have not only known men to greatly underestimate or overestimate the distance to a hostile battery and waste much time in getting the range, but I have seen them actually fire for hours under the impression that they had the range, when in fact the projectiles were striking the top of a hill a quarter of a mile beyond. It was a blunder that was by no means rare."

Such instances of incompetence were by no means limited exclusively to the Rebels. Still, when it came to big-gun warfare, the agricultural South was distinctly disadvantaged. Handicapped at the outset by a shortage of dependable ordnance and ammunition, the Confederacy was further plagued by a dearth of officers and noncommissioned officers schooled in artillery's exacting science. "Whole battalions of artillery," wrote Humphreys, "went into active service without a single man, whether officer, noncommissioned officer, or private, who knew anything about artillery."

There was a daunting amount to learn. Aspiring artillerymen—most of them unfamiliar with the technical disciplines—had to distinguish the characteristics of the different types and calibers of cannon, referred to as "pieces," and to judge when and how to use them. The pieces called guns were heavy, long-barreled, smoothbore or rifled, and ideal for hurling charges on flat trajectories over long distances. Companion weapons to the guns were the smoothbore howitzers—short, thick-barreled, large-caliber pieces that lofted projectiles in arclike trajectories, making them especially effective in rough and hilly terrain. A third type of artillery largely overlooked by the South until the spring of 1864 was the field mortar, or Coehorn. Fat, stubby, and easily portable, these weapons required only a small load of gunpowder to lob shells over nearby parapets and earthworks with awesome effect. Finally, there were siege and seacoast guns, iron behemoths capable of discharging projectiles weighing 20 to 100 pounds or more across vast distances. Ideally suited for coastal defense, these weapons included finely crafted English guns, big-bore Confederate-made rifles, and Colombiads, huge smoothbores seized from Federal coastal fortresses.

It was common practice to name a piece by the weight of the ammunition it accepted; hence, a 4.62-inch-caliber gun that fired a 12-pound load of shot came to be known as a 12-pounder. This habit persisted even as new forms of lighter ammunition were developed, leading to the incongruous situation in which the same 8-inch rifle was called both a 200-pounder and a 150-pounder.

The Confederate artillerist had to become familiar with a long list of ammunition types. Shot, a solid iron ball designed for smoothbore guns, was the oldest form of artillery ammunition. In the field, the Rebels typically used solid shot against massed troops and artillery (counterbattery fire).

Rebel artillerymen also fired projectiles that exploded above or on the target, triggered by one of two kinds of fuses, the timed fuse or the impact fuse. One type of projectile, the shell, a hollow iron container packed with black powder, was generally used for harassing fire at long range or for bombarding entrenchments and forts. Case shot, which carried a lethal payload of metal balls, was usually timed to explode above or in front of the target, showering the enemy with the pellets. Both shell and case could be fired from guns, howitzers, or mortars, and through bores that were smooth or rifled. Unlike solid shot, which wreaked havoc through sheer force of impact, shell and case destroyed their targets through blast and fragmentation. Their effectiveness was greatly hampered on the Confederate side by poor-grade gunpowder and ineffectual fuses. As Humphreys explained: "Our ammunition was inferior to that of the Federal artillery. The worst of it was that there was a great lack of uniformity in the strength of the powder, and seemingly in the time of the fuses. No reflection on the Confederate ordnance department is implied by these remarks. With the means at their disposal, their achievements were amazing; but the fact remains that our ammunition was in every way inferior. At any rate, the shell often exploded in the bore, or at the muzzle of the piece."

More reliable were canister and grapeshot, which depended only on the cannon's initial blast to be effective. Made for both smoothbore and rifled artillery, canister consisted of a thin iron can containing lead or iron balls packed in sawdust. Unfailingly lethal at 350 yards or less, canister shot sprayed from the muzzle of a cannon like a monstrous shotgun blast. At very close range, gunners would fire double canister—two charges loaded together—for twice the killing power. The innovative if poorly supplied Confederates occasionally cobbled makeshift canister together using whatever scrap they could find. A Rebel canister unearthed in recent times along the Savannah River in Georgia contained fragments of wrought-iron fence, iron shards, and door hinges.

Grapeshot, larger iron balls encased in cloth or in an iron frame, was used infrequently on the battlefield, but saw some action along the seacoast in larger-caliber guns—the 24-pounders and up.

While he was mastering artillery's odd nomenclature of pounders and five-second fuses, the Rebel artillery officer had to learn to conduct his gunners in the complex maneuvers of battery; he had to learn the knack, in Humphreys' words, of "coming into action," and of gauging "when, what, at what, how, and how often to fire."

The routine for a battery varied widely according to the branch in which it served: either "field" artillery or "heavy" artillery. A field artillery battery handled only those cannon light and mobile enough to move on the march with infantry or cavalry and maneuver on the battlefield—generally 6- and 12-pounder guns, three-inch rifles, and 12 and 24-pounder howitzers. Special mountain artillery units carried only lightweight howitzers that could be transported on muleback. When deployed with mounted troops, a battery went by the sobriquet "horse artillery." A highly mobile contingent with all the men mounted, the horse artillery provided support to cavalry engaged in quick maneuvers.

As the name would imply, heavy artillery batteries operated the large, big-bore guns and mortars, including siege and garrison cannon, that were designed to knock down, or to defend, forts and earthworks. These included seacoast artillery—the colossal, ship-killing guns and mortars whose bores catapulted watermelon-size ammunition out to sea a mile or more.

Like his Northern complement, the Southern artillerist attached to a field battery was part of a tightly structured command of men, horses, and equipment. The typical Confederate 6-pounder field artillery battery of 1861 was outfitted with four 6-pounder guns and two 12-pounder howitzers. On the march, each piece was hooked to a limber, a two-wheeled cart that carried a single ammunition chest over the axle. Each gun and limber unit was normally drawn by a team of six horses (although casualties and shortages of draft animals frequently reduced the number of horses to four). The horses, harnessed two abreast and forming "lead," "swing," and "wheel" pairs, were controlled by three drivers who rode the left horse of each pair.

Each of the six cannon was accompanied by a caisson, a two-wheeled cart consisting of a carriage with two ammunition chests and a spare wheel hitched to a limber supporting a single ammunition chest. It too had its own six-horse team. Twelve-pounder batteries tended to have two caissons per gun.

Bringing up the rear were the battery wagon, the traveling forge, and additional limbers hauling reserve ammunition. A veritable storehouse of operational supplies, the battery wagon contained more than 500 items critical to the care and maintenance of the gun unit, including oil, axes, saws, nails, tarpaulins, scythes, and a grindstone. The forge, a blacksmith's shop on wheels, carried horseshoes, washers, nails, anvils, and iron ingots, among other items.

All told, a train of 91 draft horses—84 in harness and 7 spares—was required to haul the cannon and associated paraphernalia of a single battery. For heavier artillery batteries, as many as 130 horses were needed. On the road, these lumbering processions logged a mile in roughly 20 minutes—provided they were not slowed by some unforeseen mishap. Robert Stiles, major of artillery with the Richmond Howitzers, recalled an incident during the Peninsular campaign in which his battery became mired in the spring mud of the Virginia countryside: "Our com-

pany wagon, containing a present supply of commissary and quartermaster stores and all our extra clothing, sank to the hubs and had to be abandoned. We feared for the guns and could not think of wasting teams on wagons. The danger was really imminent that the guns themselves would have to be abandoned, and the captain instructed me if a gun could not be dragged through the mud, then to let the piece drop into the deepest mud I could find, and mark the spot.

"By dint, however, of fine driving, and heavy lifting and shoving at the wheels, we managed to save our brazen war dogs," Stiles continued. "The poor horses often sank to their bellies, and I saw a team of mules disappear, every hair, under the mud, in the middle of the road. They afterwards arose and emerged from their baptism of mud, at once the most melancholy and the most ludicrous-looking objects that could be imagined. It was wretched, and yet it had its funny side."

The plodding pace of artillery on the march greatly accelerated during battle. The gunners, who usually rode atop the caissons, dreaded the jostle and tumble of the galloping carts—a sensation akin to riding a bucking bronco (later in the War, as horses failed, artillerymen frequently walked). More fearsome still was the actual artillery engagement, which, according to Major Stiles, drew deeply upon every Rebel cannoneer's reserve of "imperturbable self-possession."

Wrote Stiles: "To appreciate it to the full, it was only necessary to look at one of our guns, already overmatched, at the moment when a fresh gun of the enemy, rushing up at a wild gallop, and seizing a nearer and enfilading position, hurled a percussion shell, crashing with fearful uproar against our piece, and sweeping almost the entire gun detachment to the earth. At such a moment I have marked the sergeant or gunner of such a piece coolly disengage himself from the wreck and, stepping to one side, stoop to take his observations and make his calculations, of distance and of time, free from the dust and smoke of the explosion. Then, stepping back and bending over, aim his strained and half-disabled piece as the undisabled remnant of the detachment step over their dead and dying comrades, each in the discharge of the doubled and trebled duties now devolving upon him."

To be certain, Confederate gunners lacked neither resolve nor courage; but they did, according to Sergeant Humphreys, sorely want for practical training: "The men were carefully and regularly drilled from the start. In short, we were taught everything except the one thing that all else was a preparation for—the art of hitting."

Accurately aiming the muzzle of a cannon at a distant target was undoubtedly the most complex task charged to an artilleryman. To ensure a hit, the gunner had to first correctly estimate the distance to the enemy; then, elevate the gun's barrel to lob the projectile the exact distance; and finally, determine the effect, if any, of cross winds on the shot.

Few men, it seems, were born gunners. Said Humphreys: "Among our original gunners were some almost illiterate men, selected because they had great reputations as marksmen with the mountain rifle—men who could 'hit a squirrel's head at 50 yards.' In the course of time we learned that general intelligence and the ability to estimate distances with some accuracy were much more important than skill with a squirrel gun." Those who acquired the knack for reading distances relied largely upon their eyesight and any geometry they may have had.

A Confederate gunner had little more than trial and error to guide him in judging how much to elevate a cannon's muzzle. By 1862, however, some limber chests were issued with table-of-fire charts pasted on the inside of the lids; the charts listed the elevations required for various ranges and the number of seconds a missile would be in flight. After finding the correct elevation in degrees for the distance to his target, the gunner could then use a sight notched with an elevation scale to line up the cannon's barrel with the distant target.

While offering some aid in aiming, such table-of-fire charts were of limited value on the battlefield. They did not take into account the fact that guns of the same type and caliber performed differently according to who made them. Moreover, noted Humphreys, "The elevation, range and time of flight were all three given in round numbers. This was probably the best our ordnance department could do; but it was our place as artillerymen to modify these tables to suit ascertained facts, and to construct tables for the pieces that had none."

In the throes of battle, many men forgot what little artillery training they had received. Said Humphreys, "They would go through the motions of obtaining the range and correcting errors in assumed cases; but when it came to actual firing in the face of the enemy, they would cast all that to the winds, and begin to fire with nervous haste, taking careless aim and guessing haphazard at the necessary correction, so that they were liable after one error to err the next time as much or more in the opposite direction."

The process of firing a piece was a complex ritual, ideally involving the concerted efforts of at least four to six men. For all muzzleloading cannon the steps were the same: swabbing out the bore and vent; loading the gunpowder and projectile; aiming the piece and igniting the charge.

To clean the cannon of leftover gunpowder grains and to extinguish sparks from previous firings, a cannoneer ran a long-handled sponge down the bore and used a punch to clean out the vent at the top of the barrel through which the powder charge would be fired. While one man held a leather "finger stall" over the vent to prevent a draft that might kindle a spark, another loaded the ammunition. Solid shot, shell, and case ammunition generally came bundled in cartridge form with a wooden disk—called a sabot—between the projectile and the powder bag. The sabot centered round projectiles in the barrel and kept the ammunition's fuse pointed away from the charge. Rifle ammunition had a soft-metal sabot or band that expanded to engage the rifling in the bore when fired. In large-bore guns, the powder bag and projectile were loaded separately.

Using the opposite end of the sponge tool as a rammer, one of the crew drove the round home. As another jabbed a pick down the barrel vent to rip open the powder bag, the gunner called out orders to shift and elevate the gun for firing. The gunner then fixed a friction primer—a two-inch brass tube containing combustibles and a serrated wire—to the vent at one end, and to a rope pull, or lanyard, at the other. After confirming the correctness of the cannon's aim, the gunner commanded "Fire!" A pull on the lanyard caused the friction primer wire to drag across the ignition compound, lighting a spark that flashed down the barrel vent to the powder bag and fired the gun.

Experienced gunners could load and fire a cannon twice a minute—provided the piece itself did not malfunction. According to Humphreys, the South had more than its share of balky artillery: "The pieces themselves were often very inaccurate. We had to use guns after they were really worn out, and sometimes our new pieces were defective."

The Confederate artillery corps went into the Civil War woefully undergunned. Scattered throughout the Rebel states were a meager number of 12-pounder smoothbore howitzers, 6-pounder guns, and assorted mortars, many of which had been retired from Federal service as too feeble for warfare. By luck, Virginia had obtained a few large-bore Parrott guns—state-of-the-art rifled cannon—from the West Point foundry in 1860. Added to this small collection were 35 cannon captured during the Confederate takeover of Harpers Ferry, and a number of guns seized at Fort Sumter and other coastal forts and naval yards in the South.

To supplement its motley store of cannon, the South turned to importation and to Confederate and state manufacture. Until the Federal blockade stanched the South's brisk trade with England, the Confederacy smuggled in a steady stream of Armstrong, Blakely, Whitworth, and Clay artillery rifles. These weapons saw limited use, however, and the number of imports was never great enough to alter the course of the conflict.

With a production rate of metals only one-twentieth that of the industrialized North, the South was significantly hampered in its efforts to manufacture cannon. Early in the War, the Confederate government established foundries for artillery production in Georgia, Mississippi, Alabama, and South Carolina. These armories—despite the shortages of material and technicians—turned out a surprising quantity of weapons.

The Confederacy's largest supplier of artillery was a private armory, the Tredegar Iron Works of Richmond, Virginia. One of the finest Confederate rifles, the Brooke—the Rebel version of the Union Parrott gun—was produced there. Tredegar also manufactured a number of 12-pounders on the Napoleon pattern, smoothbore guns so reliable that, in 1862, General Robert E. Lee urged that other bronze cannon be melted down as scrap for their fabrication.

The Confederates spent much creative energy on the design and manufacture of artillery ammunition. The astounding variety of Confederate projectiles has confounded the best efforts of military historians to catalog them. Notable among Confederate smoothbore innovations, was the so-called polygonal cavity shell. This Rebel brainchild was a standard bursting shell whose interior was cast in geometric facets that, upon explosion, shattered into deadly iron polygons like a modern fragmentation grenade.

As the War progressed, Rebel ordnance designers concentrated increasingly on rifled ammunition, whose greater range and accuracy were thought to bolster the South's odds on the battlefield. The Confederates are credited with improving the ballistic prowess of the Parrott shell by reengineering its shape and length. Other, more fanciful attempts at design included the Confederate winged shot, only one round of which has survived. A rocket-shaped solid shot, it had spring-hinged metal wings that opened upon firing, ostensibly giving riflelike accuracy to the smoothbore projectile.

Unfortunately for the Confederacy, the ingenuity and unflagging grit of the disadvantaged Southern artillerists did little to win them the victory they so earnestly sought. In addition to the other shortcomings, Confederate artillery was hamstrung by its own tactics. Instead of massing the artillery of a force in battle for greatest effect against the enemy, Rebel commanders insisted on pairing individual artillery batteries with single infantry brigades. This practice, which dispersed the firepower of the big guns throughout the Confederate army, continued in the East until the winter of 1862-63, and in the West until the end of the War. Eventually, the Army of Northern Virginia created a reserve artillery capable of being deployed en masse, but this measure proved inadequate. Throughout the War, as they faced the superior, massed cannon of the North, Southern artillerists were guided by one overriding principle: loyalty to the gun. While it might not have moved the South any closer to victory, it was a principle that at times assumed heroic, and tragic, proportions.

Wrote Major Robert Stiles of his compatriots in the Richmond Howitzers: "The gun is the rallying point of the detachment, its point of honor, its flag, its banner. It is that to which the men look, by which they stand, with and for which they fight, by and for which they fall. As long as the gun is theirs, they are unconquered, victorious; when the gun is lost, all is lost. It is their religion to fight until the enemy is out of range, or until the gun itself is withdrawn, or until both it and the detachment are in the hands of the foe. An infantryman in flight often flings away his musket. I do not recall ever having heard of a Confederate artillery detachment abandoning its gun without orders."

FIELD ARTILLERY

During the Civil War, artillery attained a lethal effectiveness that did much to make the conflict one of the deadliest in history. In support of infantry attacks, the guns hurled solid shot and explosive shell into the enemy's formations and fieldworks. On the defensive, artillery blasted oncoming infantry at close range with canister. And rival gunners tried to annihilate each other with counterbattery fire.

When the War started, the Confederacy was mainly equipped with antiquated bronze-barreled smoothbore cannon. Soon, however, the Rebels began producing—and importing—more effective weapons, particularly rifled guns and the improved, powerful smoothbores called Napoleons.

This bronze six-pounder was of a design that dated back to the 1840s. Such guns, firing projectiles only 3.67 inches in diameter, were thought by Confederate and Federal artillerists to lack sufficient power and range. But they remained in use in armies on both sides, especially those in the Western theater, where newer models were scarce.

Cannon Makers for the South

Richmond's Tredegar Iron Works *(above)*, a foundry owned and managed by General Joseph Reid Anderson, cast 1,099 cannon during the War—nearly half of all the artillery pieces manufactured in the Confederacy.

**12-POUNDER
FIELD HOWITZER**

This cast-iron cannon was made by T. M. Brennan & Co. of Nashville.

10-POUNDER FIELD RIFLE

The Tredegar Iron Works in Richmond produced this cannon.

12-POUNDER FIELD HOWITZER

The short-barreled bronze gun shown above was cast by the Tredegar Iron Works.

6-POUNDER FIELD RIFLE

This iron rifle made by the Tredegar Iron Works in early 1862 has a three-inch bore.

12-POUNDER NAPOLEON GUN

Georgia's Augusta Foundry produced this cast-bronze gun, named for its inventor, Napoleon III of France.

Specialized Weaponry

Union soldiers photographed in 1865 guard a 12-pounder Whitworth breechloader captured from the Confederacy. Made in Manchester, England, and smuggled through the blockade, the steel rifles were widely used by Rebel artillery.

12-POUNDER WHITWORTH BREECHLOADER RIFLE

A spiral hexagonal bore runs the length of Whitworth rifles, which were designed to shoot similarly shaped projectiles. This unique rifling system achieved a faster spin on the projectile—and thus greater accuracy—than previous methods. The first successful Whitworths were breechloaders like the one above, shown open, but heavier-caliber muzzleloading Whitworths were also used.

COL. JOHN HASKELL

The Lethal Work of a Mobile Mortar

On July 30, 1864, as General William Mahone was preparing to renew the Confederate counterattack against Union troops in the Battle of the Crater at Petersburg, a young artillery officer named John Haskell offered his services to Mahone. Colonel Haskell had lost his right arm at Gaines' Mill in 1862, but he had lost none of his fighting spirit. Mahone suggested that Haskell move two of his compact Coehorn mortars to within 20 yards of the Crater, where they could shell the Federals with deadly accuracy.

The Coehorn was the perfect weapon for this task. It weighed only 300 pounds and was fitted with handles that enabled four men to carry it to points in the trenches that could not be reached by gun carriages. It

WHITWORTH SHELL

WHITWORTH BOLT (SHOT) AND CARTRIDGE CASE

Designed by Sir Joseph Whitworth, these twisted hexagonal projectiles and cartridge case—shown erect and on its side—were machined for a precise fit.

24-POUNDER COEHORN MORTAR, MODEL 1838

could loft an 18-pound shell over a parapet and was brutally effective at short range.

Haskell and his men moved their mortars ever nearer the Crater, stopping to lob shells over the 12-foot-high walls and reducing the powder charge after every advance. Eventually the shells rose so sluggishly, Haskell wrote, that it seemed "they could not get to the enemy"—yet they did. And once the mortars had taken a steep toll, Mahone committed his full force to the successful attack.

12-POUNDER COEHORN SHELL

Tools of the Artilleryman

SPONGE-AND-RAMMER

WORM-AND-BRUSH FOR CLEANING BARREL

Men of South Carolina's Palmetto Battalion Light Artillery stage a mock drill at their emplacement on the Stono River near Charleston in 1861. The guns appear to be light 12-pounders.

VENT PICKS (PRIMING WIRES)

GUNNER'S POUCH AND BELT

GUNNER'S HAVERSACK

Corporal T. V. Brooke of the 3d Company, Richmond Howitzers, used this haversack to carry rounds from the limber.

GUNNER'S POUCH

LANYARD

12

FRICTION PRIMERS.

C- S. Laboratory.
RICHMOND ARSENAL.
Mo., 186

FRICTION PRIMERS

The manufacturer's label on this box of a dozen friction primers—used to ignite the charge in a cannon—is marked with the date the box was packed.

The Art of Aiming

Table-of-fire charts provided gunners with vital information concerning the performance of various types of guns and ammunition, including the elevations needed for various ranges and the number of seconds the projectile would be in flight.

TABLE OF FIRE ARMS
10-PDR. PARROTT GUN
Charge, 1 lb. of Mortar Powder

ELEVATION In Degrees	PROJECTILE		RANGE In Yards	TIME OF FLIGHT In Seconds
1	Case Shot,	10½ lbs.	600	
2	Case Shot,	10½ lbs.	930	3
2¾	Shell,	9¾ lbs.	1100	3¼
3⅞	Shell,	9¾ lbs.	1460	4¾
4½	Shell,	9¾ lbs.	1680	5¾
5	Shell,	9¾ lbs.	2000	6½
6	Shell,	9¾ lbs.	2250	7¼
7	Shell,	9¾ lbs.	2600	8¼
10	Shell,	9¾ lbs.	3200	10¾
12	Shell,	9¾ lbs.	3600	12⅞
15	Shell,	9¾ lbs.	4200	16⅞
20	Shell,	9¾ lbs.	5000	21⅞

CARE OF AMMUNITION CHEST

1st. Keep everything out that does not belong in them, except a bunch of cord or wire for breakage; beware of loose tacks, nails, bolts, or scraps.

2nd. Keep friction primers in their papers, tied up. The pouch containing those for instant service must be closed, and so placed as to be secure. Take every precaution that primers do not get loose; a single one may cause an explosion. Use plenty of tow in packing.

(This sheet is to be glued to the inside of Limber Chest Cover.)

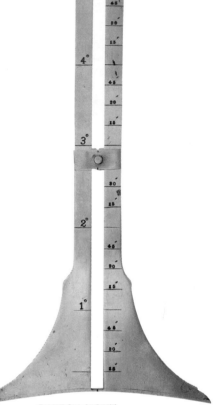

BREECH SIGHT

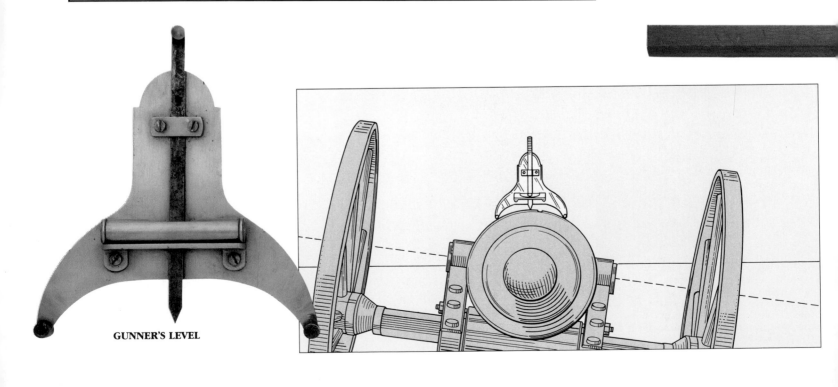

GUNNER'S LEVEL

In 1862, a Confederate gun crew mans a cannon at Wynn's Mill, a dam along the Warwick River south of Yorktown, Virginia. Casualties at Yorktown were so few that a *Harper's Weekly* artist depicted this gun solely because it killed a Union engineer who was mapping the Confederate works.

To aim a gun accurately, a gunner had to place the sight *(above, left)* on the breech of his piece so that it was absolutely vertical—a problem when the gun sat on uneven ground with its breech canted, as in the diagram at left. To find the right spot for the sight, the so-called aim point, he could use a gunner's level *(far left)*. A refinement that eliminated this procedure was a pendulum hausse *(far right)*, a sight weighted on the bottom and mounted on a gimbals so that it always hung true. To determine the elevation of the barrel, an antiquated tool called a quadrant *(right)* was sometimes used.

GUNNER'S QUADRANT

PENDULUM HAUSSE FOR 12-POUNDER GUN

PENDULUM HAUSSE FOR 3-INCH GUN

Field Artillery Projectiles

12-POUNDER CANISTER

12-POUNDER SHELL

ENGLISH BLAKELY SHELL

READ SHELL FOR 3-INCH RIFLE

READ SHELL FOR 20-POUNDER RIFLE

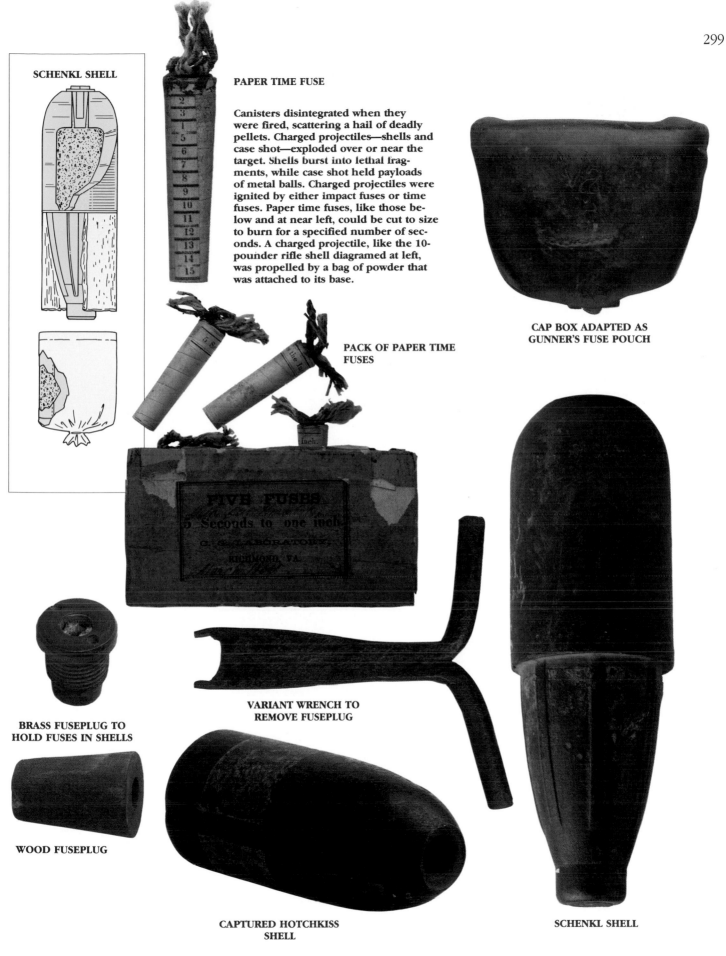

SCHENKL SHELL

PAPER TIME FUSE

Canisters disintegrated when they were fired, scattering a hail of deadly pellets. Charged projectiles—shells and case shot—exploded over or near the target. Shells burst into lethal fragments, while case shot held payloads of metal balls. Charged projectiles were ignited by either impact fuses or time fuses. Paper time fuses, like those below and at near left, could be cut to size to burn for a specified number of seconds. A charged projectile, like the 10-pounder rifle shell diagramed at left, was propelled by a bag of powder that was attached to its base.

CAP BOX ADAPTED AS GUNNER'S FUSE POUCH

PACK OF PAPER TIME FUSES

VARIANT WRENCH TO REMOVE FUSEPLUG

BRASS FUSEPLUG TO HOLD FUSES IN SHELLS

WOOD FUSEPLUG

CAPTURED HOTCHKISS SHELL

SCHENKL SHELL

COASTAL ARTILLERY

SHELL WITH SABOT

GRAPESHOT

CANISTER

The painting *(left)* by Conrad Wise Chapman, a soldier-artist with the 59th Virginia Volunteers, depicts Confederate gun crews in Charleston Harbor dueling with Federal artillery on an island a mile away. The smoothbore cannon used by Rebels for coastal defense fired huge projectiles like shell, grapeshot, and canister.

Federals display a British-made Armstrong rifle captured from the Rebels at Fort Fisher, near Wilmington, North Carolina, in January 1865. The two projectiles below were made by the Confederates for their rifles.

DAHLGREN-TYPE SHOT

ARMSTRONG SHELL

LAND/SEA MINES

The South's Infernal Machines

In October of 1862, the Confederate Congress created the Torpedo Service, which was responsible for sowing torpedoes—as mines were then called—in Southern waterways and harbors to defend against Federal warships. That the Confederacy had such weapons in its arsenals was due largely to the efforts of General Gabriel Rains of North Carolina, a pioneer in the development of the land mine. By the outbreak of the Civil War, Rains had devised two triggering mechanisms for his land torpedoes: a friction primer, set off by a tripwire that acted like the lanyard on a cannon; and the pressure-sensitive fuse shown here, rigged to detonate when struck by an object exerting at least seven pounds of pressure.

SAFETY CAP

CRUSHABLE COPPER LID

FUSEPLUG

DETONATOR

LOCKING NUT

The disassembly of a pressure-sensitive fuse used to trigger a land mine (below) reveals the firing mechanism. At assembly, the hollow locking nut was screwed into the fuseplug, and the detonator placed in the shaft so that its tip rested just below the crushable copper lid. Once sealed and loaded, the torpedo was buried with the safety cap off and the lid near the surface. Pressure shattered the detonator and triggered the explosion.

Toiling by the palisade of Fort McAllister, Georgia, after its capture by the Federals on December 13, 1864, Confederate prisoners dig up unexploded land torpedoes at the insistence of their guards.

This tin-sheathed mine was supposedly more waterproof than its wooden counterpart *(below)*. Both types exploded when a ship touched a trigger wire, which was attached to a nearby float.

The buoyant Rains keg torpedo was the most common Confederate mine. Made from small beer kegs with wooden cones added at each end for stability, it was held just beneath the surface of the water by an anchor.

A spar torpedo *(above)*, affixed to a long boom on the bow of a Confederate vessel, was the weapon of choice for use against Federal ironclads.

This cone-shaped torpedo *(left)* was anchored to float just below the surface. When the mine was struck, a weight inside fell and pulled the trigger.

The mine at right was fired when its operator, concealed on the riverbank, pulled a long lanyard. Some mines of this type were fitted with electric detonators connected by wire to shore stations.

ACKNOWLEDGMENTS

The editors wish to thank the following individuals and institutions for their valuable assistance in the preparation of this volume:

Connecticut: Southbury—Don Troiani. Southington—Dean E. Nelson.

Georgia: Atlanta—Beverly M. DuBose III; William E. Erquitt, Patricia A. Hurdle, Gordon L. Jones, Atlanta Historical Society; George Wray.

Louisiana: New Orleans—Patricia Eymard, Confederate Memorial Hall.

Maine: Kittery—John Ockerbloom.

Maryland: La Plata—William Turner. Sharpsburg—Fonda Thomsen, Textile Preservation Association.

Massachusetts: Cambridge—James Stametelos, Tony Stametelos.

Mississippi: Jackson—Mary Lohrenz, Mississippi State Historical Museum.

New Jersey: Cherry Hill—Paul Loane. Metuchen—Bob MacDonald. Morristown—Michael Kramer.

New York: Albany—Robert E. Mulligan, Jr., New York State Museum. Latham—Thomas C. Duclos, New York State Division of Military History and Naval Affairs.

North Carolina: New Bern—Will Gorgas. Raleigh—Keith D. Strawn, North Carolina Museum of History. Wilson—Betsy B. Davis; Vernon F. Moss IV.

Pennsylvania: Gettysburg—Lawrence H. Eckert, Jr., Gettysburg National Military Park; Dean Thomas. Philadelphia—Russ Pritchard, War Library and Museum.

South Carolina: Columbia—John Bigham, Confederate Relic Room and Museum.

Tennessee: Nashville—Herb Peck, Jr.

Virginia: Centreville—Louis Leigh. Fredericksburg—Bill Henderson. Richmond—Howard O. Hendricks, Richard D. Pougher, Robin Read, Museum of the Confederacy.

Washington, D.C.: Don Kloster, National Museum of American History.

West Virginia: Harpers Ferry—William L. Brown, National Park Service, Harpers Ferry Center.

BIBLIOGRAPHY

BOOKS

Albaugh, William A., III:
The Confederate Brass-Framed Colt and Whitney. Falls Church, Va.: Published by the author, 1955.
Confederate Edged Weapons. New York: Harper & Brothers, 1960.
Tyler, Texas, C.S.A. Harrisburg, Pa.: Stackpole, 1958.

Albaugh, William A., III, Hugh Benet, Jr., and Edward N. Simmons, *Confederate Handguns.* Philadelphia: Riling and Lentz, 1963.

Albaugh, William A., III, and Edward N. Simmons, *Confederate Arms.* Harrisburg, Pa.: Stackpole, 1957.

Albaugh, William A., III, and Richard D. Steuart, *The Original Confederate Colt.* New York: Greenberg: Publisher, 1953.

Alexander, John H., *Mosby's Men.* New York: Neale Publishing, 1907.

Anderson, Edward C., *Confederate Foreign Agent.* University, Ala.: Confederate Publishing, 1976.

Battle-Fields of the South. Alexandria, Va.: Time-Life Books, 1984 (reprint of 1864 edition).

Bergeron, Arthur W., Jr., *Guide to Louisiana Confederate Military Units, 1861-1865.* Baton Rouge: Louisiana State University Press, 1989.

Bernard, George S. (Ed. and Comp.), *War Talks of Confederate Veterans.* Dayton: Press of Morningside Bookshop, 1981 (reprint of 1892 edition).

Billings, John D., *Hardtack and Coffee: The Unwritten Story of Army Life.* Williamstown, Mass.: Corner House Publishers, 1980 (reprint of 1887 edition).

Blackwood's Edinburgh Magazine (January-June 1863, Vol. 93). New York: Leonard Scott, 1863.

Boatner, Mark Mayo, III, *The Civil War Dictionary.* New York: David McKay, 1959.

Brice, Marshall Moore, *The Stonewall Brigade Band.* Verona, Va.: McClure Printing, 1967.

Brown, Maud Morrow, *The University Greys.* Richmond: Garrett and Massie, 1940.

Brown, Norman D. (Ed.), *One of Cleburne's Command.* Austin: University of Texas Press, 1980.

Caba, G. Craig, *Historic Southern Saddles, 1840-1865.* Enola, Pa.: Civil War Antiquities, 1982.

Caldwell, J. F. J., *The History of a Brigade of South Carolinians.* Dayton: Press of Morningside Bookshop, 1974 (reprint of 1866 edition).

Cannon, Devereaux D., Jr., *The Flags of the Confederacy.* Memphis: St. Lukes Press, 1988.

Chamberlain, Joshua Lawrence, *The Passing of the Armies.* Dayton: Press of Morningside Bookshop, 1981.

Chamberlayne, Ham, *Ham Chamberlayne—Virginian.* Richmond: Press of the Dietz Printing Co., 1932.

Clark, Walter, *Histories of the Several Regiments and Battalions from North Carolina in the Great War 1861-'65* (Vols. 1-5). Wendell, N.C.: Broadfoot's Bookmark, 1982 (reprint of 1901 edition).

Coates, Earl J., and Dean S. Thomas, *An Introduction to Civil War Small Arms.* Gettysburg, Pa.: Thomas Publications, 1990.

Conrad, Mary Lynn, *Confederate Banners.* Harrisonburg, Va., 1907.

Cooke, John Esten, *Wearing of the Gray.* New York: E. B. Treat, 1867.

Crute, Joseph H., Jr.:
Confederate Staff Officers, 1861-1865. Powhatan, Va.: Derwent Books, 1982.
Emblems of Southern Valor: The Battle Flags of the Confederacy. Louisville, Ky.: Harmony House, 1990.
Units of the Confederate States Army. Midlothian, Va.: Derwent Books, 1987.

Dunlop, W. S., *Lee's Sharpshooters: The Forefront of Battle.* Dayton: Press of Morningside Bookshop, 1982.

Dyer, Frederick H., *A Compendium of the War of the Rebellion* (Vol. 2). Dayton: Press of Morningside Bookshop, 1979.

Editors of Time-Life Books, The Civil War series. Alexandria, Va.: Time-Life Books, 1987.

Edwards, William B., *Civil War Guns.* Secaucus, N.J.: Castle Books, 1978.

Elting, John R., and Michael J. McAfee (Eds.), *Military Uniforms in America* (Vol. 3). Novato, Calif.: Presidio Press, 1982.

Flayderman, Norm, *Flayderman's Guide to Antique American Firearms* (2d ed.). Northfield, Ill.: DBI Books, 1980.

Fuller, Claud E., and Richard D. Steuart, *Firearms of the Confederacy.* Lawrence, Mass.: Quarterman Publications, 1944.

Garofalo, Robert, and Mark Elrod, *A Pictorial History of Civil War Era Musical Instruments and Military Bands.* Charleston, W.Va.: Pictorial Histories Publishing, 1985.

Goff, Richard D., *Confederate Supply.* Durham, N.C.: Duke University Press, 1969.

Hackley, Woodford B., *The Little Fork Rangers.* Richmond: Press of the Dietz Printing Co., 1927.

Hall, Harry H., *A Johnny Reb Band from Salem: The Pride of Tarheelia.* Raleigh, N.C.: North Carolina Confederate Centennial Commission, 1963.

Hazlett, James C., Edwin Olmstead, and M. Hume Parks, *Field Artillery Weapons of the Civil War.* Newark: University of Delaware Press, 1983.

History of the Seventeenth Virginia Infantry, C.S.A. Arlington, Va.: R. W. Beatty, N.d. (reprint of 1870 edition).

Howard, McHenry, *Recollections of a Maryland Confederate Soldier and Staff Officer under Johnston, Jackson and Lee.* Dayton: Press of Morningside Bookshop, 1975 (reprint of 1914 edition).

Hoyt, James A., *The Palmetto Riflemen.* Greenville, S.C.: Hoyt & Keys, 1886.

Hunter, Alexander, *Johnny Reb and Billy Yank.* New York: Neale Publishing, 1905.

Johnson, Robert Underwood, and Clarence Clough Buel (Eds.):
Battles and Leaders of the Civil War (Vol. 4). New York: Century, 1888.
From Sumter to Shiloh. New York: Castle Books, 1956.

Kirwan, A. D. (Ed.), *Johnny Green of the Orphan Brigade.* Lexington: University of Kentucky Press, 1956.

Krick, Robert K., *Lee's Colonels.* Dayton: Press of Morningside Bookshop, 1979.

Lasswell, Mary (Ed.), *Rags and Hope: The Recollections of Val C. Giles, Four Years with Hood's Brigade, Fourth Texas Infantry, 1861-1865.* New York: Coward-McCann, 1961.

Lewis, Richard, *Camp Life of a Confederate Boy.* Gaithersburg, Md.: Butternut Press (reprint of 1883 edition).

List of Field Officers, Regiments and Battalions in the Confederate States Army, 1861-1865. Mattituck, N.Y.: J. M. Carroll, 1983.

Long, E. B., with Barbara Long, *The Civil War Day by Day: An Almanac, 1861-1865.* Garden City, N.Y.: Doubleday, 1971.

Lord, Francis A., and Arthur Wise, *Bands and Drummer Boys of the Civil War.* South Brunswick, N.J.: Thomas Yoseloff, 1966.

Lyman, Theodore, *Meade's Headquarters, 1863-1865: Letters of Colonel Theodore Lyman.* Boston: Atlantic Monthly Press, 1922.

McAulay, John D.:
Carbines of the Civil War, 1861-1865. Union City, Tenn.: Pioneer Press, 1981.
Civil War Breech Loading Rifles. Lincoln, R.I.: Andrew Mowbray, 1987.

McCarthy, Carlton, *Detailed Minutiae of Soldier Life in the Army of Northern Virginia, 1861-1865.* Richmond: Carlton McCarthy, 1882.

McKim, Randolph H., *A Soldier's Recollections.* New York: Longmans, Green, 1910.

McMorries, Edward Young, *History of the First Regiment*

Alabama Volunteer Infantry. Montgomery, Ala.: Brown Printing, 1904.

Madaus, Howard Michael:
The Battle Flags of the Confederate Army of Tennessee. Milwaukee: Milwaukee Public Museum, 1976.
The Warner Collector's Guide to American Longarms. New York: Main Street Press, 1981.

Manarin, Louis H., and Lee A. Wallace, Jr., *Richmond Volunteers.* Richmond: Westover Press, 1969.

Mosby, John S., *Stuart's Cavalry in the Gettysburg Campaign.* New York: Moffat, Yard, 1908.

Murphy, John M., *Confederate Carbines and Musketoons.* Dallas: Taylor Publishing, 1986.

Nichols, Edward J., *Toward Gettysburg: A Biography of General John F. Reynolds.* University Park: Pennsylvania State University Press, 1958.

Nisbet, James Cooper, *Four Years on the Firing Line.* Jackson, Tenn.: McCowat-Mercer Press, 1963.

Nye, Wilbur Sturtevant, *Here Come the Rebels!* Baton Rouge: Louisiana State University Press, 1965.

O'Connell, Robert L., *Of Arms and Men.* New York: Oxford University Press, 1989.

Olson, Kenneth E., *Music and Musket.* Westport, Conn.: Greenwood Press, 1981.

Owen, William Miller, *In Camp and Battle with the Washington Artillery of New Orleans.* Boston: Ticknor, 1885.

Paxton, John Gallatin (Ed.), *The Civil War Letters of General Frank "Bull" Paxton, CSA: A Lieutenant of Lee and Jackson.* Hillsboro, Tex.: Hill Jr. College Press, 1978.

Peterson, Harold L., *The American Sword, 1775-1945* (rev. ed.). Philadelphia: Ray Riling Arms Books, 1965.

Porter, Horace, *Campaigning with Grant.* New York: Century, 1897.

Reilly, Robert M., *United States Military Small Arms, 1816-1865.* Baton Rouge, La.: Eagle Press, 1970.

The Returned Battle Flags. Louisville, Ky.: Passenger Department, Cotton Belt Route, 1905.

Richmond Howitzers in the War. Gaithersburg, Md.: Butternut Press (reprint of 1891 edition).

Ripley, Warren, *Artillery and Ammunition of the Civil War.* New York: Promontory Press, 1970.

Robertson, James I., Jr., *The Stonewall Brigade.* Baton Rouge: Louisiana State University Press, 1977.

Roman, Alfred, *The Military Operations of General Beauregard* (Vol. 2). New York: Harper & Brothers, 1883.

Scharf, J. Thomas, *History of the Confederate States Navy.* New York: Fairfax Press, 1977.

Simpson, Harold B., *Hood's Texas Brigade.* Dallas: Alcor Publishing, 1983.

Smith, Daniel P., *Company K, First Alabama Regiment: Three Years in the Confederate Service.* Gaithersburg, Md.: Butternut Press, 1984 (reprint of 1885 edition).

Sorrel, G. Moxley, *Recollections of a Confederate Staff Officer.* Dayton: Press of Morningside Bookshop, 1978 (reprint of 1905 edition).

Stevens, George T., *Three Years in the Sixth Corps.* Alexandria, Va.: Time-Life Books, 1984 (reprint of 1866 edition).

Stevens, John W., *Reminiscences of the Civil War.* Powhatan, Va.: Derwent Books, 1982 (reprint of 1902 edition).

Stiles, Robert, *Four Years under Marse Robert.* Dayton: Press of Morningside Bookshop, 1977 (reprint of 1903 edition).

Sword, Wiley, *Firepower from Abroad.* Lincoln, R.I.: Andrew Mowbray, 1986.

Sylvia, Stephen W., and Michael J. O'Donnell: *Civil War Canteens.* Orange, Va.: Moss Publications, 1990.

Tennesseans in the Civil War (Part 1). Nashville: Civil War Centennial Commission, 1964.

Thompson, Samuel Bernard, *Confederate Purchasing Operations Abroad.* Gloucester, Mass.: Peter Smith, 1973 (reprint of 1935 edition).

Todd, Frederick P.:
American Military Equipage, 1851-1872. New York: Charles Scribner's Sons, 1978.
American Military Equipage, 1851-1872 (Vol. 2). New York: Chatham Square Press, 1983.

Toncy, Marcus B., *The Privations of a Private.* Nashville: Printed for the author, 1905.

Tucker, Glenn, *Chickamauga: Bloody Battle in the West.* Indianapolis: Bobbs-Merrill, 1961.

United States Navy, Office of Naval Records and Library (Comp. and Rev.), *Register of Officers of the Confederate States Navy, 1861-1865.* Mattituck, N.Y.: J. M. Carroll, 1983.

Vandiver, Frank E. (Ed.), *Confederate Blockade Running through Bermuda, 1861-1865.* Austin: University of Texas Press, 1947.

The War of the Rebellion: A Compilation of the Official Records of the Union and Confederate Armies (Series 1, 2, 3). Washington, D.C.: Government Printing Office, 1889.

Wells, Tom Henderson, *The Confederate Navy: A Study in Organization.* University: University of Alabama Press, 1971.

Wiley, Bell Irvin, *The Life of Johnny Reb.* Baton Rouge: Louisiana State University Press, 1980.

Wilson, R. L., *The Colt Heritage.* New York: Simon and Schuster, N.d.

Wright, Marcus J. (Ed.), *General Officers of the Confederate Army.* Mattituck, N.Y.: J. M. Carroll, 1983.

PERIODICALS

Humphreys, Milton W., "Notes on Confederate Artillery Instruction and Service." *Journal of the U.S. Artillery,* 1893, Vol. 2, pp. 560-588.

Jensen, Leslie D.:
"A Survey of Confederate Central Government Quartermaster Issue Jackets, Part 1." *Military Collector & Historian,* Fall 1989, Vol. 41, no. 3, pp. 109-122.
"A Survey of Confederate Central Government Quartermaster Issue Jackets, Part 1." *Military Collector & Historian,* Winter 1989, Vol. 41, no. 4, pp. 162-171.

Madaus, Howard Michael, "Rebel Flags Afloat." *Flag Bulletin,* January-April 1986, Vol. 25, nos. 1-2.

OTHER SOURCES

Madaus, Howard Michael, "Southern Cross" (Vol. 2). Unpublished manuscript. Milwaukee: Milwaukee Public Museum, N.d.

Museum of the Confederacy, *Catalogue of Uniforms: The Museum of the Confederacy.* Richmond: Museum of the Confederacy, 1987.

PICTURE CREDITS

The sources for the illustrations in this volume are listed below. Credits from left to right are separated by semicolons, from top to bottom by dashes. Photographs taken on assignment for Echoes of Glory *by Larry Sherer, assisted by Andrew Patilla, are followed by an asterisk (*).*

Cover: Courtesy W. J. Kenneth Rockwell, M.D., photographed by Chip Henderson. 3: Museum of the Confederacy, Richmond, Va., photographed by Larry Sherer. 5: Courtesy J. Craig Nannos, photographed by Larry Sherer—Museum of the Confederacy, Richmond, photographed by Larry Sherer—courtesy Russ A. Pritchard, photographed by Larry Sherer; Museum of the Confederacy, Richmond* (2)—Manassas National Battlefield Park, photographed by Larry Sherer. 6, 7: Painting by Peter F. Rothermel, State Museum of Pennsylvania, Pennsylvania Historical and Museum Commission, photographed by Henry Groskinsky. 8: Valentine Museum, Richmond. 10, 11: Western Reserve Historical Society. 13: Courtesy Bill Turner. 14, 15: Courtesy Mrs. Benjamin Rosenstock. 17: Painting by Thure de Thulstrup, Seventh Regiment Fund, photographed by Al Freni.

18: Painting by William L. Sheppard, from *Lee and Longstreet at High Tide: Gettysburg in the Light of the Official Records* by Helen D. Longstreet, published privately, Gainesville, Ga., 1905. 20: Courtesy collection of J. Craig Nannos, photographed by Larry Sherer. 22, 23: Drawings by William J. Hennessy, Jr., adapted from *Rifle and Light Infantry Tactics,* J. B. Lippincott, Philadelphia, 1863. 26, 27: Courtesy collection of Bill Turner*—courtesy collection of Paul Davies.* 28, 29: Gettysburg National Military Park Museum*—U.S. Marine Corps Museum, Washington, D.C., photographed by Fil Hunter—National Firearms Museum, NRA, photographed by Leon Dishman—collection of Richard F. Carlile; courtesy collection of Don Troiani.* 30, 31: Library of Congress—Gettysburg National Military Park Museum* (3). 32, 33: Gettysburg National Military Park Museum* (2)—courtesy collection of Michael Kramer*—Museum of the Confederacy, Richmond* (2); courtesy Herb Peck, Jr.; courtesy collection of Dean S. Thomas.* 34, 35: Civil War Library and Museum, Philadelphia*—Confederate Relic Room, Columbia, S.C.*—Fort Ward Museum, City of Alexandria, Va., photographed by Henry Beville—Museum of the Confederacy, Richmond;* Illinois State Historical Library. 36, 37: Gettysburg National Military Park Museum*—courtesy collection of Don Troiani* (3); courtesy Bob McDonald;* Atlanta Historical Society*—collection of Dean S. Thomas* (2). 38, 39: Collection of Michael Kramer* (2); Atlanta Historical Society*—courtesy Lewis Leigh, Jr.*—courtesy Russ A. Pritchard, photographed by Larry Sherer (3). 40, 41: Courtesy Russ A. Pritchard, photographed by Larry Sherer—Gettysburg National Military Park Museum*—collection of Michael Kramer* (2). 42, 43: Collection of Michael Kramer*—private collection*—Gettysburg National Military Park Museum* (2). 44, 45: Museum of the Confederacy, Richmond, photographed by Ronald H. Jennings—courtesy collection of Russ A. Pritchard* (2)—Museum of the Confederacy, Richmond, photographed by Ronald H. Jennings. 46, 47: Atlanta Historical Society* (2); courtesy collection of Dean S. Thomas* (2); collection of Richard F. Carlile—courtesy William S. Powell, frame courtesy Tom Farish, photographed by Larry Sherer—courtesy collection of John D. McAulay*—Civil War Library and Museum, Philadelphia*—Smithsonian Institution, National

Museum of American History, Washington, D.C.* 48, 49: Gettysburg National Military Park Museum*—courtesy collection of Russ A. Pritchard*—Gettysburg National Military Park Museum* (3). 50, 51: Beverly M. DuBose III*—Gettysburg National Military Park Museum*—Atlanta Historical Society*—Gettysburg National Military Park Museum*—painting by Julian Scott, courtesy 1746 Drake House Museum, Plainfield Historical Society, photographed by Henry Groskinsky. 52, 53: Museum of the Confederacy, Richmond;* courtesy collection of Bill Turner*—courtesy collection of C. Paul Loane*—courtesy J. Craig Nannos, photographed by Larry Sherer; U.S. Marine Corps Museum, photographed by Larry Sherer. 54, 55: Courtesy collection of Bill Turner; Gettysburg National Military Park Museum* (3). 56, 57: Gettysburg National Military Park Museum* (2)—courtesy Russ A. Pritchard, photographed by Larry Sherer; courtesy collection of Dean S. Thomas* (3). 58, 59: Courtesy Russ A. Pritchard, photographed by Larry Sherer—courtesy Herb Peck, Jr.; Gettysburg National Military Park Museum* (2). 60, 61: Courtesy collection of Bill Turner*—Virginia Military Institute, Lexington, photographed by Larry Sherer (2). 62, 63: Museum of the Confederacy, Richmond, photographed by Larry Sherer; New York State Division of Military and Naval Affairs, Military History Collection*—Gettysburg National Military Park Museum* (2)—Confederate Relic Room, Columbia, S.C.* (2)—private collection* (2). 64, 65: Museum of the City of Mobile, photographed by Larry Cantrell (2)—collection of State Historical Museum, Mississippi Department of Archives and History, Jackson, Gil Ford Photography; courtesy collection of Bill Turner*—Confederate Relic Room, Columbia, S.C.* (4). 66, 67: Courtesy collection of Bill Turner* (4)—courtesy Will Gorgas, New Bern Civil War Museum* (2)—courtesy collection of Russ A. Pritchard* (2). 68, 69: Gettysburg National Military Park Museum*—courtesy Tom Farish, photographed by Michael Latil; Atlanta Historical Society* (2)—Confederate Memorial Hall, New Orleans* (2)—Gettysburg National Military Park Museum.* 70, 71: Confederate Memorial Hall, New Orleans* (2)—courtesy Bill Erquitt*—Confederate Memorial Hall, New Orleans* (3)—Confederate Relic Room, Columbia, S.C.* (2). 72: Library of Congress; Museum of the Confederacy, Richmond, photographed by Larry Sherer; West Virginia Department of Culture and History, State Archives; courtesy Lynchburg Museum System, Lynchburg, Va. (2). 73: Confederate Memorial Hall, New Orleans;* Library of Congress USZ62 12995; Atlanta Historical Society* (3)—courtesy Byron J. Ihle. 74, 75: Confederate Memorial Hall, New Orleans* (2)—Gettysburg National Military Park Museum* (2)—Valentine Museum, Richmond; Museum of the Confederacy, Richmond, photographed by Larry Sherer (2); From *Die grosse Reiterschlacht bei Brandy Station, 9 Juni 1863* by Heros von Borcke and Justus Scheibert, Verlag von Paul Kittel, Berlin, 1893. 76, 77: Courtesy Will Gorgas, New Bern Civil War Museum* (4); courtesy Tom Farish; courtesy Will Gorgas, New Bern Civil War Museum* (2)—courtesy Russ A. Pritchard, photographed by Larry Sherer (2)—Atlanta Historical Society* (2); Gettysburg National Military Park Museum.* 78, 79: Museum of the Confederacy, Richmond;* New York State Division of Military and Naval Affairs, Military History Collection*—Museum of the Confederacy, Richmond;* Georgia Department of Archives and History—courtesy Will Gorgas, New Bern Civil War Museum* (2)—Museum of the Confederacy, Richmond, photographed by Larry Sherer—Museum of the Confederacy, Richmond* (2); cour-

tesy Will Gorgas, New Bern Civil War Museum* (3)—courtesy Bill Erquitt.* 80: Museum of the Confederacy, Richmond, photographed by Larry Sherer. 83: From *The Official Military Atlas of the Civil War* by George Davis, Leslie J. Perry, and Joseph W. Kirkley, compiled by Calvin D. Cowles, Fairfax Press, N.Y., 1983, courtesy Frank and Marie-T. Wood Print Collections. 86, 87: Courtesy collection of Bill Turner;* Museum of the Confederacy, Richmond* (3). 88: Atlanta Historical Society* (2)—Museum of the Confederacy, Richmond* (2). 89: Museum of the Confederacy, Richmond;* courtesy collection of Bill Turner;* De Kalb Historical Society* (2). 90, 91: Museum of the Confederacy, Richmond* (3)—Kentucky Historical Society, Military History Museum (2). 92: Atlanta Historical Society;* collection of Glen C. Cangelosi, M.D.*—Confederate Memorial Hall, New Orleans* (2). 93: All pictures Museum of the Confederacy, Richmond,* except portrait, Chicago Historical Society No. ICHi-08049. 94: Museum of the Confederacy, Richmond; courtesy Will Gorgas, New Bern Civil War Museum.* 95: Museum of the Confederacy, Richmond* (4)—courtesy Bill Erquitt;* Confederate Memorial Hall, New Orleans;* Museum of the Confederacy, Richmond* (2); Warren Rifles Confederate Museum, photographed by Michael Latil—courtesy Bill Erquitt;* Museum of the Confederacy, Richmond* (2); courtesy collection of Bill Turner. 96, 97: Vernon Floyd Moss III, Wilson, N.C.* 98: Museum of the Confederacy, Richmond;* courtesy Lee-Fendall House, Alexandria, Va. 99: Vernon Floyd Moss III, Wilson, N.C.* (6)—Atlanta Historical Society* (2). 100: Museum of the Confederacy, Richmond.* 101: All pictures Museum of the Confederacy, Richmond,* except portrait, courtesy Tom Farish, photographed by Michael Latil. 102: Virginia Historical Society Collections, Richmond; Dementi-Foster Collection, Richmond; National Archives No. 111 B 1233—Confederate Memorial Hall, New Orleans.* 103: Confederate Memorial Hall, New Orleans;* Confederate Memorial Hall, New Orleans; Confederate Memorial Hall, New Orleans.* 104, 105: Gettysburg National Military Park Museum;* Museum of the Confederacy, Richmond* (3); lower right, Vernon Floyd Moss III, Wilson, N.C.* (6). 106: Museum of the Confederacy, Richmond,* except portrait, Library of Congress. 107: Museum of the Confederacy, Richmond,* except portrait, Military Order of the Loyal Legion of the U.S. MASS Commandery, USAMHI, photographed by A. Pierce Bounds. 108: Museum of the Confederacy, Richmond,* except portrait, courtesy collection of Bill Turner.* 109: Museum of the Confederacy, Richmond* (2)—Atlanta Historical Society* (2). 110: Courtesy collection of Bill Turner; Museum of the Confederacy, Richmond* (2). 111: Museum of the Confederacy, Richmond*—courtesy Will Gorgas, New Bern Civil War Museum;* North Carolina Department of Cultural Resources, Division of Archives and History, Museum of History, Raleigh*—Museum of the Confederacy, Richmond.* 112, 113: Museum of the Confederacy, Richmond.* 114, 115: Mississippi Department of Archives and History, Jackson; Collection of Mississippi State Historical Museum, Mississippi Department of Archives and History, Jackson, Gil Ford Photography (6). 116: Museum of the Confederacy, Richmond* (3)—USAMHI, copied by A. Pierce Bounds. 117: Collection of Glen C. Cangelosi, M.D.* (2)—Confederate Memorial Hall, New Orleans* (3). 118: Courtesy Terence P. O'Leary—Museum of the Confederacy, Richmond;* courtesy Will Gorgas, New Bern Civil War Museum.* 119: Atlanta Historical Society* (2); box, lower left, Vernon Floyd Moss III, Wilson, N.C.* (9). 120, 121:

Virginia Historical Society Collections, Richmond; Valentine Museum, Richmond; Museum of the Confederacy, Richmond* (2)—Smithsonian Institution, National Museum of American History, Washington, D.C.;* Valentine Museum, Richmond; Smithsonian Institution, National Museum of American History, Washington, D.C.;* box, all Vernon Floyd Moss III, Wilson, N.C.,* except lower right, courtesy collection of Bill Henderson.* 122: Vernon Floyd Moss III, Wilson, N.C.* (6); Museum of the Confederacy, Richmond* (3). 123: From *Richard Snowden Andrews: A Memoir* by Tunstall Smith, Baltimore, 1910; Maryland Historical Society, Baltimore, gift of Charles Lee Andrews. 124, 125: Atlanta Historical Society.* 126: Courtesy Tom Farish, photographed by Michael Latil; Museum of the Confederacy, Richmond*—Library of Congress No. 262-14333, drawing by Alfred R. Waud. 127: Museum of the Confederacy, Richmond* (2)—Vernon Floyd Moss III, Wilson, N.C.* (4); National Park Service, Petersburg National Battlefield Museum—Museum of the Confederacy, Richmond. 128: Museum of the Confederacy, Richmond.* 129: Courtesy Tom Farish, photographed by Michael Latil; Museum of the Confederacy, Richmond*—Confederate Memorial Hall, New Orleans* (2). 130: Courtesy Rosenberg Library, Galveston, Tex.—courtesy Don Troiani Collection;* Confederate Relic Room, Columbia, S.C.* 131: Private collection* (2)—Atlanta Historical Society;* courtesy Tom Farish, photographed by Michael Latil. 132, 133: Museum of the Confederacy, Richmond;* Eleanor S. Brockenbrough Library, Museum of the Confederacy, Richmond, copy photography by Katherine Wetzel—Museum of the Confederacy, Richmond;* Library of Congress No. 25621 B8184-10502. 134, 135: All Museum of the Confederacy, Richmond,* except portrait, courtesy collection of Bill Turner,* and center photo, Library of Congress. 136, 137: Metropolitan Museum of Art, gift of Mrs. Frank B. Porter, 1922—courtesy Bob McDonald;* Museum of the Confederacy, Richmond* (2). 138: Gettysburg National Military Park Museum*—Museum of the Confederacy, Richmond* (2); USAMHI, photographed by A. Pierce Bounds. 139: Courtesy Bob McDonald*—Greensboro Historical Museum, photo by L. Atkinson. 140: Confederate Memorial Hall, New Orleans* (2)—lower left, Museum of the Confederacy, Richmond.* 141: Smithsonian Institution, National Museum of American History, Washington, D.C.*—Eleanor S. Brockenbrough Library, Museum of the Confederacy, Richmond, copy photography by Katherine Wetzel; Museum of the Confederacy, Richmond.* 142: Courtesy Bob McDonald* (2)—courtesy Bob McDonald. 143: Confederate Relic Room, Columbia, S.C.*—Kentucky Historical Society, Military History Museum. 144: Courtesy Michael J. Black, photographed by Robert Bailey; North Carolina Collection, UNC Library at Chapel Hill, from original courtesy Alfred T. Clifford—Museum of the Confederacy, Richmond* (2). 145: Courtesy Bob McDonald.* 146: Layland Museum, Cleburne, Tex., photographed by David Buffington; Layland Museum, Cleburne, Tex., photographed by Dr. Anne Bailey—Museum of the Confederacy, Richmond;* Layland Museum, Cleburne, Tex., photographed by David Buffington. 147: Courtesy Steve Mullinax; Museum of the Confederacy, Richmond*—Library of Congress No. B8184-10623; courtesy Jerry and Teresa Rinker. 148: Museum of the Confederacy, Richmond;* Virginia Military Institute Archives, Lexington—Museum of the Confederacy, Richmond.* 149: Private collection* (4) except portrait, private collection, photographed by George S. Whiteley IV. 150: Courtesy

Dave Mark; Museum of the Confederacy, Richmond* (2); North Carolina Department of Cultural History, Division of Archives and History, Museum of History, Raleigh.* 151: Eleanor S. Brockenbrough Library, Museum of the Confederacy, Richmond, copy photography by Katherine Wetzel—Gettysburg National Military Park Museum;* Museum of the Confederacy, Richmond.* 152: Museum of the Confederacy, Richmond.* 153: Museum of the Confederacy, Richmond;* Atlanta Historical Society* (3); Beverly M. DuBose III;* Confederate Relic Room, Columbia, S.C.* 154: North Carolina Department of Cultural Resources, Division of Archives and History, Museum of History, Raleigh, photographed by Steve Muir; courtesy Joseph Canole—Museum of the Confederacy, Richmond* (2); Museum of the Confederacy, Richmond, photographed by Larry Sherer. 155: Museum of the Confederacy, Richmond* (3); Department of Military Affairs, State of Illinois, Springfield. 156, 157: New York State Division of Military and Naval Affairs, Military History Collection;* Museum of the Confederacy, Richmond*—courtesy D. Mark Katz. 158: Museum of the Confederacy, Richmond, photographed by Larry Sherer; courtesy Tom Farish, photographed by Michael Latil—Confederate Memorial Hall, New Orleans;* Museum of the Confederacy, Richmond.* 159: Museum of the Confederacy, Richmond,* (4) except portrait, courtesy Herb Peck, Jr. 160: Confederate Relic Room, Columbia, S.C.* (2)—Confederate Memorial Hall, New Orleans;* Museum of the Confederacy, Richmond*—Museum of the Confederacy, Richmond, photographed by Larry Sherer; private collection.* 161: Private collection;* Museum of the Confederacy, Richmond* (2); courtesy Bob Walter. 162: Museum of the Confederacy, Richmond;* Gettysburg National Military Park Museum*—Museum of the Confederacy, Richmond*—Confederate Relic Room, Columbia, S.C.* 163: Museum of the Confederacy, Richmond, photographed by Larry Sherer—Confederate Memorial Hall, New Orleans*—Museum of the Confederacy, Richmond.* 164: Private collection* (2); portrait, courtesy Tom Farish, photographed by Michael Latil. 165: Virginia Military Institute Museum, Lexington, photographed by Larry Sherer; Museum of the Confederacy, Richmond*—Museum of the Confederacy, Richmond, photographed by Larry Sherer; portrait, courtesy Tom Farish, photographed by Michael Latil. 166: Confederate Memorial Hall, New Orleans*—courtesy Will Gorgas, New Bern Civil War Museum*—Museum of the Confederacy, Richmond* (2). 167: On loan to Gettysburg National Military Park Museum, courtesy State Museum of Pennsylvania, Pennsylvania Historical and Museum Commission*—private collection*—Museum of the Confederacy, Richmond; Museum of the Confederacy, Richmond, photographed by Larry Sherer (2). 168: Museum of the Confederacy, Richmond, photographed by Larry Sherer—Confederate Memorial Hall, New Orleans*—courtesy United Daughters of the Confederacy, Atlanta Chapter No. 18*—Atlanta Historical Society.* 169: Courtesy Tom Farish, photographed by Michael Latil—Museum of the Confederacy, Richmond*—Confederate Relic Room, Columbia, S.C.*—Museum of the Confederacy, Richmond.* 170: Courtesy McKissick Museum, S.C., on loan to Gettysburg National Military Park Museum* (2)—courtesy Will Gorgas, New Bern Civil War Museum;* Museum of the Confederacy, Richmond*—Confederate Memorial Hall, New Orleans;* Gettysburg National Military Park Museum.* 171: Museum of the Confederacy, Richmond;* Confederate Museum, Charleston, S.C., photographed by Thomas P. Grimball III; Confederate Memorial

Hall, New Orleans* (2); Museum of the Confederacy, Richmond.* 172: Museum of the Confederacy, Richmond* (3)—New York State Division of Military and Naval Affairs, Military History Collection* (3). 173: Atlanta Historical Society;* courtesy collection of Bill Turner—Confederate Memorial Hall, New Orleans*—Atlanta Historical Society;* Museum of the Confederacy, Richmond, photographed by Larry Sherer. 174: New York State Division of Military and Naval Affairs, Military History Collection*—Atlanta Historical Society*—courtesy collection of Don Troiani*—New York State Division of Military and Naval Affairs, Military History Collection.* 175: New York State Division of Military and Naval Affairs, Military History Collection*—Museum of the Confederacy, Richmond* (4). 176: Museum of the Confederacy, Richmond.* 177: C.S.S. *Alabama*: U.S. Navy No. NH57256—Museum of the Confederacy, Richmond* (2); box, lower right, Vernon Floyd Moss III, Wilson, N.C.* (6). 178, 179: Apalachiocola Area Historical Society; Atlanta Historical Society;* Museum of the Confederacy, Richmond*—New York State Division of Military and Naval Affairs, Military History Collection* (2)—Atlanta Historical Society* (2)—Confederate Naval Museum, photographed by Herb Cawthorne—Atlanta Historical Society* (2). 180: Courtesy Russ A. Pritchard, photographed by Larry Sherer. 184: National Archives Gift Collection, Photo No. 200(S)-CC-2288—Atlanta Historical Society;* Museum of the Confederacy, Richmond.* 185. Courtesy Russ A. Pritchard, photographed by Larry Sherer—Atlanta Historical Society.* 186, 187: Atlanta Historical Society;* Beverly M. DuBose III;* private collection, copied by Jimmy Krantz; Beverly M. DuBose III*—courtesy collection of Don Troiani;* Museum of the Confederacy, Richmond* (2)—Atlanta Historical Society;* Museum of the Confederacy, Richmond;* Atlanta Historical Society (2). 188, 189: Museum of the Confederacy, Richmond;* courtesy Dr Thomas P. Sweeney, photographed by Tom Davis—Atlanta Historical Society* (4); courtesy collection of Bill Erquitt*—Atlanta Historical Society; Museum of the Confederacy, Richmond;* Atlanta Historical Society* (6). 190: Atlanta Historical Society.* 191: Left column: Atlanta Historical Society* (3)—Museum of the Confederacy, Richmond* (5). 192, 193: Courtesy Herb Peck, Jr.; Museum of the Confederacy, Richmond* (3)—courtesy collection of Don Troiani* (2); Museum of the Confederacy, Richmond;* Confederate Relic Room, Columbia, S.C.*—Museum of the Confederacy, Richmond;* Atlanta Historical Society.* 194: Museum of the Confederacy, Richmond;* courtesy Tom Farish, photographed by Michael Latil—Museum of the Confederacy, Richmond*—courtesy collection of Don Troiani;* Museum of the Confederacy, Richmond* (3). 195: Atlanta Historical Society—courtesy Bob McDonald*—Museum of the Confederacy, Richmond* (5)—courtesy Russ A. Pritchard, photographed by Larry Sherer. 196, 197: Portrait, courtesy Georgia Department of Archives and History; Atlanta Historical Society* (2); courtesy Russ A. Pritchard, photographed by Larry Sherer—Beverly M. DuBose III;* Atlanta Historical Society*—Museum of the Confederacy, Richmond;* courtesy Russ A. Pritchard, photographed by Larry Sherer; Atlanta Historical Society*—courtesy collection of Dean E. Nelson;* Beverly M. DuBose III;* Atlanta Historical Society* (2). 198, 199: Far left, collection of Michael Kramer;* top belt, Museum of the Confederacy, Richmond*—lower belt and pouches, collection of Michael Kramer; courtesy Dr. Thomas P. Sweeney, photographed by Tom Davis; North Carolina Department of Cultural Re-

sources, Division of Archives and History, Museum of History, Raleigh;* far right, Museum of the Confederacy, Richmond.* 200: Museum of the Confederacy, Richmond* (2)—North Carolina Department of Cultural Resources, Division of Archives and History, Museum of History, Raleigh.* 201: Portrait courtesy Tom Farish, photographed by Michael Latil; Museum of the Confederacy, Richmond* (3)—lowest haversack, Atlanta Historical Society.* 202: Courtesy Bob McDonald*—Museum of the Confederacy, Richmond* (2). 203: Museum of the Confederacy, Richmond* (2)—Museum of the Confederacy, Richmond, copied by Katherine Wetzel; Museum of the Confederacy, Richmond, photographed by Larry Sherer—Museum of the Confederacy, Richmond.* 204: Museum of the Confederacy, Richmond.* 205: Courtesy Les Jensen; Museum of the Confederacy, Richmond* (2). 206, 207: Top belt, holsters, far right pack, Museum of the Confederacy, Richmond*—middle belt, Atlanta Historical Society*—lowest belt, Museum of the Confederacy, Richmond*—portrait, courtesy Steve Mullinax; Museum of the Confederacy, Richmond;* rifle pouch and knapsack, Confederate Relic Room, Columbia, S.C.*—Museum of the Confederacy, Richmond*—Atlanta Historical Society.* 208: Museum of the Confederacy, Richmond.* 209: Museum of the Confederacy, Richmond* (2)—Beverly M. DuBose III.* 210: Museum of the Confederacy, Richmond;* courtesy collection of Bill Turner*—courtesy Russ A. Pritchard, photographed by Larry Sherer; Confederate Relic Room, Columbia, S.C.* 211: Museum of the Confederacy, Richmond.* 212: Museum of the Confederacy, Richmond,* except: tobacco package, Atlanta Historical Society;* troops, Library of Congress No. B8184-4390—Princeton matches, Museum of the Confederacy, photographed by Larry Sherer—cards, courtesy collection of Dean E. Nelson.* 213: Museum of the Confederacy, Richmond.* 214: Museum of the Confederacy, Richmond;* except lower left, Atlanta Historical Society.* 215: Museum of the Confederacy, Richmond,* except: troops cooking, Austin History Center, Austin Public Library, PICA 03674—skillet, lower left, courtesy Will Gorgas, New Bern Civil War Museum.* 216: Confederate Memorial Hall, New Orleans* (2); saddle, courtesy collection of Don Troiani. 217: From *Histories of the Several Regiments and Battalions from North Carolina in the Great War 1861-65,* edited by Walter Clark, 1901; Museum of the Confederacy, Richmond* (2). 218: Museum of the Confederacy, Richmond.* 220, 221: Courtesy Old Salem, Inc., Winston-Salem, copied by Chip Henderson; Moravian Music Foundation; courtesy Old Salem, Inc., Winston-Salem, on loan by Wachovia Historical Society, photographed by Chip Henderson; Moravian Music Foundation—courtesy Old Salem, Inc., Winston-Salem, on loan by Ted C. Kerner, photographed by Chip Henderson. 222: Museum of the Confederacy, Richmond; courtesy Frank B. Holt. 223: Gettysburg National Military Park Museum;* courtesy collection of Mark A. Elrod. 224: Museum of the Confederacy, Richmond, photographed by Larry Sherer. 225: From *The Photographic History of the Civil War,* Vol. 8, edited by Francis Trevelyan Miller, Review of Reviews, New York, 1911; courtesy Will Gorgas, New Bern Civil War Museum*—Museum of the Confederacy, Richmond.* 226, 227: Courtesy Herb Peck, Jr.; Beverly M. DuBose III*—Museum of the Confederacy, Richmond* (2). 228, 229: Museum of the City of Mobile, photographed by Larry Cantrell—Museum of the Confederacy, Richmond;* Eleanor S. Brockenbrough Library, Museum of the Confederacy, Richmond, photography by Katherine

Wetzel—Kentucky Historical Society, Military History Museum, photographed by Mary S. Rezny. 230: Museum of the Confederacy, Richmond, photographed by Harold Norvell. 238: North Carolina Department of Cultural Resources, Division of Archives and History, Museum of History, Raleigh*—painting by Conrad Wise Chapman, courtesy Museum of the Confederacy, photographed by Larry Sherer. 239: War Memorial Museum of Virginia—Museum of the Confederacy, Richmond, photography by Katherine Wetzel. 240: Museum of the Confederacy, Richmond, photography by Katherine Wetzel—Confederate Relic Room, Columbia, S.C.* 241: Washington Light Infantry of Charleston, S.C., photographed by Harold H. Norvell; Museum of the Confederacy, Richmond, photography by Katherine Wetzel—Confederate Memorial Hall, New Orleans, photographed by John R. Miller; Museum of the Confederacy, photographed by Henry Beville—Virginia Military Institute Museum, photographed by Henry Beville; Smyth County Historical and Museum Society, Marion, Va., photographed by Eddie Le Sueur. 242: Museum of the Confederacy, Richmond*—North Carolina Department of Cultural Resources, Division of Archives and History, Museum of History, Raleigh;* Museum of the Confederacy, Richmond.* 243: Confederate Relic Room, Columbia, S.C.;* collection of Mississippi State Historical Museum, Jackson, Gil Ford Photography—Museum of the Confederacy, Richmond.* 244: Museum of the Confederacy, Richmond, photography by Katherine Wetzel. 245: Museum of the Confederacy, Richmond, photography by Katherine Wetzel—Museum of the Confederacy, Richmond.* 246: Museum of the Confederacy, Richmond.* 247: Beverly M. DuBose III;* National Park Service—courtesy Lewis Leigh;* Confederate Relic Room, Columbia, S.C.;* Confederate Memorial Hall, New Orleans.* 248: North Carolina Department of Cultural Resources, Division of Archives and History, Museum of History, Raleigh;* collection of Bill Turner, copied by Jeremy Ross—Museum of the Confederacy, Richmond.* 249: Courtesy of Lewis Leigh;* collection of Mississippi State Historical Museum, Mississippi Department of Archives and History, Jackson, Gil Ford Photography—Old State House Museum, Little Rock, Ark.; Confederate Memorial Hall, New Orleans.* 250: Museum of the Confederacy, Richmond, photography by Katherine Wetzel—Museum of the Confederacy, Richmond.* 251: North Carolina Department of Cultural Resources, Division of Archives and History, Museum of History, Raleigh* (2)—Fort Pulaski National Monument, National Park Service, U.S. Department of Interior. 252: Museum of the Confederacy, Richmond, photography by Katherine Wetzel—Museum of the Confederacy, Richmond*—Museum of the Confederacy, Richmond, photographed by Larry Sherer. 253: State Historical Museum, Mississippi Department of Archives and History, Jackson, Acc. No. 62.477, photographed by Gil Ford; Museum of the Confederacy, Richmond, photography by Katherine Wetzel—National Archives, Civil War No. 96. 254, 255: Courtesy collection of Bill Turner; flag, Museum of the Confederacy, Richmond, photographed by Ronald H. Jennings/

flagstaff, Siege Museum, Petersburg, Va., photographed by Larry Sherer; painting by H. E. Gassman after James A. Elder, Siege Museum, Petersburg, Va., photographed by Ronald H. Jennings. 256: Museum of the Confederacy, Richmond.* 257: Museum of the Confederacy, Richmond, photography by Katherine Wetzel—Confederate Relic Room, Columbia, S.C.;* Museum of the Confederacy, Richmond* (2). 258: Collection of Mississippi State Historical Museum, Department of Archives and History, Jackson—Old State House Museum, Little Rock, Ark. (2). 259: Old State House Museum, Little Rock, Ark.—Mississippi State Historical Museum, Mississippi Department of Archives and History, Jackson, Gil Ford Photography—Confederate Memorial Hall, New Orleans.* 260: Old State House Museum, Little Rock, Ark.—Museum of the Confederacy, Richmond, photography by Katherine Wetzel. 261: Wisconsin State Historical Society, Madison, Wis., photographed by David Busch—Confederate Memorial Hall, New Orleans;* Chicago Historical Society No. 1920.1679—Old State House Museum, Little Rock, Ark.* 262: Confederate Memorial Hall, New Orleans*—Museum of the Confederacy, Richmond.* 263: Private collection, photographed by Jim Krantz; Confederate Memorial Hall, New Orleans*—Florida State Archives; collection of Mississippi State Historical Museum, Jackson, Gil Ford Photography. 264: Museum of the Confederacy, Richmond, photographed by Larry Sherer; Tennessee State Museum, photographed by Bill LaFevor—Old State House Museum, Little Rock, Ark.; Museum of the Confederacy, Richmond, photography by Katherine Wetzel. 265: Confederate Memorial Hall, New Orleans*—from *The Photographic History of the Civil War,* Vol. 2, by Henry W. Elson, Review of Reviews, N.Y., 1911. 266: Kentucky Historical Society, Military History Museum (2); Old State House Museum, Little Rock, Ark. 267: Museum of the Confederacy, Richmond;* Civil War Library and Museum, Philadelphia*—courtesy Frank and Marie-T. Wood Print Collections. 268: Kentucky Historical Society, Military History Museum; Museum of the Confederacy, Richmond*—from *Mountain Campaigns in Georgia: War Scenes on the W. & A.* by Joseph M. Brown, 6th edition, Matthews-Northrop, 1895. 269: Museum of the Confederacy, Richmond, photographed by Larry Sherer—Tennessee State Museum, Nashville, photographed by John Frase—Museum of the Confederacy, Richmond;* Tennessee State Museum, Nashville, photographed by June Dorman. 270: Archives Division, Texas State Library, photographed by Eric Beggs. 271: Confederate Memorial Hall, New Orleans;* Old State House Museum, Little Rock, Ark.—Alabama Department of Archives and History (3). 272, 273: Collection of Mississippi State Historical Museum, Mississippi Department of Archives and History, Jackson, Gil Ford Photography; Confederate Memorial Hall, New Orleans;* Museum of the Confederacy, Richmond;* collection of Michael Kramer*—Atlanta Cyclorama, City of Atlanta, photographed by Henry Groskinsky; Confederate Memorial Hall, New Orleans.* 274: Confederate Memorial Hall, photographed by Bill van Calsem—courtesy Dr. Thomas P. Sweeney, photographed by Ralph Duke. 275: Con-

federate Memorial Hall, New Orleans*—Old State House Museum, Little Rock, Ark. (2). 276: Museum of the Confederacy, Richmond* (2)—from *Russell's Civil War Photographs* by Andrew J. Russell, Dover Publications, New York, 1982. 277: Museum of the Confederacy, Richmond*—Museum of the Confederacy, Richmond, photography by Katherine Wetzel. 278: Museum of the Confederacy, Richmond, photography by Katherine Wetzel—Washington Light Infantry of Charleston, S.C., photographed by Harold H. Norvell—Museum of the Confederacy, Richmond. 279: War Memorial Museum of Virginia—Civil War Library and Museum, Philadelphia*—Museum of the Confederacy, Richmond, photography by Katherine Wetzel. 280, 281: Painting by Richard Norris Brooke, West Point Museum Collections, U.S. Military Academy, photographed by Henry Groskinsky. 282: Manassas National Battlefield Park, National Park Service, photographed by Larry Sherer. 288, 289: Manassas National Battlefield Park, National Park Service, photographed by Larry Sherer. 290: Library of Congress—Tennessee State Museum, photographed by Bill LaFevor. 291: Gettysburg National Military Park Museum.* 292, 293: Library of Congress No. B8171-3278; New York State Division of Military and Naval Affairs, Military History Collection (4)*—Gettysburg National Military Park Museum*—from *The Haskell Memoirs* by John Cheves Haskell, edited by Gilbert E. Govan and James W. Livingood, G. P. Putnam's Sons, New York, 1960; National Park Service, Petersburg National Battlefield Museum, photographed by Larry Sherer; New York State Division of Military and Naval Affairs, Military History Collection.* 294, 295: Museum of the Confederacy, Richmond*—Fort Ward Museum, City of Alexandria, photographed by Larry Sherer (2)—Library of Congress No. B8184-10358; Museum of the Confederacy, Richmond;* New York State Division of Military and Naval Affairs, Military History Collection*—Atlanta Historical Society* (4). 296, 297: Courtesy collection of Richard Katter, copied by Larry Sherer; Fort Ward Museum, City of Alexandria, photographed by Larry Sherer; Library of Congress; Atlanta Historical Society* (3)—Fort Ward Museum, City of Alexandria, photographed by Larry Sherer; artwork by William J. Hennessy, Jr. 298: New York State Division of Military and Naval Affairs, Military History Collection.* 299: Artwork by William J. Hennessy, Jr.; courtesy collection of Don Troiani* (2)—Atlanta Historical Society*—collection of Homer Babcock, photographed by Larry Sherer; Atlanta Historical Society*—Eagle Head Arsenal, Manassas, photographed by Larry Sherer; New York State Division of Military and Naval Affairs, Military History Collection* (2). 300, 301: Painting by Conrad Wise Chapman, courtesy Museum of the Confederacy, Richmond, photographed by Larry Sherer; Library of Congress No. B8184-7073—Atlanta Historical Society, photographed by Michael W. Thomas (5). 302, 303: Box, Beverly M. DuBose III, photographed by Michael W. Thomas—courtesy Frank and Marie-T. Wood Print Collections; Beverly M. DuBose III, photographed by Michael W. Thomas; West Point Museum, U.S. Military Academy, photographed by Henry Groskinsky (5).

INDEX

A